THE AUTHENTIC
LETTERS OF PAUL

THE AUTHENTIC LETTERS OF PAUL

A New Reading of Paul's Rhetoric and Meaning

THE SCHOLARS VERSION

*For the Bill of Bills !
much thanks for carry on & on
with courage & compassion
Art Dewey
April 15
hardby ~*

TRANSLATED BY

Ar J. Seway

ARTHUR J. DEWEY

ROY W. HOOVER

LANE C. MCGAUGHY

DARYL D. SCHMIDT

POLEBRIDGE PRESS
Salem, Oregon

Cover and interior design by Robaire Ream

Library of Congress Cataloging-in-Publication Data
Bible. N.T. Epistles of Paul. English. Scholars. 2010.
 The authentic letters of Paul : a new reading of Paul's rhetoric and
meaning : the scholars version / translated by Arthur J. Dewey, [... et
al.].
     p. cm.
 ISBN 978-1-59815-019-3 (alk. paper)
1. Bible. N.T. Epistles of Paul--Criticism, interpretation, etc. I.
Dewey, Arthur J. II. Title.

 BS2643.S36 2010
 227'.05208--dc22

                                   2010037230

Table of Contents

Cameo Essays

Maps

Acknowledgments

We recall with appreciation and gratitude the learning, imagination, and courage of Robert W. Funk whose enterprising spirit initiated the work that has resulted in this book. Bob joined us for a week of work during a January recess at Texas Christian University and in several working sessions at the Westar offices in Santa Rosa. His restless discontents insisted that we keep at it until we got it right.

We owe much to Char Matejovsky for her skills as chief operating officer at Westar Institute and for her steady support and encouragement when bogging down seemed our principal attainment.

For their remarkably consistent generosity that made it possible for us to meet for numerous face to face working sessions we owe special gratitude to Jim Kasper and Lucy Hansen. They never gave up on us when despite our best efforts our pace was distressingly slow.

For his enhancement of our work with an artful cover design and for designing maps for our volume, we salute Polebridge Press designer Robaire Ream.

Our last word here belongs to Barbara (who suggested the conference calls), Elizabeth, Loann, and Judy who stayed by us through leaves of absence from domestic responsibilities and too many intrusions on the rhythms of family life because they shared our belief in the importance and worth of our project.

Readers' Note

The SV Paul Translators have provided the reader with a number of critical tools.

First, Paul's authentic letters are arranged in chronological order, rather than in the canonical order of the New Testament, so that readers may follow the historical development of Paul's correspondence with his followers. When necessary they are presented in their fragmentary condition. We have placed the probable interpolations in the letters of Paul after the authentic material. In some instances, where there is scholarly dispute, possible interpolations have been marked in the text by double brackets. We have placed single brackets around words or phrases that the SV translators have added to render Paul intelligible in North American English. Italics have been used to indicate rhetorical nuance and stress.

We have presented Cameo Essays to help throw light on significant issues. There are also references to other authentic Pauline passages as well as to the use of or allusion to the Jewish scriptures. A list of abbreviations for such references is given on the following page. At the bottom of the page of the text there are notes explaining certain textual variants, translation choices, and background information.

We have included maps so that readers can begin to get a glimpse of the vast geography behind the letters. In fact, we have provided a geographical sketch of Pomponius Mela, a contemporary of Paul. Here is a glimpse of how the "inhabited world" was possibly envisioned in the first century. We have also provided a map of the entire Roman Empire to help readers gauge the length and breadth of Paul's vision.

And we have inserted other maps to highlight Paul's spheres of activity. There is also a brief glossary of terms where our translation differs markedly from the standard versions.

Abbreviations

1,2 Cor	1,2 Corinthians
1,2 Esdr	1,2 Esdras
1,2 Kgs	1,2 Kings
1,2 Sam	1,2 Samuel
1,2 Thess	1,2 Thessalonians
1,2 Tim	1,2 Timothy
1,2,3,4, Macc	1,2,3,4, Maccabees
Deut	Deuteronomy
Eccl	Ecclesiastes
Exod	Exodus
Ezek	Ezekiel
Gal	Galatians
Gen	Genesis
Hab	Habakkuk
Hos	Hosea
Isa	Isaiah
Jer	Jeremiah
Jub	Jubilees
Lev	Leviticus
Mal	Malachi
Matt	Matthew
Num	Numbers
Phil	Philippians
Phlm	Philemon
Prov	Proverbs
Ps(s)	Psalm(s)
Rom	Romans
Sir	Sirach
Wis	Wisdom of Solomon
Zech	Zechariah

A First-century View
of the Inhabited World

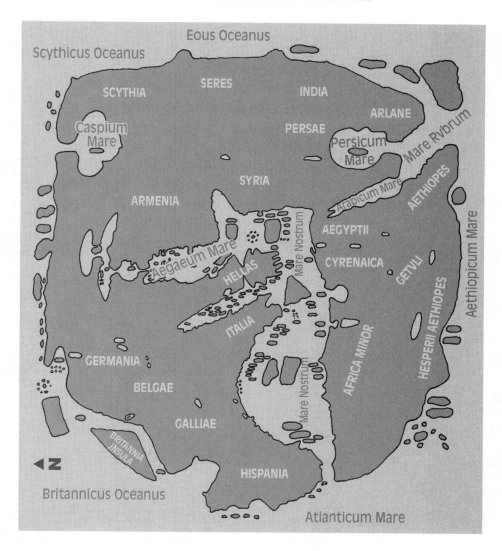

Pomponius Mela, ca. 43 CE

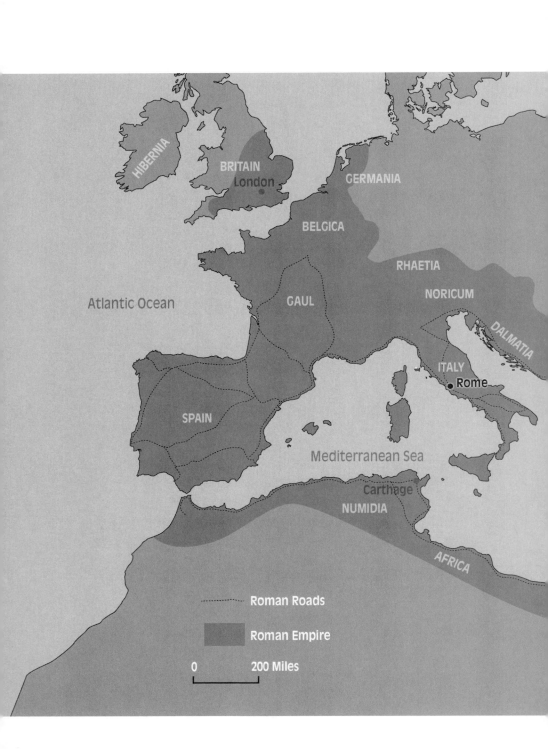

HIBERNIA

BRITAIN
London

GERMANIA

BELGICA

RHAETIA

NORICUM

DALMATIA

Atlantic Ocean

GAUL

ITALY
Rome

SPAIN

Mediterranean Sea

Carthage

NUMIDIA

AFRICA

--------- Roman Roads

Roman Empire

0   200 Miles

The Roman Empire in the First Century

Canonical vs. Authentic Paul

Canonical Paul	Authentic Paul	Non Pauline*
Romans	**Romans 1–15** *minus interpolations* **Romans 16** *minus interpolations*	*Rom 5:6–7* *Rom 13:1–7* *Rom 16:17–20* *Rom 16:25–27*
1 Corinthians	**1 Corinthians** *minus interpolations*	*1 Cor 4:6b* *1 Cor 11:2–16* *1 Cor 14:33b–38*
2 Corinthians	**A Defense of Paul's Credibility** 2 Cor 2:14–6:13; 7:2–4 **A Parody of "A Fool's Speech"** 2 Corinthians 10–13 **A Letter of Reconciliation** 2 Cor 1:1–2:13; 7:5–16 **A Collection Appeal to Corinth** 2 Corinthians 8 **A Collection Appeal to Achaia** 2 Corinthians 9	*2 Cor 6:14–7:1*
Galatians	**Galatians**	
Ephesians		Ephesians
Philippians	**A Thank-you Letter** Phil 4:10–20 **A Letter from Prison** Phil 1:1–3:1a; 4:4–9, 21–23 **Paul's Testimony and Advice** Phil 3:1b–4:3	
Colossians		Colossians
1 Thessalonians	**1 Thessalonians**	
2 Thessalonians		2 Thessalonians
Philemon 1 Timothy 2 Timothy Titus Hebrews	**Philemon**	1 Timothy 2 Timothy Titus Hebrews

* Items in italic are interpolations into an authentic letter.

Introduction

The Voiceprint of Paul

The letters of Paul delivered a distinct voice and universal vision to the first century Mediterranean world. From the outset they were complex transmissions of a complicated man addressing a variety of issues for some fledgling communities of Jesus the Anointed. Unfortunately the distinctive sound of Paul's letters has been distorted by the cacophony of later voices that have attempted to speak in his name. Indeed, modern readers of Paul are often unsympathetic to the "Paul" filtered by the tradition. *The Authentic Letters of Paul* attempts to bring the voiceprint of Paul back to the conversation.

Readers will find that the Paul of the letters is not synonymous with the Lutheran Paul, nor the Augustinian Paul. He is neither the professional theologian, nor the ecclesial misogynist. Rather, the Paul who emerges is an extraordinarily zealous Pharisaic Jew who experienced a paradigm shift so profound that it transformed the way he saw the world and all in it. This man is a thinker and rhetorician, a visionary and prophet, whose experience of God was so profound that he reimagined the conditions of existence. This is a man who was alert to the world about him, able to use metaphors that both speak to and challenge his world. This is a utopian thinker who joins in the cultural debate of his time over what constitutes the value and meaning of humanity. This is a man who has glimpsed what it means to live beyond tribal or ethnic boundaries. This is a man who can imagine those considered outsiders as equals, a man who has found freedom and meaning in the rag-tag communities of "nobodies."

This new translation is hardly the first attempt to determine the authentic Paul. The history of biblical interpretation has been consistently marked by scholarly ventures into this question. It has long been argued that the various letters attributed to Paul must be evaluated on historical-critical and literary grounds. Comparative analysis of the letters reveals that not all of them are from the same hand. By focusing on the vocabulary, phrases, social situation, Christology and ecclesial understanding of the letters scholars can detect earlier and later voices. From this analysis the Pastoral Letters (1 and 2 Timothy and Titus) prove to be not Pauline. Although written in Paul's name for the sake of claiming his authority, they are second century compositions that actually return to the values and social structures of Roman society. The distinctive voice of Paul has been replaced by a conventional voice of an authoritative command. 2 Thessalonians also shows indications of another hand. The verbatim repetitions from 1 Thessalonians along with a recalibration of an endtime scenario argue for a later attempt to rework Paul's apocalyptic vision. Both Ephesians and Colossians also show signs of a later hand. They may well have been written by disciples of Paul who were attempting to bring Paul's insights forward. Many scholars date them to the last quarter of the first century. Yet we see even in them a return to the social default of the Roman Empire. The Body of the Anointed, for example, is understood quite differently in 1 Corinthians 12 and Colossians 1. Also the role of women differs in 1 Corinthians and Ephesians. The democratic signals found in 1 Corinthians have been rechanneled along the lines of a hierarchical restoration in Colossians and Ephesians. No longer is there a call to a new regime but reconciliation to a past and eternal pattern. This leaves what is a general consensus that the extant authentic letters of Paul are: 1 Thessalonians, Galatians, 1 and 2 Corinthians, Philemon, Philippians, and Romans. We have printed the authentic letters of Paul in probable chronological order.

While the dating of the letters of Paul can be situated around the middle of the first century, a more exact figure is difficult. The usual basis for a Pauline timeline, the Acts of the Apostles, has become suspect in recent scholarship. Acts may well have been written in the early second century using the extant letters of Paul as the ground for constructing the travel narrative about Paul. This means that scholars are left with the letters themselves to determine an approximate dating. With the exception of Galatians (1:18; 2:1), there is no concern for specifying a time. The question of the dating of the letters becomes a matter of assessing the probable relation among the letters. Scholars have turned to the letters' content, style, ideas and social situation to reach a relative dating.

Yet the question of what constitutes the shape of the Pauline evidence is not only about which canonical letters Paul authored or when they were written. Scholars also have debated whether the remaining canonical format of the authentic letters preserves their original form, since some canonical letters appear to have been consolidated from letter fragments or from what originally were separate letters. It should not be forgotten that there is no extant manuscript evidence of complete letters of Paul until the third century. To presume that the original letters of Paul that survived did so without any editing or insertions is naïve. Already by the end of the first century the letters of Paul were being transmitted beyond their original locale as collections of some of Paul's letters were being circulated. The copying process was well underway. Marcion, the first Christian text critic, provides an example of this editing process, since he edits a version of the Gospel of Luke and couples it with letters of Paul to form what he calls "The New Testament" around 140 CE. Curiously 2 Corinthians in its present form does not appear until after Marcion's time. As mentioned above, from the 80s on letters were being written in Paul's name and in the second century the legendary figure of Paul became a focal point for rival interpretations of the growing Christian traditions. Moreover, a close inspection of the letters of Paul from formal, redactional, and rhetorical perspectives suggests strongly that discrepancies and other voices have been inserted in these letters.

Most recently there have been significant developments in Pauline scholarship. The social situation of the letters along with the role of the particular communities has been brought to the fore. There has been renewed interest in the kinds of communities that received Paul's correspondence. How did these communities differ, if at all, from the local clubs, associations and synagogues? How did these communities function? What social issues were they trying to address? What sort of communities of belonging were they? Of course, such communities existed within the Roman Empire. How are we to understand these letters within the echo chamber of the Empire? What happens when we read the letters of Paul against the dreams and promises of the domination of Rome?

Not to be overlooked is the fact that the letters of Paul display the marks of rhetorical finesse. Certainly Paul is no Cicero, no Demosthenes. But even the letter to Philemon under critical scrutiny reveals itself as a rhetorical gem. In fact, without a sense of the rhetorical choices Paul makes as he composes his letters, the reader will lose much of what Paul attempts to say. The questions, objections, emotional plays, the sarcasm, the elements of praise, even the prayerful thanksgivings, have to be heard within a rhetorical register. Once the reader grasps that Paul is not dictating to but attempting to persuade a community, then a different image of Paul begins to emerge.

Most notably there has been a seismic shift in our view of Paul's basic theological ground. The very way in which Paul understood Jesus and the relation of God to Jesus has been subject to renewed debate and investigation. This fascinating discussion was rekindled by questions that have been raised in recent decades about the meaning of the phrase *ek pisteōs christou* in Gal 2:16 and in several other places in Paul's letters. Since 1881 (see Cameo on Galatians 2:16, p. 65) the English translation has been "faith in Christ." However, before that time the English translation (including the King James) had been "the faith of Christ." While the grammar may allow both translations, it is significant to note that the use of the word *pistis* (trust, faith) with a name in the genitive case in the letters of Paul would argue for "the faith of Christ" (Scholars Version, "the confidence of the Anointed"). Paul uses exactly the same phrasing in Romans 4:16 where he is obviously referring to "the faith of Abraham,'" not "faith in Abraham." What happened in 1881 is that a theological agenda, focusing on a propositional theology, had gained sway. The rhetorical sound and flow of Paul's speech had been altered to fit a later theological orthodoxy.

A New Reading of Paul's Rhetoric and Meaning

The labor of translating Paul anew was undertaken by a team of Fellows of the Westar Institute. Under the inspiration of Robert Funk, former Executive Secretary of the Society of Biblical Literature and the founder of the Westar Institute, the team was asked to produce a dynamic equivalent translation of Paul, which would eventually accompany *The Complete Gospels* translations in a new edition of the New Testament and the remaining early Christian writings. *The Authentic Letters of Paul* thus represents a portion of a larger, overall project of the Scholars Version (SV). It does, however, stand on its own as a new translation of the correspondence of Paul.

This is a team translation. We began with drafts prepared by individual Fellows, who took into account the various developments in Pauline studies. We have not settled for the traditional ways of translating the material. We listened to Paul as he echoed around the Mediterranean. We sought modern advice and have taken into account the work of recent scholarship. And we worked as a team, questioning and being puzzled over every word and sentence. At first we met together for a week at a time. But, despite the positive yield of our collaboration, the pace was too slow. We also were devastated by the death of our comrade Daryl Schmidt. It took some time to regroup and rededicate our effort in Daryl's memory. We also decided to continue our work over the phone and internet. Through weekly, three hour conference calls, we worked together through each line of Paul. We did not settle for a translation until we all had tested it. What is Paul saying? How do we say this in English? What must be taken into account? What must be made explicit to get the meaning?

While much has been done regarding the historical Paul, the Paul found in numerous modern translations is still a wooden figure. Often the translation of important words is a simple transliteration. *Christos*, for example, becomes Christ. *Charis* becomes, through the Latin *gratia,* grace. But how do such transliterations deliver meaning? "Grace" carries with it all the subsequent theological debates on sanctification, while "Christ" turns into Jesus' last name. But do we understand, as readers of such translations, that the title *Christos* was given to honor a man who had been shamed and that this title rivaled those given to the Emperor? Or do we note that the benefit or favor (*charis*) is an indication that the very energy source of the world is involved; that the access and flow of divine power are available to all who trust in the Benefactor of the world?

We have not attempted to create a new Paul. Rather, we have tried to translate Paul dynamically. We do not present a literal, wooden rendering. We aim to express what Paul meant in clear North American English. We have sought a dynamic equivalence of Greek to English in order to communicate the meaning Paul wanted to convey. This means that we have not rested comfortably with a word for word strategy. At times we have had to spell out what was implied in Paul's rhetoric. We have tried to find in English ways of conveying Paul's intent.

This has meant that we have taken great pains to detect the root or basic metaphors out of which Paul thinks and communicates. People too quickly move from Paul's metaphors and images to the world of abstract theology. They do not see that, as a rhetorician, Paul thinks in and through combinations of images and metaphors. We have taken seriously, for example, his use of economic images.

We also have had to stay aware of the mythic register of his speech. Mythic speech is not simply something not factual or fanciful. Mythic speech emerges in the ancient world whenever people find themselves in situations beyond their control. They use mythic language to get a sense of orientation (where they are from and where they are going), identity, and access to the powers of the universe. The Roman Empire thrived on such mythic construction. This gave the Romans the capacity to define the power relations of the world. Paul plays off of that speech. His understanding of the Anointed Jesus in Phil 2:6ff. is understandable only on such mythic grounds (see Cameo on the "Christ Hymn" in Philippians 2:6–11, p. 193). We also can see this in the question of the translation of *hamartia,* usually rendered as "sin." The difficulty with the standard translation is that it does not catch the mythic reaches of Paul's speech. Today the word "sin" does not have a public venue; it is confined to a segregated religious habitat. Yet, Paul in Romans, for example, wants to talk about the reach and fatal grasp of a corrosive power, extending throughout time and space. Thus, we have used variations of the phrase "the seductive power of corruption" for the word *hamartia.*

We have also paid attention to a number of recent advances in understanding Paul as a rhetorician. We have taken seriously how Paul "invents" his speech through his anticipations of issues, objections, questions. We have noted at times the diatribal elements of his rhetorical technique (see Cameo on Ancient Rhetoric, p. 159). We have tried to follow and convey Paul's persuasive lines of argument. We have had to remind ourselves of the situation in which Paul found himself as he composed a letter. As we begin to read Paul this way, we can see that he is not pontificating to his audience; instead he is trying to make a persuasive case on which his listeners will have the last word and vote. We have also paid attention to the emotional vector of his speech, for this is part and parcel of a good rhetorical piece. We have tried to convey his biting sarcasm as well as his warmth and enthusiasm.

We have also had to come to grips with the fragmentary nature of the correspondence. As mentioned above, there is no extant physical evidence of an entire letter of Paul until the third century. We do know that soon after his death new letters were written in his name, collections of his letters were circulated and that editing of the letters was underway. By closely reading Paul's letters through a sustained rhetorical lens we have become acutely aware of the possible and probable interruptions in the flow of the text. Where these interruptions prove to be secondary, we have removed them from the body of the letter in question and have placed them as an appendix to the original text. We also have seen that some letters are fusions of fragmentary letters (such as 2 Corinthians and Philippians). Arguments for the fragments of each will be found in the introductions to those letters. We have decided to arrange the fragmentary letters in their probable historical order. Thus, we print not what is a later integrated letter but what remains of the original fragmentary letters. The result is startling. One begins to recognize the fragility of the actual correspondence of Paul and the industry of the subsequent tradition. Such a printing of Paul as originally separate pieces of correspondence represents a new way of imagining the historical evidence for Paul.

We have also attempted to assist the reader by providing a number of critical tools. We have presented cameo essays to help throw light on significant issues. We have provided references to other authentic Pauline passages as well as references to the use of or allusion to the Jewish scriptures. There are notes explaining certain textual variants, translation choices, and background information. We have included maps so that readers can begin to get a glimpse of the vast geography behind the letters. It is important to recognize the length, for example, that Paul intended to go (to the end of the earth, as he knew it) for the sake of what he considers the "world-transforming message." We have also provided a brief glossary of terms where our translation differs markedly from the standard versions.

Paul and the Twenty-first Century

What can a new reading of Paul contribute to our present situation? In a world verging on seeming collapse and disillusion, we come upon an older brother who has an unusual perspective. In a time when listening is not in vogue and bottom line thinking dominates, Paul delivers a different option. He takes experience seriously (both his and his communities'). He attempts to persuade not override. He risks misunderstanding. He refuses to give up on those with whom he is in solidarity. He is convinced that trust is the tissue of our life together. He speaks against those who would maintain or attempt to gain a competitive advantage over others to win the day at the expense of another. He can imagine that meaning not only can be found in the "nobodies" of the world but is the prism through which to understand the working of the planet.

The Acts of the Apostles

In searching for the historical Paul, we are immediately confronted with the question of sources: what texts are reliable historical sources for reconstructing the figure of Paul? For the SV Paul translators, the authentic letters of Paul must be the primary source, since he was the author and presumably is giving us firsthand accounts of his own actions and views.

But what about the Acts of the Apostles? Until the middle of the nineteenth century, it was assumed that Acts contains eyewitness accounts written by one of Paul's traveling companions and is therefore a reliable historical source for his missionary career. Many biographies of Paul use the chronological framework of Acts as the basic source and fit his letters into this outline, thus harmonizing what Paul says about his work with Luke's narrative and treating Acts as "the default mode" for interpreting the activities of Christian leaders during this period.

Continued on next page

Is the Acts of the Apostles a reliable historical source?

Since the time of Ferdinand Christian Baur, however, redactional studies have demonstrated that the author of Acts interpreted the events he describes in light of his theological agenda and a certain set of biases that inform his work. What launched Baur's work on the historical reliability of Acts was the stark contrast between the fragmentation of earliest Christianity reflected in Paul's letters and the utopian picture of a unified and harmonious movement painted in Acts (see 4:32a). A comparison of the account of Paul's meeting with the leaders in Jerusalem in Galatians 2:1–10 with Luke's account in Acts 15 scores this point. Paul is writing his account in the heat of a controversy with those whom he dismissively labels as "the reputed leaders of the Jerusalem assembly" (2:2b) in order to demonstrate his independence as an envoy (*apostolos*; 1:1) who was commissioned directly by God (1:15). The fact that Paul is defending himself against opponents in a conflict over his message is underlined by his sworn oath that his version is true (1:20). Such a passionate defense reflects a situation in which there was an array of Jesus groups and not a single, unified movement.

Luke's version of the meeting between Paul and the Jerusalem leaders is described very differently in Acts 15 and is often referred to as "the Apostolic Council." Here Paul is portrayed as being under the authority of "the apostles and elders" who demand that he answer the charges made against him by his opponents (15:1–2). Luke then describes an imaginary court scenario in which Paul (the defendant) is put on trial before the apostles and elders (the jury) by Christian Pharisees (the plaintiffs) (15:5–6). As a result of this "trial," a compromise judgment is reached in which two prophets, Judas and Silas, inform Paul and Barnabas and the assembly in Antioch that the nations must observe four stipulations of the Mosaic law (15:29), but are exempted from the ritual of circumcision. [Note that Paul claims in Gal 2:10 that he made no concessions to the "reputed leaders" except to remember "the poor."] In short,

Paul regards himself as one of "the Apostles" (1 Cor 15:9), whereas Luke excludes Paul from the apostolic circle and puts him under the authority of the Jerusalem hierarchy.

Why this recasting of Paul in Acts? What had changed by the time Luke composed the Acts of the Apostles? Westar's Acts Seminar has concluded that Acts best fits the historical context of the early second century battle between proto-orthodox and gnostic Christians over the legacy of Paul.[1] In this context, the author of Acts portrays Paul as an obedient Christian Pharisee and the hero of a unified and rapidly-spreading religious movement over against Marcion's portrait of Paul as a radical who was hostile to the Hebrew scriptures and the world of the flesh, and who introduced an alien god that is distinct from the earthly creator of Genesis. Though the author of Acts likely knew the letters of Paul and bases some of his narratives on information Paul provides, he does not refer to Paul's letters directly and ignores the major themes in the letters in order to enlist Paul in the ranks of the proto-orthodox cause.

Can Acts be used as a historical source for Paul's career?

If Acts as a whole is historically suspect, then it should not be the default mode for reconstructing Paul's career either. Following is a brief outline of Paul's career, based only on the autobiographical sections of his letters:

1. A circumcised Jew and member of the Pharisees (Phil 3:5).
2. Persecuted the Anointed's people (Phil 3:6a).
3. Called to be an envoy to the nations while in Damascus (Gal 1:15–17).
4. Three years of work in eastern Syria and Arabia (Gal 1:17–18a).
5. Two-week visit to Jerusalem: introduced to Cephas and James (Gal 1:18–19).
6. Travels in the province of Syria and Cilicia (Gal 1:21).
7. Eleven to fourteen years of missionary work (Gal 2:1a).

Continued on next page

8. Second visit to Jerusalem to meet with the "reputed leaders" (Gal 2:1–10).
9. Return to his mission field to collect an offering for the Anointed's people in Jerusalem (1 Cor 16:1–4; 2 Cor 8 and 9; cp. Gal 1:10).
10. Third visit to Jerusalem with the offering (Rom 15:25–32).

In contrast, Luke has altered Paul's outline in significant ways:

A. Luke turns Paul's commission to become an envoy to the nations (#3) into a religious conversion (Acts 9:17b–19).
B. Luke divides Paul's missionary work (#7) into three periods (Acts 13–14; 15:36—18:21; and 18:23—21:14), punctuated with reports to the leaders in Jerusalem.
C. Luke relocates the offering to the Jerusalem assembly from the time after Paul's missionary work (#10) to a date before Paul's "first" missionary journey (Acts 11:27–30), and changes its purpose by linking it to the famine that occurred during the reign of the Emperor Claudius between 46 and 48 CE;
D. Luke transforms the voluntary meeting between Paul and the Jerusalem leaders (#8) into a formal hearing (Acts 15);
E. Luke presents Peter as the first missionary to the nations (Acts 10:1—11:18), contrary to Paul's claim that he was commissioned to be the envoy to the nations and Peter to the Jews (Gal 2:7);
F. Luke portrays Paul as still an observant Jew (Acts 21:23–26), despite Paul's assertion that ethnic religious practices no longer are important (Phil 3:7).[2]

While some scholars still assume the historical reliability of Acts, others who recognize the inconsistencies have moved to a mediating position: they use Acts as a source for Paul's career when it does not conflict with the letters. But the SV Paul translators are persuaded that such an argument from silence is misleading in this case: Luke's theological agenda colors his entire narrative and therefore one cannot assume it is suspect in some parts and not others. Thus, the SV Paul translators recommend against using Acts, either as a whole or in part, as a historical source for Paul's career.

Conclusion

Scholars influenced by F. C. Baur's work have demonstrated that the portrait of Paul as a character in the narrative of Acts is very different from Paul as a historical figure based on his authentic letters, both in terms of the chronology of his career and the main themes of his message. The Acts of the Apostles thus should be classified among the later interpretations of Paul and not used as a historical source for reconstructing his life and work. As a result, the introductory essays and notes in this book do not utilize episodes in Acts to amplify the situations Paul addresses in his letters. References to Acts are only cited where points of difference from Paul's remarks must be noted. Our strong recommendation is that readers not resort to Acts when perplexed about the circumstances that Paul and his addresses take for granted, but attempt to fill the gaps with what is implied by the letters themselves. Only in this way can we begin to separate the authentic Paul from the often confusing, and sometimes distorted, images of him in later Christianity.

NOTES

1. See Joseph Tyson, *Marcion and Luke-Acts.*
2. See John Knox, *Chapters in a Life of Paul,* chaps. 3 and 4.

The Nations

The term "the nations" (*ta ethnē*), traditionally "the gentiles," needs to be situated within both the Jewish and Roman understanding of the world. Fraught with social implications, for Jews the term did not simply mean "foreigners," but the non-Jewish population, which would have been generally considered morally inferior by those who, through the Covenant, enjoyed a full connection with the God of Israel. People within the Covenant had a distinct advantage (in terms of access to divine power and benefits) over those outside of the Covenant.

From a Roman point of view "the nations" (in Latin, *gentes*) meant all who were not Roman. This would include Jews. The Romans also would have seen themselves as the true recipients of divine favor. Only those who would align themselves with such a favored people could expect some share in the blessings of the Roman gods. This distinction between a divinely favored people and the "others" was an underlying assumption of the ancient civilized world. Tribal thinking still reigned as people attempted to imagine one world. One tribe or people held the competitive advantage over all others before the divine.

The Galatians would have seen themselves as the nations under both aspects. Under the dominion of Rome for over two centuries, they would have been accustomed to being described as among the nations connected to Rome. With the arrival of Jewish missionaries they would have found themselves on the outside of yet another social situation. Paul's argument that the nations can enter into genuine relationship with the God of Israel in full equality with Jews would be tantamount to upsetting the social assumptions of the first century.

Paul's Correspondence to the Thessalonians

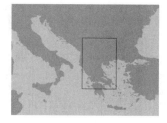

Thessalonica, a city on the Via Egnatia, was the capital of the Roman province of Macedonia.

1 Thessalonians

INTRODUCTION

1 Thessalonians as a Key to the Authentic Letters of Paul

Paul's first letter to his followers in Thessalonica is regarded by most scholars as the earliest document included in the New Testament. It is usually dated to late 50 or early 51 CE and is thought to have been written by Paul during his first stay in Corinth. It thus stands mid-point between Jesus and the Gospels: twenty years after the end of Jesus' itinerant ministry and twenty years before the first New Testament Gospel, Mark. 1 Thessalonians represents a watershed in the formation of early Christianity: the switch from a modest but intense word of mouth campaign to a loosely structured network of small communities with authority centralized in dynamic leaders like Paul. As Robert Funk notes,[1] Paul's discourse stands on the border between the oral word that establishes a new world and the written words that transmit this new world beyond its original proclamation.*

As the earliest surviving document in the history of Christianity, 1 Thessalonians established the letter as the archetypal Christian literary genre: still today written communications from ecclesiastical leaders to church groups imitate the form of a Pauline letter, for example, Martin Luther King Jr.'s "Letter from Birmingham City Jail" or papal encyclicals like Pope John XXIII's "Pacem in Terris." In particular,

---

*If one constructed a spectrum of linguistic acts ranging from oral conversations on one end to philosophical essays on the other, ancient personal letters, like modern emails, would be located on the boundary between spoken and written forms: a personal letter is the closest written form to oral speech.

1 Thessalonians created the template for all of Paul's letters. As such, the structure of 1 Thessalonians can be used to answer two nagging questions in Pauline studies: did Paul himself write all thirteen letters that are attributed to him in the New Testament? And, are all of Paul's letters in the form he wrote them or are some of them composites of several letters? The answers to these two questions about the authenticity and integrity of the letters are the first steps in the quest for the historical Paul.

Are Paul's Letters Literature?

Are personal letters even a form of literature? The early twentieth-century New Testament scholar Adolf Deissmann thought not. He assumed that because personal letters do not belong to any of the recognized genres of "high literature," they have no structure and therefore Paul's letters are chaotic and cannot be analyzed in terms of a shared literary form.[2] The discovery and analysis of thousands of personal letters from the Greco-Roman period has dramatically reversed Deissmann's assumption. Modern literary critics underscore this reversal. They argue that any piece of writing, whether from high culture or popular culture, must belong to some genre, otherwise one would not be able to contextualize that writing.

The Structure of Personal Letters in Paul's Time

Even a brief look at any of the collections of ancient letters uncovered by archaeologists in the past century shows that they were highly structured and included various conventional formulas that framed their contents.

A typical example of a personal letter from the Greco-Roman period (154 BCE) is one from Sarapion to his brothers announcing his impending marriage:

> Sarapion to his brothers, Ptolemy and Apollonios, greeting.
> If you are well, (it would be excellent); I myself am well. I

have contracted with the daughter of Hesperos and intend to marry her in the month Mesore. Please send half a chous of olive oil to me. I wrote to you in order that you may know. Farewell. Year 28, Epeiph 21.

P.Paris 43 (=U.P.Z. 66)[3]

Using this example, the standard form for personal letters from the time of Paul can be outlined and illustrated as follows:

I. Salutation
   A. Name of letter-writer(s)   "Sarapion
   B. Name of recipient(s)   to . . . Ptolemaeus and Apollonius
   C. "Greeting"   greeting.

II. Health wish/prayer   "I hope you are well . . .

III. Update for the recipient   "I have made a contract with the
     (news/information since   daughter of Hesperus and intend
     the last communication)   to marry her
                                  in the month of Mesore.

IV. Request   "Please send half a chous of
    (letter-writer asks for a   olive oil to me."
    favor or gives advice)

V. Closing
   A. Greetings to others
   B. Repeated health wish
   C. "Farewell"   "Farewell."

This example is a very terse note that is reduced to the bare structure of the personal letter form, omitting greetings to others and the repeated health wish in the closing that typically occur in most letters. As such, the constituent elements of the genre of personal letters in the time of Paul are clearly apparent here.

The Structure of Paul's Authentic Letters

In creating the template for Christian letters, Paul modifies the form of the personal letter illustrated above in light of the situation and needs of the recipients he is addressing and his calling as an envoy to the nations. A typical Pauline letter exhibits the following structure:

I.   Salutation
     A. (From) Paul (and his associates)
     B. to (name of the recipients of the letter)
     C. "Grace and peace"

II. Prayer for the recipients' faithfulness   [Thanksgiving Period]
     (including a summary of the two basic
     themes in section III)

III. (Theological) reflections on two
     basic themes: [Letter Body]
     A. The situation of the recipients
     B. Paul's authority as an envoy to
        the nations
     C. Addendum: An update on Paul's
        travel plans   [Apostolic *Parousia*]

IV. Ethical exhortations or advice   [Paraenesis]

V.   Closing
     A. Greetings
     B. Benediction

By comparing the typical form of a Pauline letter with the conventional form of personal letters illustrated above, one can see what changes Paul made in the genre. Here are a few of the main changes that are signatures of a genuine Pauline letter:

1. He changes the opening "greetings" (χαίρειν) to "grace and peace" (χάρις καὶ εἰρήνη) by dropping the Greek letter *iota* in the infinitive and converting it to a noun (from *chairein* to *charis*) and by adding the Greek translation of the Hebrew *shalom*. The result is a new Christian greeting that combines a Greek plea that the community may be blessed with divine favor ("grace") and the Hebraic expression of human goodwill and inner serenity ("peace").

2. He transforms the health wish of the common letter into a prayer of thanks for the faithfulness of the recipients. But this prayer is not simply a perfunctory gesture, as is the case of the health wish. Rather, Paul uses this second section of his

letters to introduce the two basic themes that he will elaborate in section III.

3. The two basic themes in section III (the letter body) are circular because Paul's message and the recipients' response to that message are two-sides of the same coin: whether Paul has accurately translated the world-transforming message about Jesus for Greco-Roman recipients and whether they have clearly grasped the implications of this radical message for their own lives. Paul defends the authority of his speech by pointing to the positive response of his hearers, and they in turn base their confidence in Paul's message on his claim to authority. Given the fact that Paul had never encountered the historical Jesus nor was he one of the early leaders of the Jesus movement in Galilee, he had to justify his universal message. And because his message was universal, Paul's opponents claimed it was not consistent with the pre-Pauline message by and about the Galilean visionary and teacher Jesus. Thus with every dispute that emerged from the internal dynamics of small communities in formation or from external attacks by opponents, Paul was forced to restate this dialectic between his authority as an envoy and the recipients' faithfulness in terms of the particularities of their situations.

4. As with the thanksgiving prayer (section II), so too with the addendum giving Paul's travel plans (section III.C): it has often been ignored as of no importance for the theological themes of the letters. After all, don't we usually toss the itineraries for our travels after they're completed? And here is where Robert Funk made an important contribution to Pauline studies. He argued that these travel plans are not just idle chatter and therefore of no importance to us as readers today: rather, they function to enforce Paul's authority (his promise to visit will be received as either a cause for joy or as a threat, depending on the measure of their faithfulness to Paul's message) and they reflect Paul's view that writing from a distance is a weak substitute for face to face encounters. Funk labeled these travel plans that are added to the body of

The Structure of 1 Thessalonians

I. Salutation (1:1)
    A. *"Paul, Silvanus, and Timothy*   [Senders]
    B. *"to those in Thessalonica . . .*   [Recipients]
    C. *"divine favor and peace to you.*   [Formulaic greeting]

II. Thanksgiving prayer (1:2–10): introduction of general issues in
    section III
    A. *"We always thank God . . .* (1:2)   [Opening formula]
    B. Theme A: Thessalonian situation (1:3–4, 6–8): *"imitators"* ◄
       (μιμηταί) of Paul and Jesus (1:6) and thus a *"model"* (τύπον)
       for others in Greece (1:7)
    C. Theme B: Defense of Paul's authority (1: 5, 9): *"our stay* ◄
       among you"(εἴσοδον, 1:9)
    D. Eschatological climax (1:10)   [Closing formula]

III. (Theological) reflections on the two general issues facing Paul
    (2:1–3:13)
    A. *"For you know . . .* (2:1a)   [Opening formula]
    B. Theme B: Defense of Paul's authority (2:1–12): *"our stay* ◄
       among you" (εἴσοδον, 2:1b)
       (same issue discussed four times in antithetical pattern:
       γάρ . . . ἀλλά . . .)
       1. *"For . . .* (2:1) criticism of Paul / *"but . . .* (2:2) his defense
       2. *"For . . .* (2:3) criticism of Paul / *"but . . .* (2:4) his defense
       3. *"For . . .* (2:5–7a) criticism of Paul / *"But . . .* (2:7b–8) his
         defense
       4. *"For . . .* (2:9) criticism of Paul / [but] . . . (2:10–12a) his
         defense
    C. Doxology (2:12b)   [Closing formula]
    D. Theme A: Thessalonian situation (2:13–16)
       1. repeated thanksgiving
         prayer from 1:2 (2:13a)   [Opening formula]
       2. Thessalonians are *"imitators"* (μιμηταί) of persecuted ◄
         Jesus communities in Judea (2:14)

a Pauline letter as "the Apostolic *Parousia*"*—a written substitute for Paul's promised apostolic presence.[4]

Parousia refers to the arrival and/or presence of a person, usually of
great import.

3. other models of persecution: Jesus, the prophets, Paul (2:15a; cf. 1:6–8)

E. Eschatological climax (2:16b–c): two parallel clauses

F. Apostolic *Parousia*: Paul hopes to return to Thessalonica (2:17–3:13)

    1. Paul's plans to visit were frustrated (2:18)

    2. Therefore, he sends Timothy as a substitute (3:1–5)

    3. Timothy's positive report is followed by this letter (3:6–9)

    4. Paul prays that he will still be able to visit them again (3:10)

    5. Two blessings (3:11–12) and an eschatological climax (3:13)   [Closing formulas]

IV. Ethical exhortations and advice re: Thessalonian concerns (4:1—5:24)

A. "Finally . . . we *implore* (παρακαλοῦμεν) you . . . (4:1a)   [Opening formula]

B. Theme 1: concerning the virtuous life (4:3–8)

C. Theme 2: concerning relationships with others (4:9–12)

D. Theme 3: concerning community members who have died (4:13–18)

E. Theme 4: concerning predictions of the great events to come (5:1–11)

F. Brief injunctions (5:12–24)

    1. a command to respect three kinds of community leadership (5:12–13)

    2. fourteen injunctions introduced by 2nd person plural imperative verbs (5:14–22)

    3. Eschatological climax (5:23) and a blessing (5:24)   [Closing formulas]

V. Closing (5:25–28)

A. Personal requests (5:25, 27)

B. Greetings (ἀσπάσασθε . . .) (5:26)

C. Benediction (5:28)

Any actual Pauline letter will, of course, be a fleshing out of the typical pattern based on the circumstances of the recipients of that letter. Above is a detailed outline of 1 Thessalonians, adding conventional formulas and rhetorical tropes to the typical form of a Pauline letter described previously.

Structure as a Criterion
for Authenticity and Integrity

In light of this analysis of the structure of Paul's letters, we can now return to the two perennial questions that have plagued Pauline studies: which letters attributed to Paul are authentic and are any of his authentic letters composites? Those who share Adolf Diessmann's assumption that ancient letters are chaotic have settled this question on subjective grounds: letters that reflect what a particular interpreter or religious community regards as the core of Paul's theology are taken to be authentic. But, of course, what an interpretive community regards as the core of Paul's theology is derived from the letters that are assumed to be authentic. We thus have inherited a catch-22 situation with respect to Paul: there are a variety of conflicting portraits of Paul and many contradictory claims made about his views based on the fact that the various interpreters are working from different data bases.

The work that papyrologists have done on the structure of ancient letters now offers us objective criteria for solving the nagging problems of which letters were actually written by Paul and whether any of them are combinations of the fragments of several authentic letters. Only those letters that conform to the structure of a Pauline letter described above and illustrated by the outline of 1 Thessalonians—those that contain the marks of Paul's unique changes to the conventional form of personal letters—are authentic. Moreover, any authentic letters which contain more than one example of one of the parts of a letter are probably composites of several letters (for example, if an authentic letter contains two thanksgiving periods or two letter bodies, it is very likely a combination of two letters that Paul wrote to the recipients). Using these criteria to separate the authentic letters of Paul from pseudonymous letters thus provides an important breakthrough in the quest for the historical Paul. In reconstructing Paul's views and his missionary career, one should use only the authentic letters contained in this volume as the primary source.

Is 1 Thessalonians 2:13–16 an Interpolation?

The next step in creating a data base for the quest for the historical Paul is redactional. It has long been recognized that the early collectors and later copyists of Paul's letters edited them in a variety of ways: the insertion of marginal comments into the texts, the rearrangement of sections, the addition of short connective passages and longer interpolations, and the combination of genuine Pauline fragments from different letters.[5]

One of the disputed passages is 1 Thess 2:13–16. As F. C. Baur, the founder of the modern quest for the historical Paul, pointed out in the nineteenth century, this passage implies that the Thessalonians had been persecuted (though no opponents are identified in the letter), that Paul did not participate in the persecution of Judean Christians (though Paul admits that he did in Phil 3:6), that Jews were misanthropic (a later Gentile stereotype), and that Jerusalem had already been destroyed (thus a post-70 CE situation).[6] As a result, Baur and others conclude that Paul was not the author of this passage.[7] On the other hand, concluding that 1 Thess. 2:13–16 is an interpolation would eliminate a constituent element from the typical form of a Pauline letter described above: the discussion of theme A in the letter body—the faithfulness of the Thessalonian community despite some opposition—and thus undermine the integrity of the letter's structure. Because the structural analysis of 1 Thessalonians supports the authenticity of 2:13–16, we are leaving it in the text, but placing double brackets around it to indicate that some scholars regard it as an interpolation. And we have nuanced the translation so that it makes sense in the context of pre-70 CE intra-Judaic polemics.[8]

The Rhetorical Situation

A major theme in 1 Thessalonians is the harassment, perhaps even persecution, which Paul's followers encountered from their fellow citizens. Paul mentions this theme in the introductory thanksgiving period (1:6), expands on it in the letter body (2:14–16), and relates it to Timothy's visit (3:2–5). This harassment seems to have caught the Thessalonians off guard: they evidently did not expect to be persecuted for responding to the claim that Jesus was a powerful redeemer and, indeed, God's "son" from heaven (1:10), since such claims were not different in kind from those made about the redeemer figures of the mystery religions and the divinized heroes of the civic cult. Because they were unprepared for hostile responses from their neighbors, Paul feared that they might lose the courage of their new convictions. Since he could not return immediately, Paul dispatched Timothy from Athens to see how they were faring (3:1–2). After an anxious period of waiting, Timothy returned with a glowing report about the Thessalonians: they had both weathered the persecutions (3:3–4) and had not lost their confidence in Paul's message (3:6). The rhetorical tone of 1 Thessalonians is thus celebratory, offering consolation to the Thessalonians for their suffering, praise for their faithfulness despite harassment, and encouragement in the face of continued threats. Given the ever-present dangers facing them, Paul stresses "hope" as the chief virtue they need to persevere in the face of persecution (1:3; 5:8) and invokes the promise of the impending *parousia* (arrival of the Anointed Jesus) as the foundation for this hope. As a result, the theological tone of the letter is eschatological, appealing to the future to sustain the Thessalonians through a treacherous present.

The Ancient City of Thessalonica

According to the geographer Strabo, the city of Thessalonica (called Salonica today) was created c. 315 BCE when the Macedonian ruler Cassander unified a number of the prehistoric villages in the area and named the new seaport after his wife, Thessalonikeia, the daughter of King Philip II and half-sister of Alexander the Great.[9] Following the fourth Macedonian war (150–148 BCE), the Romans annexed Macedonia, Epirus, and Thessaly, established an administrative center in Thessalonica, and constructed the Via Egnatia from Apollonia eastward to Thessalonica.[10] Thessalonica was thus the capital of the Roman province of Macedonia and a collage of various ethnic groups when Paul first arrived in 49 or 50 CE.

The religious landscape of Thessalonica in Paul's time was a mixture of ancient Greek fertility gods like Dionysus, Aphrodite, and Demeter, and more recent redeemer gods associated with the mystery religions. The remains of a Serapeum (temple of the Egyptian god Serapis, equated with Asclepius who 'saved' one from illnesses) have been discovered to the west of the city center. Coins from the end of the first century CE suggest that the Phrygian cult of the Cabiri or "twin gods" (linked to Castor and Polydeuces/Pollux, the divinized sons of Tyndareus and referred to by the Greeks as "great gods") was also strong in Thessalonica, but in the form of a singular deity, Cabirus. A temple of the Cabiri has also been discovered on the nearby island of Samothrace.[11] The confluence of Greek fertility deities and Asian redeemer gods in Thessalonica generated a notion of individual salvation from the misfortunes of this life and the promise of an afterlife freed from eternal punishment or endless reincarnations.[12] Whether Paul's message offered the same hope of salvation in the afterlife for a community member who had died before the arrival of the *parousia* as that promised in the Thessalonian mysteries seems to lie behind the concern Paul addresses in 4:13–17.

A pattern is thus evident in 1 Thessalonians that will be repeated in other Pauline letters: Paul proclaims a message about the significance of Jesus that was framed in terms of a Hellenistic-Jewish religious context; after leaving Thessalonica, he learns either from oral reports or from questions directed to him from the community that his original message had been misunderstood or was under attack; this prompts Paul to respond to these questions and concerns with a letter that restates his message in terms of the Thessalonians' particular socio-historical context. Paul was thus the first to reflect on the hermeneutical problem: to say the same thing that the followers of Jesus were saying about him in Galilee and Syria, Paul must translate it into the cultural world of his followers in the Greco-Roman world of Thessalonica. Paul realized that his message must always be articulated in terms of the particular situation of his correspondents; and this fact is what makes Paul's authentic letters personal, rather than general epistles to no one in particular.

NOTES

1. See Robert W. Funk, "Saying and Seeing: Phenomenology of Language and the New Testament," *The Journal of Bible and Religion* XXXIV, 3 (July, 1966): 213.

2. Adolf Deissmann, *Bible Studies*, trans. A. Grieve (Edinburgh: T & T Clark, 1901), 3–59.

3. A. S. Hunt and C. C. Edgar, *Select Papyri*, vol. I (Cambridge, MA: Harvard University Press and London: William Heinemann Ltd., 1959), 286–87. See also John L. White, *Light from Ancient Letters*, 73.

4. Robert W. Funk, "The Apostolic *Parousia*: Form and Significance" in *Christian History and Interpretation: Studies Presented to John Knox*, ed. W. R. Farmer, C. F. D. Moule, and R. R. Niebuhr (Cambridge University Press, 1967), 249–68.

5. Winsome Munro, "Criteria for Determining the Authenticity of Pauline Letters: A Modest Proposal" in *Westar Institute Seminar Papers* (Fall 1998): 25–30.

6. Ferdinand Christian Baur, *Paul, the Apostle of Jesus Christ: His Life and Work, His Epistles and His Doctrine*, vol. 2, trans. A. Menzies (London: Williams and Norgate, 1876), 85–89.

7. For example, Birger A. Pearson, "1 Thessalonians 2:13–16: A Deutero-Pauline Interpolation," *Harvard Theological Review* 64 (1971): 79–94 and Daryl Schmidt, "1 Thess 2:13–16: Linguistic Evidence for an Interpolation," *Journal of Biblical Literature* 102 (1983): 269–79.

8. For the argument that this passage is authentic based on Paul's apocalyptic views, see Karl Paul Donfried, "Paul and Judaism: 1 Thessalonians 2:13–16 as a Test Case," *Interpretation* 38 (1984): 242–53.

9. Strabo, *Geography*. VII, frag. 21. See also Jack Finegan, *Light from the Ancient Past* (Princeton, NJ: Princeton University Press, 1946), 271.

10. M. Cary and H. H. Scullard, *A History of Rome Down to the Reign of Constantine*, 3rd ed. (New York: St. Martin's Press, 1975), 159–60.

11. See Karl Paul Donfried, "The Cults of Thessalonica and the Thessalonian Correspondence," *New Testament Studies* 31 (1985): 336–56 and Robert Jewett, *The Thessalonian Correspondence: Pauline Rhetoric and Millenarian Piety* (Philadelphia: Fortress Press, 1986), 118–32.

12. See Robert Turcan, *The Cults of the Roman Empire*, trans. A. Nevill (Oxford: Blackwell Publishers, 1996), 24–27.

Paul's Letter to the Thessalonians

1 Paul, Silvanus, and Timothy to those in Thessalonica who are called together by God our Creator and Benefactor and our lord Jesus, God's Anointed: divine favor and peace to you. [2]We always thank God for all of you, and have you in mind when we pray. [3]Before God, our Creator and Benefactor, we constantly recall your work of confident trust, your active love and your unwavering hope in [the coming of] our lord Jesus, God's Anointed. [4]Dear friends, it is clear to us that you are loved by God and are a special people. [5]Our world-transforming message did not come to you as mere rhetoric, but with the power and presence of God, and with unqualified conviction. You recognized accurately what kind of messengers we were when we were among you for your benefit. [6]And so, you became imitators of us and of the lord when you accepted our message, though under great stress, with the joy of God's presence and power. [7]Therefore, you have become, in turn, a model for all those in Macedonia and Greece who have put their confidence and trust in God. [8]Indeed, you have made our message about the lord resound not only throughout Macedonia and Greece, but everywhere your trust in God is so widely known that we don't need to mention it. [9]These reports about you demonstrate how effective our stay was

---

1:6 *imitators:* In typical rhetorical fashion, Paul introduces the first theme of this letter with a catchword, "imitators," which is then repeated in 2:14 when Paul elaborates on this theme in the letter body.

1:9 *our stay:* The second major theme is also introduced by a catchword, *eisodon,* literally meaning "entrance," though it refers to the entire period of Paul's initial visit to Thessalonica and not just to his arrival. As a result, it is translated here as "our stay (among you)." This catchword is repeated in 2:1 at the beginning of the letter body. The two themes of the letter body are thus discussed in reverse order from their introduction in the thanksgiving prayer: ABBA. (Introducing two issues and then discussing them in reverse order is referred to as *chiasm* because it looks like the X-shaped Greek letter *chi.*)

among you: how you have turned away from lifeless images in order to serve the living and real God [10]and to wait for God's "son" from heaven, whom God raised from among the dead, Jesus, who will rescue us from the condemnation that is sure to come.

2 For you know from your own experience, friends, that our stay among you was not without power, [2]but despite having just been assaulted and insulted in Philippi, as you know, God gave us the courage to speak God's world-transforming message to you in the face of great opposition. [3]For we are not motivated by error or by insincerity or by deceit, [4]but we have been authorized by God to spread this message. We speak, not in order to please people, but to please God who already knows our intentions. [5]For, as you also know, we never used flowery rhetoric nor pretense for personal gain–so help me God—[6]nor did we look for popular acclaim, either from you or from others—[7]although as envoys of God's Anointed we could have thrown our weight around! But we treated you gently like a nanny caring for her children. [8]We were so devoted to you that we were willing to share with you not only God's message but our own lives as well—that is how much your friendship meant to us. [9]For I'm sure you remember the stress and strain we endured as we worked night and day so as not to impose on anyone while we were sharing God's message with you. [10]You are eyewitnesses—and so is God—how we treated you who were persuaded by God's message with respect, fairness, and integrity. [11]So you can't deny that we cared for each one of you as if you were our own children, [12]prodding, encouraging, and coaxing you to live in a manner

---

1:10 *"son"*: Quotation marks are placed around *son* to indicate that this is a title of honor given upon the enthronement of Jesus in the heavens. Cf. Rom 1:4.
2:1 *For you know* is the conventional formula for beginning a discussion of the main themes in the body of a letter (often called "the disclosure formula").
2:7 *gently:* We have translated the variant reading *epioi,* "gently," rather than *nepioi,* "infants."

pleasing to God, who summons you into his own kingdom and splendor.

[[¹³For this reason we have stressed how thankful we are to God that when you heard what we had to say about God, you accepted it not as a human argument, but really as the wisdom of God which enlightens and energizes you who embrace it. ¹⁴So, you became imitators, friends, of those communities in Judea for whom Jesus is God's Anointed: you have been harassed by your fellow citizens the same way that they have been by theirs. ¹⁵For their fellow countrymen killed Jesus, our lord, and their own prophets, and expelled us. They are not doing what God intended but are harming all people ¹⁶by trying to prevent us from telling all the nations of the world that they too can be rescued from certain condemnation. In this way those [who oppose my message] miss the point completely. So, condemnation has utterly overtaken them.]]

¹⁷Since we are separated from you a short time, in person but not in our hearts, we eagerly yearn to see you again face to face. ¹⁸Indeed, we tried to return to you—I, Paul, tried more than once—but our plans were frustrated. ¹⁹Who will be our pride and joy and crowning glory when we meet Jesus our lord face to face, if not you? ²⁰Yes, you are truly our pride and joy!

3 Therefore, since I couldn't leave Athens, we decided ²to send Timothy, a dear friend and fellow advocate of our message about the Anointed, both to bolster you and to allay the threats to your confidence in God ³so that none of you would be shaken by these attacks. For you surely realized that we were in danger! ⁴Remember that we warned you when we were last with you that we might be persecuted, and that's what happened, as you know. ⁵When I could not stand to worry any longer, I sent Timothy to check on your faithfulness,

---

2:13–16 Scholars are divided over whether this passage is an interpolation. See the discussion in the Introduction to 1 Thessalonians.

for fear that you had been so shaken by these threats that our work had come to nothing. [6]But now Timothy has returned to us with a glowing report of your confidence in God and your love for us, emphasizing your affectionate feelings toward us and that you miss us as much as we miss you. [7]Therefore, the news about your faithfulness has cheered us up despite all our trials and tribulations [8]because we can cope if you remain committed to the lord's service. [9]For what offering can we give to God in return for all the joy you have given us? [10]And so we pray night and day that God will allow us to see you again in person and to supply what is lacking in your understanding of what it means to trust in God. [11]May God our Creator and Benefactor and Jesus our lord direct our path straight to you. [12]And may the lord inspire in you the same kind of unfailing and abundant friendship for one another and for others as we have for you, [13]so that your intentions may remain firm in complete integrity before our Creator and Benefactor at the triumphant arrival of Jesus our lord with all who belong to him.

4 Finally, friends, we ask you—we *implore* you—[to remember] how crucial it is for you who belong to Jesus our lord to live and to serve God as we taught you. You have started living in the right way; but you should do so even more consistently. [2]For you know that what we taught you was authorized by our lord, Jesus.

[3]So, concerning the virtuous life: God wants you to keep your distance from sexual immorality. [4]Each one of you should know how to treat his own wife with respect and honor [5]and

---

4:1 *we implore:* The Greek *parakaloumen,* "we implore (you)" is the typical term for introducing the section of ethical guidelines that follows the letter body. The section of ethical guidelines and advice is called the *paraenesis* and can include both topical discussions of ethical issues and short lists of virtues and vices.

4:3, 9, 13; 5:1 Paul discusses four ethical issues or *topoi* and introduces the last three with the Greek preposition *peri,* "concerning," followed by the genitive case. This is equivalent to "RE:" in a modern memorandum.

4:4 *wife:* The literal meaning of the Greek *skeuos* is "instrument" or "vessel," although it was also used metaphorically to refer to one's wife. The verb *ktast-*

not as a sexual object as do the nations who do not know God. [6]Nor should you offend or deceive your brother in sexual matters, because the lord is one who will see that justice is done in all such matters, as we clearly warned you before. [7]For our God has not called us to loose living but to a life of virtue. [8]Therefore, anyone who rejects this is not rejecting human advice but the God who breathes the spirit of goodness into you.

[9]Concerning your relationships with one another: I don't need to add anything to the God-given precept that you should love one another. [10]You are already practicing this precept in your dealings with your fellow believers in Macedonia, but we urge you, friends, to do this extravagantly. [11]As we've urged you before: live a quiet life, mind your own business, and support yourselves, [12]so that outsiders might respect you and you might be self-sufficient.

[13]Concerning those who have died, we don't want you to be uninformed: you shouldn't mourn as do those without hope. [14]Because if we believe "Jesus died and arose," so also God will bring with Jesus all those belonging to him who have died. [15]We can assure you of this by these prophetic words from the lord:

> we who are still alive when Jesus comes will not be given preference over those who have already died.

> [16]the lord himself will descend from heaven with a loud summons, with an archangel's shout and with the trumpet of God, then those who have already died and belong to the Anointed will ascend first; [17]then those of us who are still living will be caught up with them in the clouds to greet the lord in the air. And so we will be with the lord from then on.

[18]So you should encourage each other with these prophetic words.

---

hai, "to acquire or to possess," supports the metaphorical meaning: "to treat his own wife."

4:18 *these prophetic words:* The Greek suggests the notion of two oracular utterances in v. 15b and vv. 16–17. Thus we have translated the Greek *en tois logois toutois* as "these prophetic words."

5 Concerning the chronology of the great events to come: friends, you don't need to have [anything] written to you. ²Surely you know perfectly well that the day of the lord arrives like a thief in the night. ³When everyone expects peace and security, that's just when ruin strikes without warning, or [it is] like the sudden onset of birth contractions in a pregnant woman—no one can avoid such events. ⁴But you, friends, are not in the dark so that the day [of the lord] would catch you by surprise like a thief. ⁵Rather, you are enlightened people, a people of the day. We are not denizens of the night living in the dark. ⁶Therefore, let us not sleep through life as others do, but be fully awake and in control of ourselves. ⁷"Night-people" are always asleep and drunkards are never sober, ⁸but since we are "day-people" let us always be in control of our senses and let us protect ourselves with the armor of our confidence in God and our unselfish love for one another and with a helmet of the hope of our liberation. ⁹For God has not set us up for condemnation, but intends for us to be liberated through our lord Jesus, God's Anointed, ¹⁰who died for us so that—whether we have died or are still alive—we might live together with him. ¹¹Therefore, continue to encourage one another and to support each other as you have been doing.

¹²Next, we urge you, friends, to recognize those among you who are fellow missionaries and those who care for you as members of the lord's people and those who mentor you. ¹³You should highly respect them and love them for what they are doing. In short, cooperate freely with each other! ¹⁴We also plead with you, friends: caution the unruly, encourage those who lack confidence, help the weak, be patient with everyone.

5:1 *great events:* The fourth topic concerns the dating of end-time events: Paul contrasts two different words for "time" in Greek, *kairos,* unexpected life-changing events that cannot be dated by the calendar, with *chronos,* normal historical events that can be dated.

5:2 *day of the lord:* Paul classifies "the day of the lord" as a *kairos* event, and thus it cannot be dated by the calendar.

[15]Make sure that you don't retaliate against evil, but always seek the good for each other, even for outsiders.

[16]Always be joyous; [17]live with reverence; [18]be thankful in every circumstance, for this is how God intends for you to live as members of the people for whom Jesus is God's Anointed. [19]Don't suppress charismatic fervor. [20]Don't be condescending about prophesying, [21]but test everything. Hold onto what is good [22]and keep your distance from every form of evil.

[23]And now may the true God, the God of peace, fill you with goodness; and may you be fully prepared in body, mind, and spirit for the arrival of our lord, Jesus God's Anointed. [24]The one who calls you is completely trustworthy. [25]Friends, please pray for us. [26]Embrace each other.

[27]On the basis of my authority from the lord, I solemnly charge you to read this letter to all of our friends. [28]The favor of Jesus, God's Anointed, be with you.

Scripture Parallels

1:3	4 Macc 17:4
2:4	Jer 11:20; Prov 17:3
2:16	Gen 15:16
3:11	Judith 12:8 (LXX)
3:13	Zech 14:5
4:5	Jer 10:25; Ps 79:6
4:8	Ezek 36:27; 37:14
4:13	Wis 3:18
5:1	Wis 8:8
5:3	Isa 13:8; Jer 6:24
5:8	Isa 59:17; Wis 5:18; Job 2:9 (LXX)
5:14	Isa 57:15 (LXX); Prov 14:29 (LXX)

Pauline Parallels

1:1	Gal 1:1–5; 1 Cor 1:1–3; 2 Cor 1:1–2; Phlm 1–3; Phil 1:1–2; Rom 1:1–7
1:2–10	Gal 1:6–9; 4:12–20; 1 Cor 1:4–9; 2:1–5; 2 Cor 8:1–7; 9:1–5; Phlm 4–7; Phil 1:3–11; 3:17–21; Rom 1:8–15

2:1–8	1 Cor 4:14–21; 9:15–18; 2 Cor 4:1–6; 6:1–10; 7:2–4; 10:1–6; 12:14–18; Rom 16:17–20
2:9–12	1 Cor 4:8–13; 4:14–21; 9:1–14; 2 Cor 1:12–14; Phil 4:10–20
2:17–20	1 Cor 4:14–21; 16:5–9; 2 Cor 1:15–22; 2:12–13; 7:5–13; Phil 4:1–3; Rom 15:22–29
3:1–5	1 Cor 4:8–13; 2 Cor 1:3–11; 7:5–13; 11:21–29; Phil 4:10–20; Rom 8:31–39
3:6–10	2 Cor 1:3–11
3:11–13	1 Cor 1:4–9
4:1–8	1 Cor 1:10–17; 7:1–7; 7:32–35; 7:39–40; 14:37–40; 2 Cor 10:1–6; Phlm 8–14; Rom 12:1–2
4:9–12	1 Cor 1:3:4–7; Gal 5:13–15; Rom 12:9–21; 13:8–10
4:13–18	1 Cor 15:12–28; 15:15–58; 2 Cor 4:16–5:5; Phil 3:17–21
5:1–11	1 Cor 7:25–31; 16:13–14; 2 Cor 10:1–6; Phil 2:14–18; Rom 8:28–30; 13:11–14; 14:5–12
5:12–22	1 Cor 16:15–18; Rom 12:9–21
5:23–24	1 Cor 1:4–9
5:25	Phlm 21–22; Rom 15:30–33
5:26	1 Cor 16:19–20; 2 Cor 13:11–13; Phlm 23–24; Phil 4:21–22; Rom 16:3–16
5:27	1 Cor 16:21–22; Gal 6:11–17
5:28	Gal 6:18; 1 Cor 16:23–24; 2 Cor 13:14; Phlm 25; Phil 4:23

Galatia

There has been considerable scholarly discussion over the locale of the Galatians' gatherings. The *Galatai* originally were Celtic tribes that had pushed into the Balkans in 279 BCE. Three of those invading tribes crossed the Hellespont and settled near Ancyra (in north central Turkey) in 278/277 BCE. For the next ninety years they served as mercenaries to local rulers, gaining further plunder and land. After the Romans defeated them in 189 BCE, the Galatians served loyally under Roman rule. The Galatians soon adopted Hellenistic customs and accepted Romanization (especially among their aristocracy and wealthy urban elite). Augustus later created the Roman province of *Galatia* (which included Galatia, Pisidia, Isauria, Pamphylia, Lycaonia, Paphlogonia, and Pontus Galaticus). The debate among scholars centers around the geographical location of Galatia. Does it refer to the north central part of what is now Turkey or does it refer to the southern portion of the expanded Roman province? Does the mention of the cities of Iconium, Lystra and Derbe (Acts 14) support the latter location? Additionally some have argued that it is more conceivable for Jewish missionaries to follow a southern route. However, recent research has cast doubt on the historical reliability of Acts, especially if it reflects a second century perspective and agenda. Nor should the range of Jewish missionaries be arbitrarily restricted by later Christian documents. There is, moreover, archaeological evidence of Jewish presence in Asia Minor. Nothing in the letter to the Galatians directly supports one place over the other.

The Galatian question may be better approached from another point of view. If one asks what was the religious perspective out of which the Galatians saw their world, then the prominent cult of the Mother of the Gods becomes quite helpful. Throughout central Anatolia this cult prevailed. Paul's audience would have been quite familiar with the various devotions to the "Mountain Mother." Worshipped under many different names, the Mother of the Gods was often identified with a mountain overlooking a city or

Continued on next page

village under her protection. The Mother of the Gods was an enforcer deity, dealing justice and punishing the guilty. The Mountain Mother maintained protection over written records as well as graves by delivering curses to prevent transgressions. At major cult centers the Mother of the Gods was served by young men who, in the midst of their orgiastic rituals, castrated themselves. The cult to the Mother of the Gods reached far beyond central Anatolia. She was invited to Rome near the end of the Second Punic War (204 BCE) and functioned prominently in Roman propaganda. By the time of Paul's visit Roman coins in almost every city in western and central Asia Minor present her as a protective deity in the Roman image. In some ways one can say that the question of north or south Galatia falls as one learns of the far-spread devotion to the Mother of the Gods.

Paul's Correspondence to the Galatians

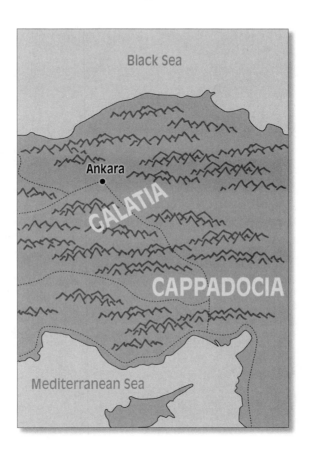

Galatia was a Roman province ranging from north central to south central Asia Minor.

Galatians

INTRODUCTION

Unlike his other correspondence Paul's letter to the Galatians begins on a disquieting note. After an initial salutation, invoking the benefits of God upon his audience, Paul registers his amazement at their abandonment of the world-transforming message that he had delivered to them (1:6). He quickly moves into a defense of his understanding of the message, detailing some incidents prior to his arrival in Galatia. He then returns to address the Galatians directly (3:1ff.) and offers them in the remainder of the letter the choice of living a life based on confidence in God or upon traditional religious practices. For Paul what is at stake is quite clear: a life of freedom, lived out of confidence in God or an existence still subject to the confining forces that dominate the present age.

Yet the situation was not that clear to the Galatians. Originally Paul had arrived in Galatia (see Cameo on Galatia, p. 37) and was well received, despite his illness (4:14). They had trusted the world-transforming message he delivered and had experienced the power and presence of God (3:1–13). Sometime after Paul left the gatherings of Galatia, other missionaries arrived and had some marked effect (1:6–7). Word about this development reached Paul and his letter attempts to address this new situation.

There has been much scholarly debate as to the identity and origins of these missionaries. In good rhetorical fashion Paul does not honor the opposition by mentioning their names or titles. Moreover, since we only have Paul's version of the situation, we must be cautious in deriving what the opposition may have proposed. Readers must work closely with the text.

By considering all the discrepancies, problems, and jumps in Paul's argument, as well as noting all the terms, images and metaphors that appear to be assumed as part of the discussion (such as "traditional religious practices," law, sons of Abraham, Moses—not mentioned but behind much of the argument, elements of the universe, power and presence of God, circumcision, feasts, world-transforming message, Jesus), we can begin to construct a profile of the unknown missionaries that had such an effect upon the Galatians' gatherings.

It would appear that upon their arrival in Galatia the missionaries made initial headway with the Galatians by following up on Paul's missionary initiative. Notice that neither Jesus nor the power and presence of God are a matter of dispute. Rather, what seems to be at issue is the connection of this foundation with "traditional religious practices." The missionaries apparently interpreted Paul's message and the Galatians' experience in light of Jewish tradition. Thus, they claimed that Jesus' "confidence in God" is a testament to his "faith," namely Judaism. Moreover, the initial presence of God experienced by the Galatians can be magnified and amplified within the fullness of the rich Jewish tradition. Jesus would fall into the category of Jewish heroes of whom Moses is the greatest. God's raising of Jesus would confirm not only the trust of Jesus but the worth of the tradition in which he lived.

To insure the retention of God's presence the Galatians would be encouraged to enter more fully into this ancient tradition, that is, into the law and Covenant. By observing the particular aspects of the tradition, they then can be assured that their life is virtuous and pleasing to God. Circumcision as well as keeping religious festivals would not be mere externals but indications of entering the eternal Covenant. This Covenant, moreover, was given not only to Moses but also to Abraham. And just as Abraham was once of the nations (see Cameo on the Nations, p. 14) and became the first Jew (through circumcision), so now the Galatians can do likewise. The Galatians can become the true sons of Abraham, heirs of the Eternal Covenant. Entering this Covenant would not be a regression into some provincial religion, but an entrance into the oldest and most powerful one. By accepting the message of Jesus the Galatians had already begun to turn to the true religion, to the universal Covenant of the Jews.

Why would the Galatians be swayed by the opposition's position? It is crucial for the modern reader to realize that what was "new" or "novel" in the ancient world was not considered in a positive light. Rather, in an honor/shame culture the matter of patrimony and lineage was paramount. The oldest tradition was seen as most desirable; it contained the heroes of excellence within it. We can see this, for example, in the Roman linkage of the emperor Augustus with the ancestor Aeneas. Second, traditions were seen as storehouses of power, which could be tapped by experts for the benefit of the many. Thus, these missionaries could open up the vast powers and rituals of the Jewish tradition for the Galatians. The Galatians would then be assured of the continuing access to the benefit flow from the Divine Benefactor. This was no theoretical matter. The entire ancient economy rested on the notion of divine benefits and favors. The sacrificial systems were set up to insure the maintenance of this benefit cycle. Therefore, access to the oldest tradition meant the ability to access the benefits needed to survive in the ancient world.

In addition, some scholars have argued that these missionaries might have been syncretists, who included some elements of the Galatians' former religious practices within their understanding of Judaism. The missionaries wanted to set the Galatians' original experience of Paul's message within the larger frame of current religious tradition. Whether or not this was the case, it is crucial to ask: what was the religious situation of the Galatian audience before Paul's arrival? Recently it has been argued that many of the specific issues of the letter can be clarified by the prevalent religious tradition within central Anatolia, the homeland of the Mother of the Gods. His audience would have been well versed in the various devotions to the Mountain Mother. Worshipped under many different names, the Mother of the Gods was often identified with a mountain overlooking a city or village under her protection. The Mother of Gods was an enforcer deity, dealing justice and punishing the guilty. The Mountain Mother maintained protection over written records as well as graves by delivering curses to prevent transgressions. At major cult centers the Mother of the Gods was served by young men who, in the midst of their orgiastic rituals, castrated themselves. The cult to the Mother of the Gods reached far beyond central Anatolia. She was invited to Rome near the end of the Second Punic War (204 BCE) and functioned prominently in Roman propaganda. By the time of Paul's visit Roman coins in almost every city in western and central Asia Minor present her as a protective deity in the Roman image.[1]

It is against such a predilection for a dominating religious tradition that Paul makes his case and offers a vision of two alternate ways of living. Immediately in the opening lines of the letter Paul makes it quite clear that he was "not appointed by any human authorities" (1:1), nor was his insight from God mediated through some human (1:12). His message to the Galatians is not a report that sustains the status quo; rather, it proclaims deliverance into the new world (6:15) already underway in what God has done for Jesus (1:4). Paul's vision, in brief, is discontinuous. What God has done has signaled the end of the "present evil age" (1:4). Paul envisions a future opened in freedom, not a present linked to the dominating past. The unnamed missionaries, on the other hand, work out of a model of continuity, which prizes linkage with the powers and glories of the ancestral past.

Paul's argument throughout Galatians bears the note of radical discontinuity. Consider how he uses terms in contrast and opposition. This is not unusual in ancient rhetoric. But by observing how Paul constellates the terms he uses, we can begin to grasp his particular angle of argument. His contrasts are quite extensive: human/divine, temporal/eternal, human approval/divine favor, traditional religious practices/confidence in God, mediators/one God, uncircumcised/circumcised, the nations/Jews, old identity/new identity, written/oral, curse/blessing, promise/law, minor/adult, Jew/Greek, slave/freeborn, male/female, dominated/liberated, son of a free woman/son of a slave woman, Mount Sinai/ heavenly Jerusalem, life of subjection/life of freedom, self-serving desires/living in God's power, present evil age/new world. It is crucial to see that Paul's opposition would not see these terms necessarily in contrast. Rather, they actually could accommodate both sides of most of these terms within the dimensions of their ancient framework. It is Paul's apocalyptic insight of a divine breakthrough, ushering in the new age, which gives him the impetus to see such words in such stark contrast.

Paul's Breakthrough

After taking the Galatians to task for abandoning the message he delivered to them, as well as rejecting any different message, Paul begins to make his argument with what appear to be personal remarks (1:10–2:21). He reiterates that he has not received his insight from any tradition or teacher. He then gives his audience the only direct information we have from him about how he understands his personal breakthrough.

Paul describes his former behavior as a practicing Jew. In his estimation he went beyond most of his contemporaries in the observance of Jewish traditions. Saying that he was "notably zealous" for his ancestral traditions supports his remarks in Phil 3:5–6. As a Pharisee Paul's concerns over purity matters would have had their basis in his understanding of the purity and integrity of the God of Israel. His harassment of communities of Jesus believers may have come from the fact that some early Jesus communities (Syrian) were celebrating the death of Jesus as a hero and, in so doing, were invoking the God of Israel. From Paul's perspective such an association of God with a criminal who had been shamefully executed is tantamount to blasphemy. His concern for the integrity of God may well have fueled his attempts to wipe these communities out. Beyond this extrapolation from Pharisaic concerns, there is little that can be known.

Moreover, what happened to Paul that made him change his mind is also based on his fragmentary remarks. Paul characterizes what happened to him as a prophetic experience. He uses traditional prophetic language to describe what he sees as a prophetic call ("when the One who designated me before I was born and commissioned me to be an envoy"). Paul never saw himself as a "convert" as some would say today. He never stopped being a Jew (cf. Rom 9:3), although he has moved beyond his Pharisaic self-understanding. Instead, he takes up the vision of the Jewish prophets in their call to the nations. It could be said that what had actually changed was Paul's vision of God. Somehow his vision of God's integrity was transformed by seeing what God had done for Jesus. In accepting this shamed criminal the God of Israel had taken an outrageous step. God had accepted the impure. From that changed understanding of God, Paul concludes that a new chapter of God's action has begun. Paul sees his task as announcing this vision. Because God had accepted this shamed nobody, Paul could understand that his mission was to go to those nations whom the Jews, generally speaking, regarded as morally inferior peoples and thus at a distinct religious disadvantage. Paul had undergone a paradigm shift in his understanding of God and the nations (see Cameo on the Nations, p. 14).

Jerusalem and Antioch

Moving beyond the account of his personal breakthrough, Paul mentions his two visits to Jerusalem. He does this to establish that his message was not beholden even to the legendary leaders of the Jesus movement. His first visit came three years after his pivotal insight; it appears to be short and limited to meeting with Cephas and James. His second visit, fourteen years later, seems to reflect a more formal situation.

Accompanied by Barnabas and Titus, Paul privately communicated to the leaders of the Jerusalem community to make sure that they do not miss the meaning of his work among the nations (2:2). There evidently were others at the meeting who demanded that the inclusion of the nations into fellowship entailed full initiation into the traditions of Judaism. Paul asserts not only that the leaders did not require the circumcision of Titus but also they actually agreed that Paul's mission was to the nations and theirs to "the circumcised" (2:9). From Paul's recounting the only condition in this agreement was the injunction that the poor of Jerusalem be remembered (2:10).

It is later at Antioch that it becomes clear that not everyone understood the Jerusalem agreement in the same way. Upon his arrival in Antioch, Cephas shares the table fellowship with people from the nations. When representatives of James appeared on the scene, many of the Jewish followers of Jesus, who had been eating with the nations (including Cephas and Barnabas), began to eat at separate tables in order to maintain purity requirements. Paul perceived this action as duplicitous and called Cephas to account (2:14–17). It is here that Paul raises the critical point about being acceptable to God. Drawing upon his God-given insight and experience with the nations, Paul contends that divine acceptance comes not from reliance on traditional religious practices but from confidence in God like that of Jesus, God's Anointed (2:16; see Cameo on Galatians 2:16, p. 65). It is significant that Paul does not indicate whether his argument carried the day. His silence on the matter strongly suggests that he lost. Indeed, his later movement into territories outside of Antioch would also appear to confirm this. Nevertheless, Paul uses only selected portions of his past in order to establish his argument for the Galatians' ears. He attempted to counter what the opposition may have argued before the Galatians, namely, that they represented the proper way of entering into a relationship with the traditions and God of Israel. Paul's experience ran counter to the argument of continuity. Rather, his God-given breakthrough, along with the Jerusalem leaders' acceptance of his mission to the nations, argued in support of his understanding of the entailments of his message.

Addressing the Galatians

Paul directly confronts the Galatians with a series of rhetorical questions (3:1–5; see Cameo on Diatribe, p. 257). Inductively working as he often does in his correspondence, Paul tries to get the Galatians to remember the basis of their experience of God's presence and power. He then brings in the figure of Abraham. The choice of Abraham was quite strategic. It may well have been part of the opposition's argument, for Abraham in Jewish tradition stood for the archetypal figure of proselyte conversion. Here was the legendary non-Jew who heard the call of God and entered into a covenant with God. Indeed, the sign of his entering the covenant was circumcision (Genesis 17).

Paul chose to interpret the Abraham tradition in another fashion. First, he focuses (3:6) upon Gen 15:6, stressing the confident trust of Abraham, not his circumcision. Second, in personifying Jewish scripture as announcing beforehand God's promise, Paul brings in the entailments of blessing and curse in the Covenantal tradition. The oral promise plays against the written tradition that details the requirements of observing the law. Those who cannot honor all that is required incur a curse. Paul has begun to spin out the two possibilities of existence (already intimated in 2:16) for the Galatians. In 3:13 Paul further displays his rhetorical finesse by tying the death of Jesus with the written curse of the law ("Anyone who is crucified is accursed"). From Paul's perspective the shame-filled execution of Jesus literally embodied the curse written in the law. In fact, as if in reverse magic, the blessing promised to Abraham comes about precisely through this one who meets his end in trust (3:14, cf. 3:22; 4:4–5). Both Abraham and Jesus demonstrate to the Galatians that unconditional trust is the acceptable way of life.

Paul still had to deal with the question of the status of the law. By distinguishing God's promises from the law, Paul was able to argue that the law not only came later (3:17) but also was temporary. Instead of an eternal source of God's power, the tradition of the law is characterized at best as a means for restraining undisciplined behavior. Paul even diminishes its capacity to that of the slave accompanying children to school (3:24). Such an argument was probably aimed at the opposition's claim that the law delivered by Moses had an eternal validity. Notice that in order to further downplay the importance of the law Paul never mentions Moses, the Lawgiver, by name. Instead, Paul countered with the Galatians' own experience of liberation. Their baptismal song ("no longer Jew or Greek, no longer slave or freeborn, no longer 'male and female'") reiterated their experience of trust in God. They have already become Abraham's offspring, adopted children of God. Having attained genuine adulthood, there is no reason for return to some former, pediatric condition (3:25; 4:7, 9).

The Choices before the Galatians

In order to underline the two options facing the Galatians' decision, Paul spells out in allegory the difference between living according to the promise and living under the curse (4:21–31). For many readers this allegory has been quite troublesome. How was it possible for Paul to link Hagar, the slave woman, with Mount Sinai and then Jerusalem? Indeed, if this was the rhetorical flourish of his argument, how can Paul conclude on such an ambiguous note? In fact, once the cult of the Mother of the Gods is recalled, the association makes for a compelling argument. The connection to Mt. Sinai comes from the Anatolian association of mountains with the Mother goddess. But Paul has reduced the Mountain Mother to a slave figure. At the same time the city of Jerusalem would come under "her" protection. Such an imaginative combination would have been understandable to a Galatian audience. Paul thus can ask: Will the Galatians align themselves with the figure of the slave woman, embodying the fate of a conquered nation, or with the heavenly "mother Jerusalem," representing a life of freedom?

He exhorts his listeners to remain in the freedom brought about through God's Anointed (5:1) and urges them not to be persuaded by those who would advocate religious practices that are part of the passing age. The very evidence of such freedom is found in the selfless love they show one another. The very presence and power of God, not the requirements of the law's tradition, will guide their discernment. Paul then concludes the letter with a final list of encouragements (6:1–10).

In 6:11–17 Paul interrupted the writing of his scribe and took a pen in hand. He adds his own brief but pungent remarks, decrying the intentions of those who would advocate the Galatians' circumcision. Paul declares in 6:15 that a new age has occurred, transcending the usual categories of the age that is ending. Such an insight about the new condition of human existence will be picked up with a new metaphorical play in 2 Cor 5:16–21.

NOTE

1. For the groundbreaking work on this insight see: Susan Elliott, *Cutting Too Close for Comfort: Paul's Letter to the Galatians in Its Anatolian Cultic Context* (JSNTSup 248; London/New York: T & T Clark, 2008).

Paul's Letter to the Galatians

1 Paul, an envoy, not appointed by any human authorities nor by any individual but by Jesus, God's Anointed, and by God, Creator and Benefactor, who raised Jesus from among the dead, [2]and from all my associates, to the communities [of the Anointed] in Galatia. [3]May favor and genuine peace from God our Great Benefactor and from our lord Jesus, God's Anointed, be yours. [4]In accordance with God's purpose to rescue us from the present evil age, Jesus devoted his life to free us from our sinful fate. [5]Highest praise to God whose new world never ends! Amen!

[6]I'm amazed by how quickly you have abandoned the one who called you by the favor of God's Anointed and have embraced an entirely different message. [7]There is no other world-transforming message, but there are people who are confusing you and want to pervert the truth about God's Anointed.

[8]Even if one of us, or for that matter a messenger from heaven, were to advocate a message different from the one we delivered—they must be rejected and shunned! [9]We told you before and now I repeat it: anyone who champions a message

---

1:1–5 This is a standard letter opening for Paul.

1:2 *Galatia:* See Cameo on Galatia, p. 37.

1:6 *I'm amazed* . . . Paul dramatically changes what would have been the expected thanksgiving. See Introduction.

1:8 *messenger from heaven:* In Greek the word is *angelos*. It has been traditionally translated as "angel."

1:8, 9 *They must be rejected and shunned.* The Greek reads literally "Let a curse fall on them." The use of *anathema* (curse) was a public way of shaming and ostracism. Paul is delivering a curse on those who would distort the world-transforming message. Such curse language would have been familiar to the Galatian audience. The Mother of the Gods would deliver curses as a preventive caution to protect followers, graves, and documents.

other than the one you heard from us—they must be rejected and shunned!

[10]Am I now trying to win a popularity contest, or to win God's approval? If I were still looking for human approval, I would not be the Anointed's slave.

[11]Let me make it clear, friends, the message I announced does not conform to human expectations. [12]I say this because it was not transmitted to me by anyone nor did anyone teach it to me. Rather, it came to me as an insight from God about Jesus as God's Anointed.

[13]Surely you've heard of my own behavior as a practicing Jew, how aggressively I harassed God's new community, trying to wipe it out. [14]I went way beyond most of my contemporaries in my observance of Judaism, and became notably zealous about my ancestral traditions.

[15]However, when the One, who designated me before I was born and commissioned me to be an envoy, surprising all human expectations, chose to make his son [16]known through me with the intent that I would proclaim God's world-transforming news to the nations, I did not rush off to consult with anyone. [17]Neither did I set out for Jerusalem to get the approval of those who became envoys for God's Anointed before I did. Instead, I left for Arabia and afterward returned to Damascus.

[18]Then, three years later I went up to Jerusalem to get acquainted with Cephas, and I stayed with him for two full weeks. [19]I did not meet any of the Anointed's other envoys except James, our lord's brother. [20]*What I am writing to you is not a lie, so help me God!* [21]Afterwards I traveled to the regions of Syria and Cilicia. [22]The communities in Judea for whom Jesus is God's Anointed had no idea what I looked like. [23]They knew

---

1:13–16 Here we have information about Paul's earlier life as well as his perspective on his new prophetic understanding. Also note: Phil 3:1b–6. See Introduction and Cameo on What Happened to Paul, p. 149.
1:17 *Arabia* refers to the Nabataean Kingdom, whose capital was Petra.

me only by reputation: "The one who used to harass us is now advocating 'the faith' that he once tried to wipe out." ²⁴And so they praised God because of me.

2 Fourteen years later I returned to Jerusalem with Barnabas and took Titus along. ²I went in response to divine direction. There I expressly communicated in private to those who were reputed to be leaders of the Jerusalem assembly the world-transforming message that I preach to the nations so that those leaders would not fail to grasp the point of the race I've been running. ³In fact, they did not require my companion Titus, though a Greek, to be circumcised. ⁴But some, pretending friendship, infiltrated the meeting to undermine our freedom in God's Anointed, Jesus, and to enslave us again. ⁵However, we did not cave in to their demands for a moment, for we were determined to preserve the truth of God's world-transforming message for you Galatians.

⁶In fact, those who were reputed to be leaders—it makes no difference to me what they were, since God does not pay attention to reputation—the reputed leaders added nothing to what I had to say. ⁷On the contrary, they recognized that God had entrusted me with the task of announcing God's world-transforming message to the uncircumcised, just as Peter had been entrusted with taking it to the circumcised. ⁸For it was evident that the God who worked through Peter as envoy to the circumcised worked through me as envoy to the rest of the world. ⁹When they realized that God had given me this special role, James, Cephas and John, the reputed pillars [of the Movement] extended the right hand of fellowship to Barnabas and me and agreed that we should go to the

---

2:1–10 Many scholars equate the meeting presented in Acts 15 with Paul's account of the meeting in Jerusalem. However, there are numerous discrepancies between them. These problems are not aided by the strong probability that the Acts account comes from a second-century hand. The unnamed infiltrators are often linked with the representatives of James in 2:12. If this is so, they must have had a very different take on what happened at the meeting.

nations and they to the circumcised. ¹⁰Their only condition was that we remember the poor—something I was eager to do.

¹¹Nonetheless, when Cephas came to Antioch, I confronted him publicly because he was clearly in the wrong. ¹²Before representatives of James came to Antioch, Cephas would eat with those from the nations. But when they arrived, he avoided and kept his distance from those people because he feared those who were advocating circumcision. ¹³In turn, the rest of the Jewish followers also began to waffle, with the result that even Barnabas was carried away by their duplicity. ¹⁴But when I saw they were behaving in a way that was inconsistent with the meaning of God's world-transforming message, I challenged Cephas in front of the whole group. I said:

> If it is all right for you, a Jew, to live like somebody from the nations and not practice Jewish customs, how can you possibly insist that people from the nations adopt Jewish practices? ¹⁵We may be Jews by birth and we may look at people of the nations as ignorant and corrupt, ¹⁶but we now see that no one becomes acceptable to God by relying on traditional religious practices. We gain this acceptance only through a confidence in God like that of Jesus, God's Anointed. So we put our confidence in God along with the Anointed, Jesus, in order to be acceptable to God based on a confidence like that of God's Anointed, rather than by relying on traditional religious practices. The truth of the matter is "no one will be acceptable to God" on the basis of traditional religious practices. ¹⁷If it then turns out that in our desire to be acceptable to God in the way that the Anointed was, we are regarded as ignorant and corrupt, does that mean that God's Anointed is

---

2:10 *the poor:* The meaning of "the poor" is debated. Was "the poor" a name for the Jerusalem community of Jesus followers? or was it a reference to the needy members of that community? Was this collection of money understood as a gesture of unity, the essential equality of Jews and the nations before the One God, both by the Jerusalem community and Paul, or did only Paul see it in this way?
2:12 The situation turns on the matter of the purity rules of table fellowship.
2:16 See Cameo on Galatians 2:16, p. 65.

responsible for turning us into ignorant and corrupt people? Of course not!

[18]The point is, if I now endorse what I previously rejected, then I am demonstrating that I have no integrity. [19]In fact, my old identity, defined by religious customs, passed away, so that a new God-given identity could come to life. I was crucified with the Anointed. [20]The person I used to be no longer lives. God's Anointed lives in me; and the bodily life I now live, I live by the same confident trust in God that the "son of God" had. He loved me and gave up his life for my benefit.

[21]I do not set aside God's generosity as if it didn't matter [as some do]. If acceptance by God comes about through traditional religious observances, then God's Anointed died for no reason!

3 You clueless Galatians! Who has cast an evil eye on you, putting you under a spell? Your own eyes saw Jesus, God's Anointed, graphically portrayed on a cross. [2]Tell me this: Did you experience God's presence and power by relying on traditional religious practices or by being convinced by what you heard? [3]How stupid can you be? Do you really think that what was begun by God's presence and power can be completed by a merely earthly life? [4]Has everything you experienced meant nothing to you? Surely it meant something! [5]Is the one, who empowers and works miracles among you, able to do so because you rely on traditional religious practices or because you are convinced by the message you heard?

[6]You're in the same situation as Abraham. [As scripture says]: "Abraham put his trust in God, and God counted that the right thing to do." [7]From this you ought to draw the conclusion that Abraham's heirs are those born of confidence in

---

3:1–5 The series of rhetorical questions, sharply delivered, is indicative of *diatribal* speech (see Cameo on Diatribe, p. 257). As is typical of Paul, he works inductively, attempting to get his listeners to remember their experience.

God. [8]Indeed, scripture anticipated what is happening right now, namely that God acknowledges that the nations are right to put their confidence in God. Scripture announced this beforehand to Abraham when it says, "Because of you all the nations will be blessed." [9]For that reason those who put their confidence in God are blessed just like Abraham.

[10]On the other hand, whoever relies on traditional religious practices is under a curse, because it is written, "Everyone who does not honor all the things written in the book of the law by observing them is accursed." [11]It is clear that no one is acceptable to God by relying on traditional religious practices. As scripture says: "The one who lives on the basis of confidence in God gets it right." [12]But the religious practices spelled out in the book of the law are not derived from confidence in God; so it is written, "Those who observe its requirements will have to live by them." [13]God's Anointed freed us from the curse of subjection to the law, by becoming a curse for us, since it is written, "Anyone who is crucified is accursed." [14]This was done so that Abraham's blessing might come to the nations by belonging to the Anointed Jesus, and so that we might receive the promise of God's presence and power through putting our unconditional trust in God.

[15]My friends, I'll use an example from daily life: once a person's last will is recorded, no one else is able to annul or alter it. [16]Now the promises of inheritance were made to Abraham "and to his offspring." Scripture does not say, "and to offsprings," as though there were many of them, but it says,

---

3:8 Paul personifies the Jewish scriptures. The sacred scroll speaks to her listeners and indicates that the tradition can be understood in terms of promise or curse. Personification was another element in diatribal discourse. The use of curse in the cult of the Mother of the Gods would have echoes here.

3:13 Paul creatively connects the crucified Jesus with the written curse of Deuteronomy. By reading the verse from Deuteronomy against the image of the one "graphically portrayed on a cross" (3:1) Paul makes two points. Jesus has become literally a curse (cf. 2 Cor 5:21). Second, since God has accepted this crucified one, there is a movement beyond the curse. Thus Paul can move to the blessing that surprisingly emerges out of that cursed condition.

"and to your offspring" in the singular which refers to God's Anointed. [17]Here is what I mean: the commitment to Abraham, validated by God, is not something invalidated 430 years later when the law came, as though God reneged on the promise made earlier. [18]After all, if that inheritance were grounded in the law, then it would no longer be based on a promise. But God gave it as a gift to Abraham by way of a promise.

[19]Then why the need for the law? It was provided to restrain our undisciplined behavior until the arrival of the offspring to whom the inheritance was promised. The law was transmitted by divine messengers through a human mediator. [20]But a mediator implies that more than one was involved. [But God alone made the promise,] since God is one.

[21]Does this mean the law is opposed to God's promises? Absolutely not! If there were a law that had the power to create life, then our acceptance by God would indeed be based on the law. [22]But the scripture confined everything under the seductive power of corruption, in order that the promise that has come to fruition in Jesus the Anointed's complete confidence in God might be extended to those who share the same confidence. [23]Now before this kind of confidence in God arrived, we were under the surveillance of the law, held in bondage until the awaited disclosure of such confidence.

[24]In effect, then, the law served as our disciplinarian until God's Anointed came, so that we would become acceptable to God on the basis of our compete confidence in God. [25]Now that this mature confidence in God can be ours, we no longer have need for a disciplinarian. [26]Indeed you are all now God's adult offspring through the kind of confidence exemplified by God's Anointed, Jesus. [27]So, everyone of you who has been baptized into solidarity with God's Anointed has become invested with the status of God's Anointed. [28]You are no longer

---

3:24 Paul utilizes the metaphor of a slave who accompanied children to school.
3:28 This may well be a baptismal formula or song known to the Galatians. It celebrates a transcendence of the normal social and political categories.

Jew or Greek, no longer slave or freeborn, no longer "male and female." Instead, you all have the same status in the service of God's Anointed, Jesus. [29]Moreover, if you now belong to God's Anointed, that also makes you Abraham's offspring and—as promised—his heirs.

4 Let me put it this way: An heir who is still a minor, even though destined to inherit the whole estate, is no better off than a menial servant, [2]but remains under the care of overseers and household managers until the time set by the father. [3]It is the same with us; when like children we knew no better, we were dominated by the cosmic powers that controlled human fate. [4]However, when the time for growing up arrived, God's "son" was sent into the world, born of a woman, subject to the Jewish law, [5]in order to emancipate those who were under the law, so that we might become God's "children" through adoption. [6]Now because you are adopted, God sent into your hearts the same filial attitude toward God that was in Jesus, that can call God, "Abba! Father!" [7]So as a result, you are no longer menial servants, but through what God has done you have become adopted as "children" and that means heirs.

[8]In the past, when you had no knowledge of God, you were dominated by powers that were not really divine. [9]Now that you know God, or rather, God knows you, how can you return to those impotent and impoverished cosmic powers, let alone wish to be their menial servants again? [10]For example, you are still involved in observing days and months, seasons and years, as if that determined your fate! [11]I'm afraid my efforts on your behalf have been a waste of time.

4:5 In the Roman world adoption would have meant that the one adopted had the same rights and privileges as the biological heir. It does not imply second class status.

4:9–10 *cosmic powers . . . seasons and years:* The ancient calendars (whether solar or lunar) mapped the mythic course of time and space. The keeping of festivals allowed people to participate in the major course and rhythm of the universe. Even the Jewish calendar would honor the order set by God.

¹²I plead with you, my friends, to become like me, because I became like you [as one outside the law]. You did not shun me then, ¹³for as you recall, it was while I was ill that I first delivered God's world-transforming message to you. ¹⁴Although my illness was trying for you, you neither disdained nor scorned me; instead you welcomed me as God's own messenger, as you would the Anointed Jesus himself.

¹⁵What happened then to that warm endorsement you gave me? I can testify that if you could have, you would have plucked out your own eyes and given them to me. ¹⁶Have I now become your enemy by telling you the truth? ¹⁷Others are paying you plenty of attention, but not for your own good; they want to keep you away [from me], so that you will pay attention only to them. ¹⁸It's always good to be well regarded in a good cause—and not only there when I'm with you. ¹⁹My dear children, I'm having labor pains all over again with you, waiting until God's Anointed is formed in you! ²⁰I only wish I could be there with you now and could soften my tone of voice. I am at my wits' end about you!

²¹Those of you who want to live under law, tell me: Don't you hear what the law says? ²²Scripture says that Abraham had two sons, one by a slave woman and the other by a free woman. ²³The difference was that the son of the slave was born naturally, the son of the free woman through God's promise. ²⁴This is all allegorical: these women represent two

---

4:14 *my illness:* Paul's illness could well have been a reason for the Galatians to reject him and his message. He would not convey the appearance of a successful missionary.

4:21–31 See Introduction. The notion of a heavenly *metropolis* has roots in both Greek and Jewish thought. The Greeks often speculated on the ideal community while Jewish apocalyptic entertained the possibility of a renewed community coming in the future from the creative hand of God. Moreover, at this time certain key cities served as metropolitan hubs for surrounding territories. Rome, of course, would be the primary instance. More specifically, Paul is playing upon the Galatians' association of mountains with protecting goddesses. Here Paul is subverting the honorable connection of the Mother goddess with a known mountain by using the slave figure of Hagar. Paul links Hagar to Mt. Sinai, an association unknown in Jewish speculation.

covenants. The one from Mount Sinai, who bears slave children, corresponds to Hagar. [25]This Hagar is Mount Sinai in Arabia; but she also corresponds to the present Jerusalem; she is in slavery with her children. [26]In contrast, it's the heavenly Jerusalem that is free—that's the one who is our mother. [27]In fact, scripture says:

> Celebrate, you barren woman without children,
> break out into shouting, you without labor pains,
> because the barren woman will have more children
> than does the woman with a husband.

[28]Now you, friends, are just like Isaac, you are children born by God's promise. [29]But just as it was back then, so too now: the child conceived naturally tries to harass the one conceived by God's power. [30]Yet, what does scripture say? "Expel the slave woman and her son; because the slave woman's son will not share the inheritance with the free woman's son." [31]The conclusion, my friends, is that we are not children of the slave woman but of the free woman.

5 God's Anointed set us free so that we could live free; so stand your ground, and do not be subject again to the yoke of slavery.

[2]Now look! I, Paul, am telling you: if you get circumcised, God's Anointed can't do anything for you. [3]I tell you as emphatically as I can once again: every person who gets circumcised will have to observe the law in its entirety. [4]You've cut yourself off from the Anointed, you who want to be accepted by God through relying on the law. You have deprived yourselves of God's great gift. [5]We, on the other hand, are the ones who by the power of God and on the basis of a complete confidence in God are looking forward to the consummation of our hope. [6]For those who belong to God's Anointed Jesus, neither the status of circumcision nor the lack of it makes any difference; only confidence in God made effective through love matters.

[7]You were running in the right direction. Who impeded you from accepting the truth? [8]That bad advice did not come from the one who first called you. [9]Remember the proverb, a little bit of leaven corrupts the whole batch of dough. [10]Our lord makes me confident that you will not disagree with my view. In any case, those stirring up trouble among you will have to answer for it, whoever they are. [11]As for me, my friends, if I were actually still advocating circumcision, why am I still being harassed? For in that case the scandal of the cross is removed. [12]I wish that those who stir you up over circumcision would go all the way themselves and have everything cut off!

[13]On the other hand, friends, you were called to a life of freedom. Don't use your freedom as a license for self-indulgence but, out of love, serve one another. [14]After all, the whole law is summed up in one injunction: "You are to love your neighbor as yourself." [15]But if you bite and nip at each other, watch out that you don't eat each other up.

[16]Here's my advice: be guided by the presence of God's power, and do not give into sensual desires. [17]The impulse to be self-serving works against what God's power and presence inspire, and God's power and presence work against the impulse to be self-serving. These two are opposed to each other in such a way as to prevent you from doing what you want to do. [18]If you are guided by God's power and presence, you are not restrained by the leash of the law. [19]The results of giving in to self-serving desires are obvious: sexual immorality, moral corruption, flagrant indecency, [20]idol worship, sorcery, bitter hostility, violent conflict, jealousy, fits of anger, selfish ambition, divisiveness, factionalism, [21]envy, drunkenness, orgies, and other such vices. I warn you again, just as I did before: people who engage in such activities will not inherit God's empire.

5:16–23 The lists of vices and virtues are a commonplace in the ancient world.

[22]The evidence that God's power is present among us is seen in our selfless love, joyous demeanor, and genuine peace, our long-suffering patience, warm-heartedness, and moral integrity, our trustworthiness, [23]gentleness, and self-control. There is no law against such virtues. [24]Those who belong to God's Anointed, Jesus, have crucified their former way of life along with its passions and desires. [25]If God's power has given us life, we should live in accordance with God's power. [26]Let's not have any swelled heads, name-callers or backstabbers among us.

6 Friends, if someone is found to have strayed off course in some way, you, who really experienced God's power and presence, must gently get that person back on track. And at the same time look out for yourselves so that you also won't be tempted.

[2]Shoulder each other's loads, and in this way you will carry out the "law of God's Anointed."

[3]Indeed, if people think they're something special when they're not, they are deluding themselves. [4]You should be brutally honest about your own conduct, and then you will keep your boasting only to yourself and not impose it on somebody else.

[5]We all must carry our own load.

[6]When you receive instruction, you must give a share of your worldly goods to your teacher.

[7]Don't deceive yourselves: God cannot be sneered at. As everyone knows, "People reap what they sow."

[8]If you sow to sustain your earthly life, you will from that earthly life reap corruption, but if you sow for a God-empowered life you will from that power reap unending life.

[9]Don't give up on doing the right thing; the day will come when we'll reap our harvest, so don't despair.

[10]In conclusion, as long as we have the opportunity, we should keep doing what's right for the benefit of all, and espe-

cially for those with whom we share our confidence and trust in God.

[11]p.s. (Notice how large the letters are when I write to you in my own hand!) [12]Those who are pressuring you to be circumcised seek only to make themselves look good and then only to avoid being harassed for the Anointed's cross. [13]These advocates of circumcision do not observe the law themselves, yet they want you to get circumcised so they can take pride in your altered flesh. [14]As for me, I absolutely refuse to take pride in anything except the cross of our lord, Jesus, God's Anointed—the same cross that crucified this world for me and me for this world. [15]Because being circumcised or not being circumcised does not matter; what matters is a new world.

[16]Peace and mercy upon those who lead their lives by this principle, as well as on the Israel of God.

[17]From now on, don't give me any more grief! I have the scars of Jesus on my body.

[18]May the favor of our lord, Jesus, God's Anointed, be yours, friends. Amen!

6:15 *new world:* The Greek (*ktisis*) refers to a new foundation, such as a new settlement or city. It also is used in the Septuagint to refer to the act of creation. See 2 Cor 5:16–21 where Paul expands on this image, playing out the notion of a new regime.

Scripture Parallels

1:15	Isa 49:1
2:1ff.	Acts 15
2:6	Deut 10:17
2:16	LXX Ps 142(3):2
3:6	Gen 15:6
3:8	Gen 12:3
3:10	Deut 27:26; 28:58
3:11	Hab 2:4
3:12	Lev 18:5

3:13	Deut 21:23
3:16	Gen 13:15; 17:8; 24:7
3:17	Exod 12:40
3:19	Lev 26:46;
3:28	Gen 1:27
4:6	Mark 14:36
4:22	Gen 16:15; 21:2, 9
4:27	Isa 54:1
4:30	Gen 21:10
5:12	Deut 23:1
5:14	Lev 19:18
6:1	Matt 18:15
6:7	Job 4:8; Prov 22:8

Pauline Parallels

1:1–5	1 Thess 1:1; 1 Cor 1:1–3; 2 Cor 1:1–2; Phlm 1–3; Phil 1:1–2; Rom 1:1–7
1:4	1 Thess 1:10; Rom 12:2
1:5	Rom 16:27
1:6	2 Cor 11:4
1:6–12	1 Thess 2:1–8
1:7	Gal 5:10; 2 Cor 11:13
1:13–14	1 Cor 15:9; 2 Cor 11:21b–23; Phil 3:4–6; Rom 11:1
1:15–16	1 Cor 9:1; 1 Cor 15:8–9; 2 Cor 12:1–5
2:10	2 Cor 8:4; 9: 1; Rom 11:25–28
2:14	Rom 2:17–24
2:16	Rom 3:20, 28
2:19–20	2 Cor 5:16–17
3:6–9	Rom 4:1–8
3:15–18	Rom 4:13–15
3:19	Rom 5:12–21; 7:7–24
3:21–25	Rom 3:9–20; 7:7–24
3:26–29	1 Cor 12:12–13; Rom 10:12
4:1–7	Rom 8:9–17
4:8–11	1 Thess 1:9–10; 1 Cor 12:2
4:12–20	1 Thess 1:5–7; 2:7–12; 1 Cor 2:1–5; 4:14–21; 2 Cor 7:5–13

4:21–31	Rom 9:6–13
5:6	1 Cor 7:18–19; Rom 2:25–29
5:9	1 Cor 5:6
5:14	Rom 13:9
5:16–26	Phil 4:8–9; Rom 8:1–8
6:1–6	2 Cor 2:5–11; 13:5–10; Rom 15:1–6
6:7–10	1 Cor 15:42–50
6:11	1 Cor 16:21; Phlm 19
6:15	1 Cor 16:19; 2 Cor 5:17
6:18	1 Thess 5:28; 1 Cor 16:23–24; 2 Cor 13:14; Phlm 25; Phil 4:23; Rom 16:20

Galatians 2:16

2 [16]but we now see that no one becomes acceptable to God by relying on traditional religious practices. We gain this acceptance only through a confidence in God like that of Jesus, God's Anointed. So we put our confidence in God along with the Anointed, Jesus, in order to be acceptable to God based on a confidence like that of God's Anointed, rather than by relying on traditional religious practices. The truth of the matter is "no one will be acceptable to God" on the basis of traditional religious practices.

The Confident Trust of Jesus

One of the most crucial texts for interpreting Paul is Gal 2:16. English translations prior to the twentieth century, including the Authorized Version (KJV), had consistently rendered the term "the faith of Jesus." A shift occurred with the American Standard Version in 1901 (anticipated in the 1881 Revised Version) to "faith in Jesus," which still endures in all prominent translations (see below).

The case for translating "the confidence in God like that of Jesus, God's Anointed" includes the consistency with which Paul uses this kind of genitive construction with the noun *pistis* ("faith/trust"). In the logic of Paul's argument, a directly parallel construction is used when Paul appeals to "the trust/faithfulness of Abraham" in Rom 4:12, 16. Indeed,

Continued on next page

no other reading seems possible there. The further test is then how well this understanding fits other contexts. In the references to Abraham a more appropriate alternative to "faithfulness" is "trust" or even "unconditional trust." The classic text from Gen 15:6 that Paul quotes in Rom 4:3 is best translated "Abraham put his trust in God." When Paul re-quotes that text in Rom 4:9 he inserts the noun *pistis* ("faith/trust") to describe Abraham's act of "unconditional trust," which is then the referent for its repeated use in 4:11, 12, 13, 14, 15. Scholars Version thus uses "trust" or "confidence" or "reliance" throughout the discussion of Abraham in Romans 4. Since this so clearly provides the support for Paul's argument at the end of Romans 3, the analogy between Abraham and Jesus requires a similar translation in Romans 3: "the confidence of Jesus."

Translation History of Gal 2:16

Tyndale (1525)	by the fayth of Jesus Christ
Great Bible (1539)	by the fayth of Jesus Christ
Geneva Bible (1560)	by the faith of Jesus Christ
Bishops' Bible (1568)	by the faith of Jesus Christ
Rheims (1582)	by the faith of Jesus Christ
King James (1611)	by the faith of Jesus Christ
(RV 1881) ASV 1901	through faith in Jesus Christ
RSV (1946)	through faith in Jesus Christ
TEV 1966	through faith in Jesus Christ
JB 1966/NJB 1986	[through] faith in Jesus Christ
NAB 1970/NABR 1986	through faith in Jesus Christ
NIV 1973	by faith in Jesus Christ
NRSV 1990 Note	or *the faith of Jesus Christ*
Anchor Bible (J. L. Martyn, 1997)	the faith of Jesus Christ
Jewish N. T. (D. H. Stern, 1989)	through the Messiah Yeshua's trusting faithfulness

Cotton Patch Version (Clarence Jordon, 1968):

> We know that a man can't get right with God by walking in our Southern way of life. It is only as we *live the way of Christ Jesus*. Now all of us have put our faith in Christ Jesus, so as to be made right by our Christian faith and not by our Southern traditions, because custom never made a saint out of anyone.

Paul's Correspondence to the Corinthians

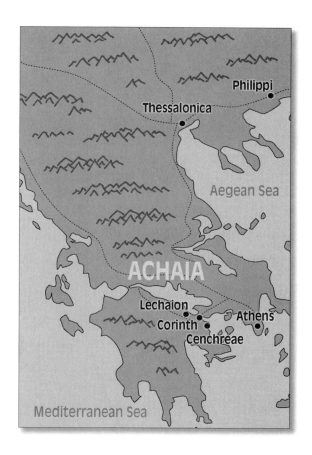

Corinth was the capital of the Roman province of Achaia.

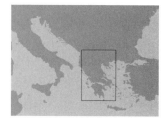

1 Corinthians

INTRODUCTION

The Location and History of Corinth

The ancient city of Corinth was located at the southwestern end of the four to six mile wide isthmus that is the land link between the northern and southern regions of Greece. Corinth was founded by Dorian people in the tenth century BCE who migrated into the territory of Greece from the north, conquering as they went. By the fifth century BCE a rivalry had developed between Corinth and Athens that fed the conflicts which led to the outbreak of the Peloponnesian War in 431. The war brought about the fall of Athens and the end of its empire.

In the second century BCE Corinth was the principal member of the Achaean Confederacy which attempted to resist the expansion of Roman power, an effort that resulted in the total destruction of the city by a Roman army led by the consul Lucius Mummius in 146 BCE. For the next hundred years Corinth lay in ruins. In 44 BCE, however, Julius Caesar refounded the city and populated it with freed slaves. In 27 BCE Caesar Augustus named Corinth the capital of the Roman province of Achaia and appointed a proconsul to reside in the city as the provincial governor.

The new Corinth soon became the fourth most important city of the Roman Empire, after Rome, Alexandria, and Ephesus. Its location at the base of the isthmus made it the crossroads for trade and transport between northern and southern Greece, and also for the transshipment of cargo between the Aegean (east) and Ionian (west) seas. The long voyage around the Peloponnesus was time-consuming and at times dangerous. Transshipping goods across the isthmus was an attractive alternative. A major engineering project initially constructed in the late seventh or early sixth century BCE made transshipment across the isthmus efficient and economical: a road paved with stone on which a large trolley could haul small ships across the isthmus to the sea on the other side. Two grooves in the pavement prevented the trolley from rolling off the road. Known as the *diolkos*, (literally, "the haul-across") this roadway remained in use until at least the first century CE. Some sections of it are still visible today.

From the early sixth century BCE Corinth also hosted the biannual Isthmian games, second in importance only to the quadrennial Olympic Games. The games were held even during the century that the city was in ruins and continued to be held every other spring during the period when Paul came to Corinth in the course of pursuing his mission. These games drew large "holiday" crowds that swelled Corinth's already considerable commercial activity.

The Roman Corinth that Paul knew thus benefited from its strategic location as much as did its Greek predecessor. It was a large, bustling, and wealthy commercial center with a population even more diverse than that of the earlier Greek city. A city founded with an initial population of freed slaves may also in Paul's time have been home to a population with upwardly mobile social aspirations that seem to be reflected in a number of the issues Paul addresses in this letter.

Paul's Initial Visit to Corinth

Paul came to Corinth during his first missionary travel to the eastern coast of the Aegean Sea. Paul himself refers to his itinerary for this trip in a letter to the Thessalonians. He had previously visited Philippi where he had succeeded in gaining a hearing and a following, as his letters to the Philippians show; but where he had also been assaulted and insulted (1 Thess 2:2). He then proceeded to Thessalonica where he apparently had somewhat better success and where he stayed for some time to instruct and encourage those who responded to his message (1 Thess 2:1–12). He next headed south, pausing in

Athens from where he sent Timothy back to Thessalonica to see how the new gathering of the Anointed's people was faring. We have no information about how long Paul stayed in Athens nor with what result. Although Luke's imaginative tale in Acts 17 attempts to fill this gap, Paul himself makes no mention of Athens in any subsequent letter. There is no evidence that he was able to attract a following there.

From Athens Paul continued south to Corinth, from where he evidently wrote a letter to the Thessalonians (which we know as 1 Thessalonians) after Timothy and Silvanus (the Latinized form of Silas) had rejoined him there (1 Thess 1:1; 2 Cor 1:19).

The Date of Paul's Visit and of 1 Corinthians

Many scholars have thought that the story of Paul's hearing before the Roman proconsul Gallio in Acts 18:12–17 furnished information about an external event that makes it possible to establish with certainty a date that can serve as a base for reconstructing the chronology of Paul's mission. The publication in 1905 of fragments of an inscription found by French archaeologists at Delphi that refers to Gallio as proconsul (of Achaia) made it possible to date Gallio's term of office either in 50–51 or 51–52 CE. It follows that if Paul appeared at a hearing before Gallio, it must have happened in one of these term-years, most likely 51–52 CE. (Proconsuls usually served a one-year term beginning July 1.)

However, the recent findings of Westar Institute's Acts Seminar (and other scholars) have reduced this alleged chronological certainty to the status of a dubious uncertainty. Whereas earlier scholarship had usually regarded Luke's story of Paul's appearance before Gallio as a report of an actual historical event, it now appears more probable that Luke has created that piece of narrative based on his own supposition. It is a recurrent pattern in the Lukan composition we know as the Acts of the Apostles that when Jesus is proclaimed as

God's Anointed, Jews stage a fierce and public protest. That is
the pattern in the Gallio episode also. It thus appears that in
portraying Paul before Gallio, Luke has composed a story that
fits into the literary and theological plot of his narrative. But
Paul never mentions Gallio or a hearing before the tribunal in
Corinth in any of his letters. So what many of us have previously regarded as a known and historically documented inci-
dent, Luke appears to have composed as a plausible tale. Luke
may have calculated that Paul's initial visit to Corinth could
have overlapped with Gallio's term as proconsul and thus justified an inferential tale about what, in his view, typically happened in response to Paul's preaching. He clearly believes that
such enraged public protest repeatedly happened in response
to Paul's message. But even in that case, Luke's plausible tale
of Paul's hearing before Gallio falls well short of being the basis for an "absolute chronology" for Paul's mission.[1]

Paul's own chronological comments furnish a better basis
for estimating the date of his first visit to Corinth. In Galatians
1 and 2 Paul says that seventeen years after the change in
his religious orientation and calling to be God's envoy to the
nations, he had visited Jerusalem to meet with the leaders of
the Anointed's people there. This information is useful, but it
still only enables us to resolve the question of the date of Paul's
visit to Corinth approximately. We do not know the exact date
of Paul's change in religious orientation and calling. Was it as
early as 31, or as late as 35 CE? Further, scholars who have made
a serious attempt to reconstruct Paul's chronology disagree
about just how long a time Paul's reference to seventeen years
actually was: did Paul use "round numbers" to include parts
of years—as was often done in antiquity—so that the actual
extent of time was only about fourteen full years rather than
seventeen? Or was the interval in fact a full seventeen years?

The purposes of this brief introduction can be sufficiently
served if we note that, although the vexed problem of Pauline
chronology is still a matter of scholarly debate, there is fairly
wide consensus among scholars that the meeting with the

leaders of the Anointed's people in Jerusalem, to which Paul refers in Galatians 1 and 2, probably took place in 49 CE. Following that meeting Paul went to Antioch for a brief period where a serious public disagreement between Paul and Peter occurred (Galatians 2), after which Paul took a trip through Galatia and then on to Philippi, Thessalonica, Athens, and Corinth to carry out his calling as God's envoy to the nations. This itinerary probably placed Paul in Corinth in 50 CE. After a stay of about eighteen months, Paul went to Ephesus where he stayed for about three years. While he was in Ephesus, Paul wrote several letters to the Corinthians between 52 and 55 CE, of which this letter was the second about which we know. In 1 Cor 5:9 Paul mentions an earlier letter, but it was not preserved.

The Contents of the Letter

In this initial visit, Paul is thought to have remained in Corinth for about eighteen months, so he had a considerable period of time to educate those whom he attracted to the new gathering of the Anointed's people about what it ought to mean to order their lives in accordance with what he proclaimed as God's world-changing news. He also no doubt sought to inform their thinking about their commitments and their prospects, in view of his expectation that "the world in its present form is passing away" (1 Cor 7:31).

The issues Paul addresses in this letter indicate that a number of the people who had been attracted to the group Paul founded there either did not yet grasp the implications of the message he proclaimed, or were resisting those implications because their aspirations led them to think and behave differently. Paul's comment in 1 Cor 16:8 indicates that he wrote this letter from Ephesus, where he has found a good opportunity to proclaim his message even though he has also met with opposition. Paul wrote this letter, first of all, in response to reports he has received from members of the community in Corinth whom he identifies only as "Chloe's people" (1:12).

They may have been household slaves or business partners of the woman named Chloe, but whether she lived in Corinth or in Ephesus is not clear. The Corinthians to whom Paul wrote evidently knew who she was, so it is plausible that the Corinthian community or some part of it met in her house; but that is only one possible inference. In 16:17 Paul refers to other members of the Corinthian community who had come to spend some time with him in Ephesus, but he does not say anything further about Chloe or her people either in this letter or in the several letters he wrote to the Corinthians later.

Chloe's people had told Paul that rivalries had surfaced in the Corinthian community: groups of people had chosen to follow one leader of the Jesus movement as superior to the others as a way of gaining distinction for themselves. They also aspired to superior eloquence and "wisdom," as forms of excellence that elevated them above others. Paul tells them that such divisiveness is contrary to the equality and unity that ought to characterize the communities for whom the Anointed Jesus is lord.

Paul has also heard that one man in the Corinthian community is having sex with his father's wife (chap. 5), that some see nothing wrong with consorting with prostitutes (chap. 6), or with suing each other in a court of law (chap. 6). That's not all. Paul addresses an additional series of issues that have been raised among the Corinthians: whether one should eat meat that has been sacrificed as part of a pagan rite (chap. 10); misconduct among participants in the Lord's Supper (chap. 11); the value of various gifts that the presence and power of God inspires in the community (chaps. 12 and 14), and the credibility of the idea of the resurrection of the dead (chap.15).

The history of scholarship on 1 Corinthians includes many scholars who were inclined to see Corinth's reputation as a notoriously licentious city reflected in the attention Paul pays in this letter to problematic sexual behavior. "Not for every man is the voyage to Corinth, "went one proverbial saying, implying that ship captains (and probably seamen too) often spent too much of their pay on the city's prostitutes. The first-century BCE geographer Strabo says that "the temple of Aphrodite was so rich that it owned more than a thousand temple-slaves, prostitutes, whom both men and women had dedicated to the goddess. And therefore, it was also on account of these women that the city was crowded with people and grew rich."[2] The Athenian comic poet Aristophanes is credited with inventing the word, "to Corinthianize" to refer to fornication. But the wit of Aristophanes and the writ of Strabo and other Athenian writers about Corinth's alleged reputation for sexual license all refer to the Greek city that was destroyed in 146 BCE, not the refounded Roman city that Paul visited.*

The probability is that all of the problematic notions and behaviors that Paul addresses in this letter are traceable to the predilection of some participants in the Corinthian community to interpret Paul's message as legitimizing what they regarded as a quest for "spiritual" elevation and liberation. Paul tries very hard in this letter to persuade them to turn away from their obsession with distinguishing themselves and toward the personal maturity and social responsibility that builds up the community.

Comments Inserted into Paul's Letter

In the centuries following his lifetime Paul's letters were intensively studied in search of usable religious meaning and extensively copied. According to Kurt and Barbara Aland,[3] the letters of Paul are preserved in seven hundred seventy-

---

*Most scholars today regard Strabo's reference to a temple complex that was home to 1000 women devoted to sacred prostitution as an uninformed conjecture on Strabo's part. There is no archaeological evidence of such a large temple complex in the remains of the ancient city. The temple of Aphrodite at the top of the AcroCorinth is only a small shrine. There is no evidence that sacred prostitution was ever practiced anywhere in ancient Greece. All of the writers who characterized Corinth as a licentious city were Athenians who were expressing their disdain for the commercial city.

nine extant manuscripts that date from the second/third to the sixteenth century CE.

Comparisons among the earliest of these hand-copied manuscripts show that differences among them do exist and occasionally some errors were made by the copyists. In a few cases, additions appear to have been made to the original text by a copyist who wanted to advocate what he thought Paul should have said, or what he thought Paul would have said, if he were to deal with the situation of the church at that later time. Two passages in 1 Corinthians appear to be such interpolations: they disrupt the flow of Paul's argument and reflect a view that is noticeably different from the view for which Paul argues elsewhere in his letters. The first is 11:2–16, in which it is argued that women must wear their hair up in public as a sign of their subordination to men. The second is 14:33b–38, in which women are forbidden to speak in public meetings of the Anointed's community. A third passage also calls for some comment: the rhetoric of the much-loved chapter 13 is unlike anything else that we have in Paul's letters. Is Paul quoting an ode to love authored by some other early Christian, or by a pagan author? Or has someone slipped this passage into Paul's text, where it seems to disrupt the argument that moves from chapter 12 to chapter 14?

Finally, there is a phrase in 4:6 and a "closing remark" in 16:22 that both appear to be interpolations. A rationale for the judgments the Scholars Version translators have made about these apparent additions to or insertions in Paul's text are found either in a note at the point where they occur in the letter, or in the appendix where we have located the longer interpolations.

Why Is This Letter Important?

What gives this letter to the Corinthians its fascination and importance is that we can watch early Christianity's most extraordinary leader in the process of instructing and admonishing his converts on what it means to live what we have come to call "a Christian life." ("Christianity" and "Christian" were terms not yet in use in Paul's time. Because of their brevity and familiarity we use them here as a matter of convenience.) Paul belongs to the first "Christian" generation. He has no "Christian" scriptures or tradition to draw upon as he makes his case. He is constructing a theological and ethical argument in the course of writing the letter. He is "making it up" as he attempts to deal with the concrete questions and behaviors about which the Corinthians have asked him, in the light of God's world-transforming news. He does draw upon his Jewish tradition, but always as it must be recast in light of "an insight from God about Jesus as God's Anointed" that he refers to in Gal 1:12 as the basis of his new religious orientation and his calling to be God's envoy to the nations. It's no wonder that so many in the first centuries of "Christian" history regarded his letters as more than just today's mail, and so saved them and copied them so that they could be widely read and preserved for readers in generations to come—something Paul never anticipated.

NOTES

1. For a well-inforfmed, readable discussion of the results of recent scholarship on Acts, see Richard Pervo, *The Mystery of Acts: Unraveling its Story* (Santa Rosa, CA: Polebridge Press, 2008). The full report of the Acts Seminar is forthcoming from Polebridge Press.

2. Strabo, Geography 8.20c; cited in Jerome Murphy-O'Conner, *St. Paul's Corinth* (Wilmington, DE: Michael Glazier, Inc., 1983), 55.

3. Kurt Aland and Barbara Aland, *The Text of the New Testament* (Grand Rapids, MI: William B. Eerdmans, 1987), 78–81.

Paul's First Letter to the Corinthians

1 Paul, by God's will summoned to be an envoy of the Anointed Jesus, and our brother Sosthenes, [2]to the gathering of God's people in Corinth who are dedicated to the service of the Anointed Jesus, and called to be people of complete integrity along with everyone everywhere who appeals to the name of our lord, Jesus the Anointed, their lord and ours.

[3]May you have favor and peace from God our Creator and Benefactor and Jesus the Anointed, our lord.

[4]I thank God all the time for the generous favor God has shown to you through the Anointed Jesus. [5]You have been richly endowed with speech and knowledge of every kind. [6]Our testimony about the Anointed has indeed been confirmed among you, [7]so you do not lack any gift as you wait for the coming of our lord, Jesus the Anointed. [8]And God will sustain you to the end, so that you will be beyond reproach on that day when our lord, Jesus, God's Anointed, appears. [9]God is faithful and is the one who has called you into fellowship with God's "son," Jesus the Anointed, our lord.

[10]I plead with you by the authority of our lord, Jesus the Anointed, to reach agreement with one another, to end the divisions among you, and to restore yourselves to good order by being united in thought and purpose. [11]Some of Chloe's people have told me, my friends, that you are divided into factions. [12]I put it this way because you are all saying, "I follow Paul," or "I follow Apollo," or "I follow Peter," or "I follow the Anointed." [13]The Anointed is not divided, is he? Paul was not crucified for you, was he? Nor were you baptized in the name of Paul, were you? [14]I baptized none of you, thank God,

---

1:13 Reading *not divided* with P[46] and other mss.

except Crispus and Gaius, [15]so none of you can say that you were baptized in my name. [16]I also baptized Stephanas and his family; beyond that I don't remember whether I baptized anyone else or not. [17]The Anointed did not send me out to conduct baptisms, but to proclaim God's world-transforming message not, however, by means of pretentious speech that would rob the Anointed's cross of its significance.

[18]The message about the cross is utter nonsense to those who are heading for ruin, but to us who are bound for salvation it is the effective power of God. [19]I remind you that it is written in the scriptures,

"I will bring to ruin the wisdom of the expert,
And I will confound the intelligence of the best and the brightest."

[20]Where does that leave the expert? Where does that leave the scholar? Where does that leave the pundit of this age? Has not God shown the world's wisdom to be foolish? [21]Since in the larger scheme of God's wisdom the world did not come to acknowledge God through its own wisdom, God decided to save those who embrace God's world-transforming news through the "nonsense" that we preach. [22]At a time when Jews expect a miracle and Greeks seek enlightenment, [23]we speak about God's Anointed *crucified!* This is an offense to Jews, nonsense to the nations; [24]but to those who have heard God's call, both Jews and Greeks, the Anointed represents God's power and God's wisdom; [25]because the folly of God is wiser than humans are and the weakness of God is stronger than humans are.

[26]Consider your own situations when you were called, my friends. Not many of you were considered wise in the eyes of the world, not many of you were people of power and influence, not many of you were descendants of the nobility; [27]but God has chosen people the world regards as fools to expose the pretensions of those who think they know it all, and God has chosen people the world regards as weak to expose the

pretentions of those who are in power. [28]God has chosen people who have no status in the world and even those who are held in contempt, people who count for nothing, in order to bring to nothing those who are thought to be really something, [29]so that no human beings might be full of themselves in the presence of God. [30]It is God's doing that you belong to the people of the Anointed Jesus. God has made him our wisdom and the source of our goodness and integrity and liberation. [31]So, as scripture says, "If you have to take pride in something, take pride in what God has done."

2 When I came to you, my friends, I did not try to impress you with exceptional eloquence or extraordinary learning when I spoke about the hidden truth of God's will. [2]I resolved that I would not claim to know anything while I was with you except Jesus God's Anointed, *crucified*. [3]I came to you in human weakness and with apprehension and trepidation. [4]My rhetoric and my message did not feature weighty words of wisdom, but was accompanied by visible evidence of God's presence and power, [5]so that you would put your confidence not in human wisdom but in the power of God.

[6]Now of course I do have something to say about wisdom, when I am with those who can fully comprehend it, but it's not a wisdom of this age nor of those who rule it at present, all of whom are destined to be deposed. [7]I am talking about a hidden and mysterious wisdom of God which God intended before time began: to raise us to the glory of God's presence. [8]None of the rulers of this age knew anything about this. If they had known, they would not have crucified the one who has become our exalted lord. [9]However, as scripture says,

> "No eye has ever seen, no ear ever heard,
> nor has the human mind ever imagined
> what God has prepared for those who love him."

1:28c *those who are:* Literally "the things that are." The phrase here refers not to "things" but to the attributes of persons.

¹⁰But these things have been shown to us by God's presence and power; because the wisdom of God searches out everything, even the deep and hidden purposes of God. ¹¹Who knows the things that constitute human life except by the capacity to comprehend that is hidden within a human being? So also, no one knows the things that God intends except the hidden wisdom of God. ¹²We have not received as a special gift the capacity to understand the nature of this world, but the capacity to comprehend the things that God has generously given to us. ¹³And we speak about these things not in terms derived from the instruction of human wisdom, but by the instruction of God's presence and power, interpreting the hidden wisdom of God for those who can comprehend it. ¹⁴People who are concerned only with worldly affairs do not respond to the hidden wisdom of God. It makes no sense to them. They are unable to comprehend such things, because the hidden wisdom of God is discerned only by people who can recognize it. ¹⁵Such discerning people can judge the value of everything, but they themselves cannot be judged by other human beings. ¹⁶As the scripture says,

"Who knows the mind of the Lord;
Who will instruct him?"

But we have the mind of the Anointed.

3 I could not speak to you as discerning people, my friends, but as people preoccupied with worldly concerns, as mere toddlers in the Anointed's new way of life. ²I offered you milk, not solid food, because you were not up to it. And you are not up to it even now. ³You are still preoccupied with mundane interests. As long as there is rivalry and contention among you, are you not still preoccupied with mundane interests and behaving in a way that is all too common? ⁴When one of you says, "I follow Paul," and another says, "I follow Apollos," isn't your behavior merely common and ordinary? ⁵Who is Apollos, after all? And who is Paul? We are servants through whom you came to put your trust in God's world-transforming message in accordance with the role God assigned to each of us. [6]I planted, Apollos watered, but God's power is what made it grow. [7]So neither the one who plants nor the one who waters is important; it's God's power to make things grow that is important. [8]The one who plants and the one who waters have the same aim and each will be rewarded for the work each has done. [9]We are co-workers for God; you are God's field, God's building project.

[10]Because of the generous favor God has given to me, I laid the foundation like a skillful master builder; now someone else is building on it. Each builder must pay careful attention to how he builds on it. [11]No one can put down another foundation than the one that has already been laid: Jesus the Anointed. [12]The sort of material each builder uses—gold, silver, precious stones, wood, hay, straw—[13]is going to become evident. The day of judgment will expose it, because it will be revealed by fire. The fire of final judgment will put the quality of each builder's work to the test. [14]If what someone has built on the foundation survives the test, that builder will be rewarded; [15]but if the work of a builder is consumed by the fire, that builder will forfeit his reward; he himself will be saved, but only as one who has been through a fire. [16]All of you know, don't you, that you are God's temple and God's presence and power dwells among you? [17]If someone does damage to the temple of God, God will destroy that one; for the temple of God is worthy of the deepest respect, and that is indeed what you are.

[18]Don't be deceived. If any of you thinks that you are wise in the eyes of this age, you will have to become foolish, before you can become truly wise. [19]Because what this world counts as wisdom is folly in the eyes of God. As scripture says, "God ensnares the wise in their own craftiness," [20]and "the Lord knows that the designs of the wise will come to nothing." [21]So you must not place your confidence in human leaders, because everything is yours, [22]whether Paul, Apollos, Cephas, or for that matter, the world, life, death, the present, the

future—everything is yours, and you are the Anointed's and the Anointed is God's.

4 So one should think of us as persons in the Anointed's service and as stewards who are entrusted with the secret purposes of God. ²I might add here that what one wants in a steward is someone who will be reliable. ³Now I couldn't care less if I am judged by you or by some court of law. But I don't judge myself either. ⁴I am not aware of having done anything wrong, but that does not mean I am acquitted. The lord is the one who judges me. ⁵So don't pass judgment on anything before the right time for it, when the lord comes. He will bring to light everything done in the dark and expose the motives of all human hearts; and then each of us will receive God's commendation.

⁶I have applied these remarks to Apollos and myself for your benefit, so that you could learn by these references to us not to inflate your own importance by preferring one of us over the other and pitting us against each other. ⁷Who thinks you are so exceptional? What do you have that you did not receive? And if you have received everything you have, why do you brag as if you had achieved something on your own? ⁸Already you have it all! Already you have become rich! You have become kings without any help from us! I wish that you really were kings so that we could reign with you. ⁹But it seems to me that God has placed us envoys last in the parade, like men condemned to death. We have become a spectacle for the whole world, both for heaven's messengers and for humankind. ¹⁰We are made to look like fools for the sake of the Anointed, but you are the Anointed's wise men; we are weak, but you are strong; you are well thought of, we get no respect. ¹¹Right up to this very moment we are hungry and thirsty and poorly clothed, cuffed around, have no place to call home, and are worn out by the hard work we do with our own hands. ¹²When we are abused, we bless; when we are harassed, we put up with it; ¹³when we are slandered, we are conciliatory.

We have been treated as if we were the scum of the earth, the filth everyone wants to get rid of, and still are.

[14]I am not writing this to make you feel ashamed, but to caution you as my dearly loved children. [15]Even if you have innumerable mentors in the community of the Anointed, you don't have many fathers, and I became your father in the community of the Anointed Jesus when I presented God's world-transforming message to you. [16]For that reason I urge you to regard me as your model. [17]It was for this purpose that I sent Timothy to you. He is my dear and faithful child in the service of the Lord. He will remind you of my views on our life as people who belong to the Anointed Jesus, just as I teach them everywhere in every community of the Anointed.

[18]Because they imagine that I am never going to visit you again, some have become inflated with self-importance. [19]But I am going to visit you soon, if the Lord wills it, and I will find out for myself not only what these pretentious people have to say, but also whether their rhetoric has any transforming power. [20]For the Empire of God is not just about talk; it's about the power that transforms the world. [21]So what do you prefer? Shall I come to visit you with a stick, or with affection and gentleness?

5 It is common knowledge, I hear, that there is immoral sexual behavior among you and of a kind that is inadmissible even among pagans: that one of you has a sexual relationship with his father's wife. [2]And you are proud of it! Should you not rather be so aggrieved that you would expel the one who has done this from your company? [3]Although I am physically absent, (as you hear these words) I am truly present, and I have already passed judgment, as if I were physically present,

---

5:3, 4 *I have already passed judgment, as if I were physically present, on the man who has engaged in such behavior in the name of the lord Jesus:* SV reads this verse as it stands in the Greek. The man who has a sexual relationship with his father's wife evidently justified his action by invoking the freedom he brazenly claims

on the man who has engaged in such behavior ⁴in the name of the lord Jesus. When you are assembled and hear me speaking through this letter, with the power of our lord Jesus ⁵you must turn this man over to the realm of Satan until he has put an end to his fleshly passion so that his life may be restored on the day when the lord comes for the final judgment.

⁶Your bragging about this is not good. Don't you know that a little bit of leaven affects the whole batch of dough? ⁷Clean out the old leaven so that you can be a fresh batch of dough, because unleavened is what you are supposed to be. The Anointed, our "Passover lamb," was sacrificed ⁸so that we would celebrate the feast of our liberation not with the old leaven of vice and base behavior, but with the unleavened bread of integrity and truth.

⁹When I said in the letter I wrote to you that you should keep your distance from sexually immoral people, ¹⁰I did not mean that you should have nothing at all to do with immoral people in society, or with people motivated by greed, or who cheat and steal, or who worship phony gods. In that case you would have to go clear out of this world. ¹¹What I meant was that you should keep your distance from any so-called brother or sister, if they are sexually immoral, or motivated by greed, or worship phony gods, or use abusive language, or are habitually drunk, or cheat and steal. You should not even eat with such a person. ¹²Judging outsiders is not my business, is it? But judging insiders is your business, isn't it? ¹³God will judge the outsider. As scripture says, "Expel the immoral person from your midst."

---

is warranted by Paul's message about God's anointed. Other translations, missing this point, turn the phrase around: "I have already passed judgment, as if I were physically present, in the name of the lord Jesus on the man who has engaged in such behavior."

5:5 *you must turn this man over to the realm of Satan:* That is, expel him from the community.

5:9 Paul refers to an earlier letter that has not been preserved which preceded 1 Corinthians. Thus 1 Corinthians is historically 2 Corinthians.

6 Does one of you who has a grievance against another dare to run the risk of filing suit in a pagan court of law rather than bringing it before the people devoted to serving God? ²Don't you know that the people devoted to serving God will judge the world? If you are going to serve as judges of the world, are you incapable of deciding the smallest disputes? ³Don't you know that we are going to judge heaven's messengers, never mind everyday matters? ⁴So if you have such everyday disputes, why do you designate those who are not respected by the community of the Anointed as your judges? ⁵I say this to your shame. Is it really the case that there is no one among you wise enough to decide between one brother and another, ⁶but that one brother takes the other to court before outsiders?

⁷To take each other to court is already a defeat for you. Would it not be better to be wronged? Or to be cheated? ⁸But as it is you are the ones who are doing wrong and cheating, and you are doing this to your brothers and sisters! ⁹Don't you know that wrongdoers are not going to inherit the Empire of God? Don't let anyone mislead you; neither those who consort with prostitutes nor those who follow phony gods, neither adulterers nor promiscuous people, nor pederasts, ¹⁰neither the thieving nor the greedy, neither drunkards nor those who engage in verbal abuse nor swindlers are going to inherit the Empire of God. And these are what some of you were. ¹¹But you have been cleansed, you have a new relation with God through the name of the lord, Jesus the Anointed, and through the presence and power of our God.

¹²[Some of you say,] "I am free to do anything I want"; but not everything is good for me. "I am free to do anything I want"; but I am not going to let anything dominate me. ¹³[Some of you say,] "Food is for the belly and the belly for food," but God is going to do away with them both. In any case, the body is not intended for sexual indulgence, but is intended for the lord, and the lord is intended for the body. ¹⁴God raised up the lord and God will raise us up by divine

power. ¹⁵Don't you know that your bodies are parts of the body of the Anointed? So then, shall I take members of the Anointed's body and join them with the body of a prostitute? Certainly not! ¹⁶Don't you understand that the one who unites with a prostitute becomes one body with her? Scripture says, "The two of them will become one flesh." ¹⁷On the other hand, the one who is united with the lord has completely identified with him. ¹⁸So stay clear away from sexual promiscuity. Every other offense that a person may commit has to do with something outside the body; but the sexually promiscuous commit an offense against their own bodies. ¹⁹Don't you realize that your body is a temple of the presence and power of God within you that is God's gift to you, and that you do not belong just to yourself? ²⁰You have been ransomed at a price. So honor God by what you do with your body.

7 Now about the matters you raised in your letter: I do think it is better for a man to abstain from sexual intercourse with a woman. ²But because sexual immorality is so prevalent I think that each man should have sexual intercourse with his own wife and each woman should have sexual intercourse with her own husband. ³The husband should give his wife what he owes her, and likewise the wife should give her husband what she owes him. ⁴The wife does not have authority over her body, her husband does; and the husband does not have authority over his body, his wife does. ⁵Don't withhold yourselves from each other, except perhaps for a little while by mutual consent so that you may have the leisure you need to pray; then come together again so that Satan will find no opportunity to tempt you because of your lack of self-control. ⁶But I offer this advice as a concession, not as a command. ⁷I wish that everyone were like me in this regard; but we all have

---

7:1 Paul has thus far addressed issues conveyed to him in an oral report by "some of Chloe's people" (1:11). Now he turns to issues that were raised in a letter he had received from the leaders of the Corinthians.

our own special gift from God, one has a gift of this kind, another has a gift of that kind.

[8]My advice to the unmarried men and widows is that they are better off if they remain single as I am. [9]But if they cannot control themselves they should get married; it is much better to marry than to be burning with sexual desire.

[10]To the married my instruction (not mine, but the lord's) is that a wife should not divorce her husband—[11]but if she is already divorced, she should remain unmarried or be reconciled with her husband—and that a husband should not leave his wife.

[12]We have no teaching from the lord addressed to those in other situations, but my advice is that if a member of the community has a wife who is not a member of the Anointed's community and she is willing to live with him, he should not leave her. [13]And if a woman has a husband who is not a member of the community and he is willing to live with her, she should not leave her husband, [14]because the husband who is not a member is consecrated through his wife and the wife who is not a member is consecrated through her husband. Otherwise your children would be outsiders, but this way they belong to God. [15]But if the partner who is not a member of the community insists upon it, a divorce should be granted. The brother or sister is not bound in such cases. God has called us to live in peace. [16]After all, wife, what do you really know about whether you will save your husband; or what do you really know, husband, about whether you will save your wife?

[17]Except for this case, each of you should continue to live the life the lord has apportioned to you as you were when God called you. This is the rule I follow in all the communities of the Anointed. [18]Were you circumcised when you were called? Don't have surgery to undo it. Were you uncircumcised when you were called? Don't have yourself circumcised. [19]It makes no difference whether you are circumcised or uncircumcised. What matters is doing what God commands us. [20]Each of you should remain as you were when you were called. [21]Were you

a slave when you were called? Don't let that concern you. On the other hand, if you are able to become a freedman, take advantage of it. ²²The point is this: anyone who was a slave when called to be one of the lord's people is one of the lord's freedmen, and likewise anyone who was free when called is the Anointed's slave. ²³You were bought at a price; don't become slaves to human beings. ²⁴Each of you, my friends, should remain as you were before God when you were called.

²⁵I have no specific instruction from the lord about people who have not yet married, but I offer my opinion as one who is trustworthy because he has been favored by God's mercy. ²⁶This is what I think is advisable because of the urgency of this time: that it is better for a man to continue as he is. ²⁷Are you bound in marriage to a woman? Don't seek a divorce. Are you without a wife? Don't seek to be married. ²⁸But if you marry, you are doing nothing wrong and if a virgin marries, she is doing nothing wrong. But those who marry will have the demands of earthly life to deal with, and I am sparing you that. ²⁹This is what I mean, friends: this period of opportunity [for our mission] is coming to an end. In what is left of it those who have wives should live as if they did not have them, ³⁰and those who mourn as if they have nothing to be sad about, and those who rejoice as if they have nothing to celebrate, and those who buy things as if they have no possessions, ³¹and those who deal with the world as if they have no use for it; because the world in its present form is passing away.

³²I would like you to be free from day to day cares. The unmarried man is concerned about the lord's business, how he might please the Lord. ³³The married man is concerned about earthly life, how he might please his wife. His interests are divided. ³⁴The unmarried woman and the virgin are concerned about the lord's business, so that they may be completely devoted in body, heart, and mind, but the married woman is concerned about earthly life, how she might please her husband. ³⁵In saying this I am trying to be helpful to you. I do not want to impose a restriction on you, but want your devotion to the

lord to be admirable and constant and undistracted. [36]But if a man thinks that he is not treating his fiancée honorably, if he is past self-control and it has to be, he should do what he wants: they should marry. There's nothing wrong with that. [37]But any man who has made up his mind and is under no necessity, but has his desire under control and has decided in his own mind to keep his fiancée a virgin will do well. [38]So then, the man who marries his fiancée does well but the man who does not marry his fiancée will do better.

[39]A woman is bound as long as her husband lives; but if her husband dies, she is free to marry anyone she wishes, as long as he belongs to the lord. [40]But she will be happier if she remains as she is, in my opinion. And I think that my opinion is consistent with what we know about the wisdom of God.

8 Now on the issue of the meat of animals sacrificed to so-called divinities, I am well aware that "we are all in possession of knowledge"; but whereas knowledge puffs up, love is what builds up. [2]If someone thinks he knows something, he does not yet know what he needs to know. [3]But if someone loves God, this one is known by God. [4]With regard to eating the meat of animals sacrificed to so-called divinities, we know that such images have no reality in the world and that there is only one who is really God. [5]Even if there are many so-called gods whether in heaven or on earth, as indeed there are many "gods" and many "lords," [6]nevertheless for us,

> There is one God, our Creator and Benefactor
> from whom all things are and for whom we live
> and one lord, Jesus the Anointed
> through whom all things are and through whom we live.

[7]But not everyone understands this. Because they are so accustomed to the idea, some still eat the meat as if it were offered to real divinities, and their conscience is compromised, since they have misgivings about this. [8]Food will not bring us

---

8:6 This may well reflect a pre-Pauline creedal formula.

into God's presence. We lose nothing if we do not eat, we gain nothing if we do. [9]But see to it that your right to decide about this does not create a problem for those whose conscience is unsettled. [10]If someone whose conscience is unsettled sees you, "one who has knowledge," reclining at table in a temple of one of the so-called divinities, won't such a person be induced to participate in these ritual occasions also? [11]Such a vulnerable person is brought to ruin by your "enlightenment" — a brother for whom the Anointed died. [12]So when you do something that harms your brothers and sisters and injures them because their consciences are unsettled, you commit an offense against the Anointed. [13]Therefore if meat from a sacrifice causes my brother or sister to stumble, I will never eat such meat again, so that I will never cause my sister's or brother's downfall.

9 I'm a free man, am I not? I'm an envoy, am I not? I have seen Jesus our lord, haven't I ? You are the result of my work in the lord's service, aren't you? [2]If in the opinion of others I am not an envoy, to you I certainly am, because you are the certification of my authenticity in the lord's service.

[3]This is how I respond to my critics. [4]Am I not entitled to be provided with food and drink? [5]Do I not have the right to be accompanied by a wife as do the other envoys and the brothers of the lord and Cephas? [6]Or are Barnabas and I the only ones who are supposed to pay their own way? [7]Does anyone ever serve in the army at his own expense? Does anyone ever plant a vineyard and not eat its fruit? Does anyone ever tend a flock and not drink its milk? [8]Am I merely appealing to common sense, or does scripture say the same thing? [9]It is written in the law of Moses: "Don't muzzle an ox while it is threshing grain." Is God just concerned about oxen, [10]or is God actually speaking for our benefit? It was written for our benefit, because the plowman should plough in hope and the thresher should thresh with the hope of sharing the crop. [11]If we have sown heaven's benefits among you, why is it a big deal if we reap some of your earthly goods? [12]If others share

in this legitimate claim on you, do not we even more? But we have not made use of this legitimate claim; we put up with anything in order to avoid creating a hindrance to our proclamation about God's Anointed. [13]Are you unaware of the fact that those who work in the temple service get their food from the temple, and that those who officiate at the altar of sacrifice receive a share of the sacrificial offerings? [14]In the same way the lord commanded that those who proclaim the news about God's Anointed should receive their living from their work of proclamation. [15]But I have never made use of these legitimate claims, nor am I writing this so that they will be given to me. I would rather die than have someone rob me of what I pride myself on. [16]If I proclaim the news about God's Anointed, that's not something for me to be proud of. I was compelled to do it. I would be in terrible trouble if I refused to proclaim that news. [17]If I do this voluntarily, I am entitled to be rewarded for it. But if I do this involuntarily, it is because I have been entrusted with a responsibility. [18]So what is my reward for this? That when I preach I get to offer the news that I proclaim free of charge, and make no use of the legitimate claims to which proclaiming this news entitles me.

[19]Although I am free from servitude to anyone, I have made myself the servant of everyone in order to win over as many as I can. [20]To the Jews I behaved like a Jew so that I might win over Jews. To those who are subject to the Mosaic law I behaved as if I were under that law, not because I really was subject to that law, but to win over those who are. [21]To those not subject to the Mosaic law I behaved as one not subject to it, not because I am not subject to the law of God, but because I am subject to the law of the Anointed, so that I might win over those who are not subject to the law. [22]To the weak I behaved as if I were weak, so that I could win over the weak. I have accommodated myself in all sorts of ways to all sorts of people so that by all these means I might save some. [23]I do all of this for the sake of God's world-transforming news, so that I might have a share in its benefits.

²⁴You surely know that all of the runners in the stadium are in the race, but only one wins the prize. So you should run to win. ²⁵All who engage in athletic competition discipline themselves about everything. They do that to receive a perishable prize, but we for an imperishable one. ²⁶For that reason I don't run as if I had no goal in mind nor do I box just to punch the air. ²⁷But I punish my body and make it submit to my aim, so that after I have preached to others I myself do not fail to qualify.

10 Friends, I don't want you to be unaware of the fact that our ancestors were all under the cloud and walked through the sea. ²They were all baptized into [the community of] Moses in the cloud and in the sea, ³and all ate the same numinous bread ⁴and drank the same numinous drink. For they were all drinking from the numinous rock that was following them and that rock was the Anointed. ⁵But God was not pleased with most of them, since "they were laid low in the desert." ⁶Now these things have become a cautionary tale to teach us not to hanker after evil things as they did. ⁷Don't become devotees of pseudo-divinities, as some of them did, as when the scripture says, "The people sat down to eat and drink and began to play around." ⁸We should not indulge in illicit sex; some of them did and twenty-three thousand of them fell dead in a single day. ⁹We should not put God to the test; some of them did and they were killed by snakes. ¹⁰We should not whine and complain; some of them did and they were cut down by the "grim reaper." ¹¹These things that happened are cautionary tales, written down to instruct us upon whom the end of the ages has come. ¹²So anyone who thinks he is standing firm should take care that he does not fall. ¹³No temptation has overtaken you that is not common to human experience. God is faithful and will not allow you to be tempted beyond what you can cope with, but with the temptation will provide the way out so that you can get through it.

¹⁴The point is, my dear friends, that you must keep your distance from the worship of pseudo-divinities. ¹⁵I appeal to you as sensible people: make your own judgments about what I am saying. ¹⁶The cup of God's gracious benefits that we consecrate means that we are involved in the blood of the Anointed, doesn't it? The bread that we break means that we are involved in the body of the Anointed, doesn't it? ¹⁷That there is one loaf means that we who are many constitute one body, because we all partake of the one loaf. ¹⁸Consider the case of earthly Israel: those who eat the sacrifices are involved in the altar of sacrifice, aren't they? ¹⁹What is my point? That meat sacrificed to a pseudo-divinity really is what it is alleged to be, or that an idol is what it is alleged to be? ²⁰Not at all. My point is that such sacrifices are actually offerings to demons and not to God. I don't want you to become involved with demons. ²¹It is just not possible for you to drink both the cup of the lord and the cup of demons; it is just not possible for you really to participate in the table of the lord and the table of demons. ²²Do we want to provoke the lord's jealous anger? Do we really suppose that we are stronger than he is?

²³"We are free to do anything we want,"[as some of you say;] but not everything is good for you. "We are free to do anything we want," [as some of you say;] but not everything strengthens the community. ²⁴You should not seek your own welfare, but that of your neighbor. ²⁵You should feel free to eat anything sold in the meat market without raising a question about it for reasons of conscience. ²⁶After all, "the earth is the Lord's, and so is everything in it." ²⁷If someone who is not a member of the Anointed's community invites you to dinner and you would like to go, you should feel free to eat whatever is served without raising a question about it for reasons of conscience. ²⁸(But if someone says to you, "This meat has been offered in a sacrifice," then you should decline to eat it out of consideration for the person who pointed this out and for reasons of conscience. ²⁹When I refer to conscience I mean his, not yours.) Why should my freedom be decided by someone

else's conscience? ³⁰If I partake with gratitude, why am I condemned for what I thank God for?

³¹So whether you eat or drink or whatever else you do, do everything to honor God. ³²Avoid giving offense to both Jews and Greeks and to the gathering of the people of God ³³just as I try to please all people in everything I do by seeking not what will benefit me, but will benefit many, so that they may be saved. **11** ¹Follow my example as I follow the Anointed's.

11 ¹⁷I do not applaud you in connection with the instruction I am going to give you now, because you gather together not for the better but for the worse. ¹⁸First of all, I hear that when you meet as a community there are divisions among you and to some extent I believe it. ¹⁹[You evidently think that] it is necessary for there to be factions among you so that you will be able to see who the genuine people among you are. ²⁰When you gather together in one place it's not the lord's supper that you eat. ²¹When you eat you serve yourselves first, so some are left out while others get drunk. ²²Don't you have houses where you can do your eating and drinking? Are you not showing disrespect for the gathering of the people of God and humiliating those who have to do without? What shall I say to you? Shall I applaud you? In this case, I do not applaud you.

²³Here's why: I received from the lord the same thing I passed on to you, that on the night when he was handed over, the lord Jesus took bread ²⁴and after he gave thanks he broke it and said, "This means my body broken for you. Do this to remember me." ²⁵And in the same way he took the wine cup after the meal and said, "This cup means the new covenant ratified by my blood. Whenever you drink this, do it to remember me." ²⁶So every time you eat this bread and drink this

---

11:2–16 In the judgment of the SV translators this passage is probably an interpolation into Paul's text and therefore appears in the appendix to 1 Corinthians in this translation. See the explanatory note there.

cup you are proclaiming the death of the lord until the day when he returns.

[27]It follows that anyone who eats the bread or drinks the cup without considering its meaning will be guilty of demeaning the body and the blood of the lord. [28]A person should think about what he is doing before he eats the bread and drinks from the cup. [29]All who eat and drink without recognizing that the community is the body of the Anointed eat and drink judgment upon themselves. [30]This is why many of you are weak and sick and why some have died. [31]If we were in the habit of judging ourselves accurately, we would not suffer such judgment. [32]But when we are judged by the lord, we are being disciplined so that we will not be condemned with the world.

[33]So then, my friends, when you gather to eat [the lord's supper], wait on one another. [34]Any of you who thinks only about his own hunger should eat at home, so that your gathering together does not bring condemnation upon you! I will give you direction about the remaining matters when I come to see you.

12 I don't want you to misunderstand the gifts that come from God's presence and power, my friends. [2]You know that when you were pagans you were always misguidedly drawn to speechless idols. [3]So I want you be aware of the fact that no one whose speech is inspired by God says, "Jesus be damned," and that no one is enabled to say, "Jesus is lord" except by the authentic power of God.

[4]There are different gifts, but the same power of God, [5]and there are different kinds of service, but the same Lord, [6]and there are different activities, but the same God makes them all effective in everyone. [7]Some expression of God's power is given to each of us for the benefit of all. [8]The ability to speak

---

11:33 Early gatherings of the Anointed undoubtedly did eat common meals together (see, e.g., Gal 2:11–12). But in this passage it is observance of the lord's supper, not a community supper that Paul is concerned about.

wisely is given to one through God's power, the ability to speak knowledgeably to another in accordance with the same divine power, [9]to another deeds of faith by the same divine power, to another gifts of healing by the one divine power, [10]to another the ability to do powerful deeds, to another prophecy, to another the ability to distinguish the gifts that are inspired by God's power from those that are not, to another different forms of ecstatic speech, to another the ability to interpret ecstatic speech. [11]One and the same power of God makes all of these effective and assigns them to each person individually as God pleases.

[12]Just as the body has many parts and all of the parts, even though there are many of them, are still parts of one body, so is the body of the Anointed. [13]For we were all baptized by the same power of God into one body, whether we were Jews or Greeks, slaves or free, and we were all invited to imbibe the same divine power. [14]The body does not consist of only one part, but of many. [15]If the foot were to say, "Because I'm not a hand, I'm not part of the body," that's no reason to suppose that it's not part of the body, is it? [16]And if the ear were to say, "Because I am not an eye, I am not part of the body," that's no reason for thinking it isn't part of the body, is it? [17]If the whole body consisted of an eye, how would it hear? And if the whole were an ear, how would it be able to smell anything? [18]But in fact God has put each of the parts in the body to accomplish what God intended. [19]If everything consisted of just one part, there would be no body, would there? [20]But the fact is, although there are many parts, there is one body. [21]It's just not possible for the eye to say to the hand, "I have no need of you;" or for the head to say to the feet, "I have no use for you." [22]But in many respects the parts of the body that seem to be less important are the most necessary, [23]and the parts of the body that we think are undignified we treat with more respect, and we clothe our private parts with a greater degree of propriety [24]than our more presentable parts require. But God unified the body by giving the inferior part greater value,

²⁵so that there would be no division in the body, but that the parts would care about each other. ²⁶If one part is in pain, all parts suffer; if one part is honored, all parts celebrate.

²⁷All of you together are the body of the Anointed and individually you are members of it. ²⁸And God has made some appointments in the community of the Anointed: first envoys, second prophets, third teachers, then those who work wonders, then those who know how to heal, helpers, administrators, and those who can speak in various kinds of ecstatic utterance. ²⁹Are all envoys? Is everyone a prophet? Are all teachers? Are all wonder-workers? Are all healers? ³⁰Do all engage in ecstatic speech? Does everyone interpret? But I urge you to aspire to the more important gifts. And I can point out a way that is even more excellent than having any of these gifts.

13 In Praise of Love

[[if I were fluent in human and heavenly tongues
  but lacked love
  I'd sound like a hollow gong
  or a crashing cymbal

²if I could interpret oracles
  had the key to all the sacred rites and secrets
  and every insight
  if I had all the confidence in the world
  to move mountains
  but lacked love
  I'd be nothing

³if I parted with all that I owned
  if I offered my body to the sacrificial flames
  but lacked love
  it would do me no good

⁴love takes its time
  makes itself good and useful

13:1–13 There is substantial disagreement among scholars about the authorship of this passage. Some think Paul wrote it; some think that Paul adapted it from a non-biblical source; some think it is a later interpolation into Paul's letter. See the Cameo on 1 Corinthians 13, p. 113.

love doesn't envy
it doesn't boast
it doesn't bluster

⁵it doesn't make a scene
it doesn't look after its own interests
it doesn't throw fits
it doesn't dwell on the negative
⁶it takes no pleasure in injustice
but is delighted by the truth

⁷love upholds everything
trusts in everything
hopes for everything
endures everything

⁸love never falls away
though oracles will cease
tongues will fall silent
insight will fall short

⁹we know bits and pieces
in bits and pieces we deliver oracles

¹⁰but when the whole picture emerges
the bits and pieces will disappear

¹¹when I was very young
I talked like a child
thought like a child
reasoned like a child
when I grew up
I put an end to childish ways

¹²now we look at a reflection quite obscure
then we'll gaze face to face
now I know only bits and pieces
then I shall know as I am known

¹³so then confidence hope love
these three endure
but the greatest of these is
love]]

14 Pursue the more excellent way of love, and eagerly desire the spiritual gifts, especially that you may prophesy. ²People who engage in ecstatic speech are not speaking to us but to God. No one understands what they are saying; they are inspired to utter things that are unintelligible. ³Those who prophesy speak to us for our instruction and growth, our encouragement and consolation. ⁴Those who speak ecstatically build themselves up, but those who prophesy build up the community of the Anointed's people. ⁵I would like all of you to be able to speak ecstatically, but I especially want you to be able to prophesy. The one who prophesies is greater than the one who speaks ecstatically, unless someone interprets so that the community of the Anointed may receive something constructive.

⁶Listen, friends, if I meet with you and speak in an ecstatic language, how will I be of any use to you unless I offer some God-given insight, or some piece of knowledge, or some prophecy or teaching?

⁷Similarly, when inanimate objects such as a flute or a harp make a sound, if they don't play distinct notes, how will anyone know what music is being played? ⁸And if the bugle's call is unclear, who will prepare for battle? ⁹So also if in your ecstatic speech you make unintelligible sounds, how will anyone know what you are saying? You will be speaking into the air. ¹⁰It may be true that there are many types of language in the world and that none of them is incapable of conveying meaning. ¹¹But if I do not understand the force of the language, he will be speaking gibberish to me, and I will be speaking gibberish to him. ¹²That's the way it is in your case also. Since you are so enthusiastic about charismatic empowerment, try hard to become more and more accomplished in building up the Anointed's community.

¹³It follows that the person who is given to ecstatic utterance should pray for the ability to interpret it. ¹⁴If I pray in an ec-

static language, my heart is praying but my mind is idle. ¹⁵So what am I going to do about this? I am going to pray with my heart and pray with my mind also. I am going to sing with my heart and sing with my mind also. ¹⁶Otherwise, if you praise God with your heart, how can those who are outsiders say the amen after your thanksgiving, when they don't know what you are saying? ¹⁷You are offering a fine prayer, but no one else derives any benefit from it. ¹⁸I thank God that I engage in ecstatic speech more than any of you. ¹⁹But in the community of the Anointed I would rather speak five intelligible words in order to teach others than ten thousand words in unintelligible ecstatic speech.

²⁰Friends, don't be infantile in your thinking. Be infants with regard to evil, but in your thinking be adults. ²¹In scripture it is written: "by strange languages and by the lips of foreigners I will speak to this people, and not even then will they listen to me, says the Lord."

²²What this means is that ecstatic language is an omen not for members but for non-members, and prophecy is an omen not for non-members but for members. ²³If then the whole community of the Anointed has come together in one place and everyone is speaking in ecstatic languages and outsiders or non-members come in, will they not say that you are mad? ²⁴But if everyone is prophesying and some non-members or uninitiated persons come in, they will be convicted by all, called to account by all, ²⁵the secrets of their hearts are exposed; and so they will fall on their faces and worship God and declare that "God really is present among you."

²⁶So what should you do, my friends? When you gather together and you each have a hymn, a bit of instruction, a God-given insight, an ecstatic utterance, an interpretation, everything should be done for the benefit of the community. ²⁷If someone breaks out in ecstatic speech—two or at most three at the same time—one of you should interpret. ²⁸But if no interpreter is present, they should remain silent in the meeting

and speak to themselves and to God. [29]Two or three prophets should speak and the others should ponder what they say. [30]If an insight from God comes to someone else sitting alongside, the first speaker should be quiet. [31]All of you can prophesy if you speak one at a time, so that all may learn and be encouraged. [32]When and how prophets speak is under the control of the prophets, [33]because God is not a God of disorder but of peace.

[39]So, my friends, be eager to prophesy and don't forbid ecstatic utterance, [40]but everything should be done appropriately and in an orderly way.

15 I want you to understand better the meaning of the world-transforming message I preached to you, my friends, the message that you received and is the ground on which you stand. [2]It is also by that message that you are being rescued, if you hold on to the terms by which I presented it, unless you embraced it without thinking about what you were doing. [3]I passed on to you as of paramount importance what I also had received:

> that the Anointed died to free us from the seductive power
> of corruption
> according to the scriptures,
> [4]and that he was buried, and that he was raised "on the
> third day"
> according to the scriptures;

14:33b–38 In the judgment of the SV translators this passage is very probably an interpolation into Paul's text and therefore appears in the appendix to 1 Corinthians in this translation. See the explanatory note there.

15:4 *on the third day:* "The third day" is an idiomatic expression, not a literal number. It appears in Hos 6:2, where it means "after a short time," not three days later. In their Easter stories Matthew and Luke have turned this indefinite reference into a definite number: day three. Paul, however, never says that Jesus was raised from the dead three days following his crucifixion, and apparently had never heard the story about the discovery of the empty tomb on Easter morning. He never mentions it. The reference to "the third day" in the early creedal formula Paul quotes here retains the indefinite character it has in Hosea: "after a short time."

⁵and that he was seen by Cephas, then by the twelve; ⁶then he was seen by more than five hundred brothers and sisters at the same time. Most of them are still alive today, but some have passed away. ⁷Then he was seen by James, then by all the envoys. ⁸Last of all, as to one in whose birth God's purpose seemed to have miscarried, he was seen by me as well. ⁹For I am the least worthy of the envoys; I do not deserve to be called an envoy because I tried to put the community of the Anointed out of business. ¹⁰But the generous favor of God has made me what I am, and God's generosity to me has not been wasted. On the contrary, I have worked harder than any of them. I don't mean that I have done this all on my own; on the contrary, it was because God's generous favor was working with me. ¹¹So it doesn't make any difference whether it was I or they; this is what we present and this is what you embraced.

¹²Now if our message is that the Anointed has been raised from among the dead, how can some of you possibly be saying that there is no such thing as the resurrection of the dead? ¹³If there is no such thing as the resurrection of the dead, then the Anointed has not been raised either. ¹⁴And if the Anointed has not been raised, then our message has lost its credibility and so has your faith. ¹⁵We will be exposed as making false statements about God, because we have testified falsely that God raised the Anointed whom God did not raise, if it is really true that the dead are not raised. ¹⁶As I said, if the dead are not raised, then the Anointed has not been raised either. ¹⁷If the Anointed has not been raised, your faith is worthless and you are still not free from the seductive power of corruption, ¹⁸and in that case those who have died believing that they belonged to the Anointed have perished. ¹⁹If for this life only we are hoping in the Anointed, then we are the most pathetic people in the whole world.

²⁰But in reality the Anointed has been raised from the dead as the first fruits of the harvest of the dead. ²¹Because death

came into being through one human being, so also the resurrection of the dead has come through one human being. [22]For just as all who share Adam's humanity die, so also all who share the humanity of the Anointed will be brought to life. [23]But each of these in their proper order: the Anointed, the first fruits, afterwards at the Anointed's coming, those who have become his people. [24]Then comes the end of all things, the time when the Anointed hands the sovereignty back to God our Creator and Benefactor, after he has put down every ruler and every authority and power. [25]It is necessary for the Anointed to exercise the sovereignty until "he has put all of God's enemies under his feet." [26]The last enemy to be put down is death. [27]God has put everything under the Anointed's authority. Now when it says that everything is made subject to his authority, obviously the one by whom everything is subjected is excepted. [28]But once all things are subjected to him, then the "son of God" himself will become subject to the one who put everything under his authority, so that God may be the one who rules everything everywhere.

[29]If this is not the case, what do those who are being baptized on behalf of the dead think they are doing? If the dead are not raised at all, what's the point of being baptized on their behalf? [30]And why am I putting my life at risk all the time? [31]I face death every day—that's the real measure of the confidence I have about your prospects, my friends, thanks to the Anointed Jesus our lord. [32]If I had to fight wild beasts, so to speak, at Ephesus, what good does that do me? If the dead are not raised, "Let us eat and drink, because tomorrow we will be dead." [33]Don't let anyone mislead you. "Keeping bad company is the ruin of good character." [34]Come to your senses and straighten up your life. Some of you are without any knowledge of God. I say this to shame you.

15:33 The quotation is from a well-known proverb thought to have originated with Menander in *Thais*, fragment 218 (Loeb Classical Library, *Menander*, 1.356).

³⁵But someone will ask, "How are the dead raised? With what kind of body do they come back?" ³⁶Stupid man, what you sow does not come to life unless it dies. ³⁷And what you sow is not the body which it will be; what you sow is a bare seed, it could be of wheat or one of the other grains. ³⁸God gives it the body God intended, and to each kind of seed God gives its own kind of body. ³⁹Not all flesh is the same, but there is one kind of flesh for humans, another for animals, another for birds, and another for fish. ⁴⁰There are also heavenly bodies and earthly bodies; but the splendor of the heavenly is of one kind and the splendor of the earthly is of a different kind. ⁴¹The splendor of the sun is of one kind and the splendor of the moon of a different kind, and that of the stars yet another. In fact, one star differs from another in its splendor.

⁴²And so the dead will come to life like that: sown in corruption, raised incorruptible; ⁴³sown in a condition of humiliation, raised in a state of splendor; sown in a condition of weakness, raised in a state of power. ⁴⁴Sown with a body fit for earthly life, they are raised with a body fit for life in God's new world. If there is such a thing as a body fit for earthly life, there is also such a thing as a body fit for life in God's new world. ⁴⁵As scripture says. "The first Adam was created for earthly life," the last Adam became a life-creating power. ⁴⁶The body fit for life in God's new world was not first, but the body fit for earthly life; then the body fit for life in God's new world. ⁴⁷The first human was a lump of earth, an earthly man; the second human is from heaven. ⁴⁸As was the earthly man, so are those who are earthly, and as is heavenly man so are those who are

---

15:44 *A body fit for earthly life:* The phrase *(soma psychikon)* is often translated incorrectly as "a physical body." The sense of this phrase includes both the body and the "life-breath" that animates the body. Unlike neo-Platonists Paul does not see the body's animating force as immortal in itself.

15:47 Paul regards both the first and the second humans—the first Adam and the second Adam—as prototypes: the first of their kind and the model for all who follow them.

heavenly. [49]Just as we have borne the likeness of the earthly man, so we will also bear the likeness of the heavenly man.

[50]What I am saying, my friends, is this: flesh and blood is not capable of inheriting the coming Empire of God, no more than the corruptible can inherit the incorruptible. [51]Listen, now; I am going to tell you a wondrous secret: We are not all going to die, rather we are all going to be transformed, [52]in an instant, in the blink of an eye at the sound of the last trumpet-signal. The trumpet will sound and the dead will be raised incorruptible and we [too] will be transformed. [53]Because this perishable man must be clothed with the imperishable, and this mortal man must be clothed with immortality. [54]And when the perishable is clothed with the imperishable and the mortal is clothed with immortality, then the saying that is written will come true:

Death has been engulfed by victory.
Where, O Death, has your victory gone?
What's happened, O Death, to your fatal sting?

[56]The law is what makes the seductive power of corruption so lethal. [57]But thanks be to God for giving us the victory [over corruption and death] through our lord Jesus the Anointed.

[58]So then, my dear friends, stand firm, let nothing shake you. See that your work for the lord is always increasing, because you know that your labor for the lord will not come to nothing.

16 Now about the money we are collecting for God's people in Jerusalem, you should follow the directions I gave to the communities of the Anointed in Galatia. [2]On the first day of every week each of you should put aside and save up whatever your prosperity may permit, so that contributions need

---

15:53 *must:* Paul's use of this term reflects his view that the course of human history is being played out in accordance with God's plan—hidden from view until the disclosure of God's world-changing news about God's Anointed.

not be solicited when I come. ³And when I arrive, I will send those whom you have approved, with letters of introduction, to convey your gift to Jerusalem. ⁴If it seems worthwhile for me to go also, they will go with me.

⁵I will come to see you once I have made my way through Macedonia, because I am planning to go through Macedonia, ⁶and I may possibly stay with you a while or even spend the winter with you, so that you may help to send me on my way wherever I may go. ⁷I don't want to see you right now just in passing, because I am hoping to spend some time with you, if the Lord permits it. ⁸But I'm going to stay in Ephesus until Pentecost, ⁹because a large and promising door is open to me even though we have many opponents.

¹⁰If Timothy comes to see you, make sure that he has nothing to fear while he is with you, because he is engaged in the lord's work just as I am. ¹¹No one should treat him with disrespect, rather I ask that you help him on his way in peace so that he can return to me. I am expecting him with the brothers.

¹²Now about our brother Apollos, I have strongly encouraged him to come to see you along with the brothers. He is firm about not wanting to visit you right now, but he will come to see you when he has a good opportunity.

¹³Be alert, be unwavering in your confidence and trust in God, have courage, be strong. ¹⁴Do everything with love.

¹⁵I think you know that Stephanas and his household were the first in Achaia to respond to God's world-changing news and that they have devoted themselves to the service of God's people. ¹⁶I urge you, my friends, to accept direction from such people and from everyone who works and labors with them.

¹⁷I am very pleased that Stephanas and Fortunatus and Achaicus have come because they had made up for what you were not able to do. ¹⁸They have refreshed both my spirit and yours. So give recognition to such people. ¹⁹The communities of the Anointed in Asia send their greetings. Aquila and Prisca send their warm fraternal greetings to you as does the

gathering that meets in their house. ²⁰All of the brothers and sisters here send you their greetings. And you should greet and embrace each other.

²¹I, Paul, greet you in my own handwriting. ²²Anyone who does not love the lord should be avoided and shunned. *Marana tha.* ²³The favor of the lord Jesus be with you. ²⁴My love to all of you who belong to the Anointed Jesus.

16:22 Such a harsh curse in the middle of an otherwise gracious conclusion has no parallel in the benedictions in Paul's other letters. Further, Paul does not use either the Greek term for love here (*phileo*) or the Aramaic exclamation *Marana tha* in any other letter. This odd sentence jarringly disrupts the flow of the benediction in vv. 21, 23–24. These peculiar features of this harsh statement give one reason to suspect that it may have been inserted by a later transcriber of Paul's letter.

Scripture Parallels

1:19	Isa 29:14
1:31	Jer 9:23–24
2:9	Isa 64:4
2:16	Isa 40:13
3:19	Job 5:13; Ps 94:11
5:7	Exod 12:3–8, 21; cp. Mark 14:12; Luke 22:7
5:13	Deut 17:7
6:16	Gen 2:24
9:9	Deut 25:4
9:14	Cp. Luke 10:7
10:5	Num 14:29–30
10:7	Exod 32:4,6
10:8	Num 25:1–9
10:9	Num 21:5–6
10:10	Num 16:13–14; 41–49
10:26	Pss 24:1; 50:12
11:23–25	Mark 14:22–25; Matt 26:26–29; Luke 22:14–20
11:25	Jer 31:31
14:21	Isa 28:11–12

15:25	Ps 110:1
15:32	Isa 22:13
15:45–47	Gen 2:7
15:54–55	Isa 25:8 LXX; Hos 13:14

Pauline Parallels

1:1–3	1 Thess 1:1; Gal 1:1–5; 2 Cor 1:1–2; Phil 1:1–2; Phlm 1–3; Rom 1:1–4, 7
1:4	1 Thess 1:2; Phil 1:3; Phlm 4; Rom 1:8
1:31	2 Cor 10:17; Gal 6:14
4:9	2 Cor 2:14–16
6:9–11	Gal 5:19–21; Rom 1:26–27
7:11–12	1 Thess 4:3–5
7:19	Gal 5:6; 6:15
8:6	Rom 11:36
8:7–13	Rom 14:13–21
9:1–2	2 Cor 3:1–3
9:3–6; 15–18	1 Thess 2:9–10; 2 Cor 11:7–9; Phil 4:10–18
9:24–27	Phil 1:12–14
11:1	1 Thess 1:6; Phil 3:17; 4:9;
12:4–13; 27–31	Rom 12:3–8
15:21–23; 42–50	Rom 5:12–14
15:24–27	Phil 3:20–21
15:51–52	1 Thess 4:16–17
16:1–4	2 Cor 8:1–7; 9:–5; Rom 15:26–28
16:5–9	2 Cor 1:16–18; 23–24; 2:1–4
16:10	2 Cor 8:16–24; Phil 4:19–24
16:19	Rom 16:3
16:20	1 Thess 5:26; 2 Cor 13:12–13; Rom 16:16
16:21	Gal 6:11
16:23	1 Thess 5:28; Gal 6:18; 2 Cor 13:14; Phil 4:23; Phlm 25; Rom 16:20b

INTERPOLATIONS

1 Corinthians 4:6b

An Explanatory Comment

Harvard Professor John Strugnell, in a private conversation with Arthur Dewey, suggested that "not to go beyond what is written in the scriptures" in v. 6 was probably a comment originally written in the margin that was later inserted into the text. The SV translators agreed that this comment disrupts the rhetorical continuity of Paul's statements, was very probably not originally part of Paul's letter, and have therefore deleted it from this translation.

4 ⁶. . . "not to go beyond what is written [in the scriptures]"

∽

1 Corinthians 11:2–16

An Explanatory Comment

Several features of this passage strongly suggest that it is a later insertion, not part of Paul's letter. The most important is the argument it makes for the social subordination of women. Such an argument is compatible with the interpolated statement in 14:33b–38, but contradicts Paul's affirmation of the equal status of men and women in Gal 3:26–28 and throughout 1 Corinthians 7. Secondly, the appeal to following Paul's "practices" and maintaining "all of the traditions" that he had passed on to the Corinthians is the way the later Pastoral Letters of 1 and 2 Timothy and Titus speak about such things, but not the way Paul speaks about himself or about tradition. Paul does exhort his readers to imitate him (1 Cor 4:16; Phil 3:17; 4:9) and refers to tradition that he had received regarding the lord's supper (1 Cor 11:23–25) and regarding Jesus' resurrection (1 Cor 15:3–5), but these are not traditions about social behavior like that which this passage insists upon. Thirdly, the argument of this passage disrupts Paul's argument: 11:17–34 continues Paul's discussion of the ordinary meal practices in chapter 10 and extends it to the inappropriate sacred meal (lord's supper) practices of some of the Corinthians, whereas 11:2–16 breaks up this continuity by introducing a totally different topic.

11 [2]I applaud you for following all my practices and for faithfully maintaining the traditions just as I passed them on to you. [3]Now I want you to know that the Anointed is the head of every man, a man is the head of every woman, and God is the head of the Anointed. [4]Any man who prays or prophesies in public with a head-covering brings shame on his "head," [5]and any woman who prays or prophesies with her hair not done up in public brings shame on her "head." She may as well have had her head shaved. [6]If a woman goes without doing her hair up, she might as well cut her hair off; but if it is indeed shameful for a woman to clip her hair or shave her head, then she should put her hair up. [7]A man shouldn't put his hair up, since he is the "image and reflection" of God; but woman is the reflection of man, [8]because man did not come into being from woman, but woman from man. [9]And man was not created for woman, but woman for man. [10]That is why a woman ought to wear her hair in a way that acknowledges her status because that is how heaven's messengers act. [11]But in the eyes of the lord, no woman exists apart from a man and no man exists apart from a woman, [12]because just as a woman was originally made from man so also man now comes into being through woman; and everything comes from God. [13]You be the judge: is it fitting for a woman to pray to God with her hair down and disheveled? [14]Doesn't nature itself teach us that it's shameful for a man to let his hair grow long, [15]but that if a woman lets her hair grow long she gains honor. Long hair is given to her to use as a covering. [16]But if anyone wants to be contentious about this we have no other practice nor do the churches of the people of God.

∾

1 Corinthians 14:33b–38

An Explanatory Comment

There are substantial reasons for regarding this passage as an interpolation into Paul's letter. The notion that women should be prohibited from speaking in the public gatherings of the Anointed's community is contrary to the equality of men and women that Paul strongly affirms in Gal 3:26–28 and throughout the seventh chapter of 1 Corinthians. This passage claims that this prohibition is a commandment of the Lord in the law (reading v. 37 as repeating the claim of v. 34). Paul, however, nowhere argues that social customs embedded in Mosaic law are mandatory for the nations. Further, there is no known "saying of the lord," i.e. of Jesus, which commands women to be silent in such gatherings. The regulation advocated here is comparable to what is found in the pseudo-Pauline letters of 1 and 2 Timothy, and Titus, which are the work of an early second-century author who claims the authority of Paul. This passage also interrupts the coherence of Paul's argument in this chapter on the relative value of ecstatic speech and prophetic speech. This part of Paul's argument reads coherently if this passage is deleted as an insertion into Paul's original text. That coherence is disrupted by the insertion of this passage, which is not representative of Paul's thought. Finally, the location of this passage varies in the early manuscripts: vv. 34–35 are located after 14:40 in some of the Latin versions and the Western texts.

14 ³³. . . As in all the churches of God, ³⁴the women should be silent during the meetings. They are not permitted to speak, but must be subordinate, just as scripture says. ³⁵If there is something they want to know, they should ask their own husbands at home, because it is a disgrace for a woman to speak out in a meeting of the congregation. ³⁶Or do you think that the word of God originated with you? Or that it has come only to you? ³⁷If any of you thinks you are a prophet or are inspired by the spirit, you should recognize that what I am writing to you is a command of the lord. [38]Anyone who ignores this will be ignored.

Did Paul Write 1 Corinthians 13

Whether or not this chapter was authored by Paul or was even part of the original form of this letter are much debated questions. Several features of this beloved passage make it look like an insertion. In its vocabulary and structure, it is unlike any other passage in Paul's authentic letters. For instance, contrary to what is typical of Paul's language throughout his letters, there is no mention of God or of God's Anointed in this passage, nor is the love that is celebrated in this passage said to be the love of God or the love of God's Anointed. Further, the connections with what precedes this chapter (12:31) and with what follows it (14:1) are a bit forced and rather awkward. Chapter 12 is a discussion of gifts that are inspired by God's presence and power. Chapter 14 is a discussion of the gifts of ecstatic speech and prophetic speech. In the view of some scholars, chapter thirteen's lyrical praise of love disrupts Paul's discussion of special gifts in chapters 12 and 14, and is therefore likely to have been inserted into Paul's text by a later transcriber.

It is sometimes noted that the Greek term *pistis* (traditionally, "faith"; SV "confidence" [in God]) is used here in a way that differs from the predominant way it is used in Paul's letters. Paul most frequently uses the term *pistis* to refer to "confidence and trust in God." In this passage (13:2, 13) *pistis* refers to a person's special gift or attribute: the power to do miraculous or extraordinary deeds. But this usage of the term is not quite as unusual as it may seem. In two other passages in his Corinthian correspondence the term *pistis* occurs with the same sense it has here, namely 1 Cor 12:9 and 1 Cor 8:7. Further, in Gal 5:23 the term *pistis* occurs in a list of the "evidence that God's power is present among us" where it refers to "trustworthiness;" and in Gal 1:23 Paul quotes the remark that Jesus' followers in Judea made about

Continued on next page

him—that the man who had once persecuted them was now proclaiming "the faith" (*tēn pistin*). These Judeans were using the term *pistis*, with the definite article, as a name for their religious orientation.

So *pistis* is used by Paul with some variation of meaning, including reference to the power to do miraculous or extraordinary deeds to which the term refers in 1 Cor 13:2 and 9. While this usage of the term is infrequent in Paul, it does not furnish compelling evidence of the non-Pauline origin of this passage. The principal reasons for suspecting that the passage may not have originated with Paul are that its placement in the text appears to disrupt the argument Paul begins in chapter 12 and continues in chapter 14, and its unusual poetic structure and lyrical language.

A number of scholars continue to regard this chapter as part of Paul's original letter, some because they regard it as the climax of Paul's argument about the gifts that come from God's presence and power discussed in chapter 12 (because love transcends such gifts), others because they judge it to be a Pauline digression in which he draws upon his background in Hellenistic Judaism (which might account for the atypical vocabulary and style of the passage). Since scholarly opinion is so divided, SV translators have chosen to retain the chapter as part of the text of Paul's letter rather than consign it to the appendix, even though its status as part of Paul's letter remains uncertain.

2 Corinthians

INTRODUCTION

The Corinthian correspondence presents the reader with a remarkable opportunity. Unlike any other material in the New Testament, these letters provide a window onto how an early Jesus community was actually developing. Paul's correspondence with the Corinthians documents his sustained efforts over a significant period of time to negotiate with and advise that most energetic and surprising community.

However, it is not simply the case that there are only two letters to the Corinthians. What we call "First Corinthians" was actually a second letter (1 Cor 5:9). The matter becomes more complicated when what is traditionally known as "Second Corinthians" is read with a critical eye. The Second Letter to the Corinthians does not appear to be a unified piece. Rather, a close reading of the material delivers a problematic picture. Numerous discrepancies and inconsistencies abound. Some scholars have tried to overcome such observations by noting that there is no evidence of the fragmentary nature of Second Corinthians in the textual tradition. However, this argument is rather specious since the earliest text we have of Second Corinthians comes from the third century. Moreover, the earliest mention of anything from what we know as Second Corinthians comes from about 140 CE. If Paul wrote the Corinthian correspondence in the mid fifties of the first century, there was then a considerable amount of time in which a number of shorter letters could have been combined into one major letter.

The Question of Unity

It is incumbent then to see how a careful reading of 2 Corinthians raises many troubling issues. The question of the unity of 2 Corinthians must be considered at the outset in order to reach some determination of the intent of the extant evidence.

Many scholars have often pointed out that 2 Cor 6:14–7:1 presents a distinct body of material. The language, issues, and tone dramatically interrupt the letter. The dualistic language is more akin to that found among the Dead Sea Scrolls. The unyielding homiletic approach of these verses contrasts sharply with the more personal appeal in 6:13 and 7:2ff.

Yet the discrepancies with 2 Corinthians do not end there. Although the letter starts off with a rousing note of reconciliation (1:3–7), 2:14 abruptly changes the momentum of the letter. Another thanksgiving has been inserted into what was a developing letter of reconciliation. What follows in 2:14–6:13, 7:2–4 stands in contrast to the tone, language, and rhetoric of the letter's beginning. A conflict apparently is budding, yet Paul seems to be confident in resolving the matter. Indeed, he seems to be using some of the terms of his opposition in making his case. Although Paul uses scripture to demonstrate his point, the format of this section seems closer to a political speech than a letter of reconciliation.

This political section falls off at 7:4. From 7:5 to the end of the seventh chapter we are back to the matter of communal reconciliation. The opposition mentioned in 2:14–6:13, 7:2–4 has disappeared.

Chapter 8 brings another change in tone, content, and rhetoric. The note of reconciliation is not present. This section is a letter of appeal for the collection for Jerusalem. The collection for the Jerusalem community has in no way been prepared by chapter 7. In addition, Titus had just returned from Corinth in chapter 7, while in chapter 8 he seems already to have departed.

Chapter 9 also can be seen as a distinct letter fragment. It contains different episodes regarding the collection for Jerusalem. It is addressed to all of Achaia. Moreover, the delegation mentioned in chapter 8 already has departed (9:3–5).

Paul is sending out other delegates. The format looks very much like a homiletic tract.

The difficulties of 2 Corinthians continue with chapter 10. At first blush this section (chap. 10–13) seems to be dealing with problems similar to 2:14–6:13; 7:2–4. But something has changed. Paul is no longer confident of his position with the Corinthians. He appears on the verge of losing them. There seems to have been a visit by Paul and a subsequent explosion. This section, moreover, does not at all connect well with the chapters immediately preceding. There is a decided change in tone and style. The topics are quite different. It does not function as a fitting conclusion to a plea for a collection. Scholars have pointed out that this material sounds much more like a philosophical apology, employing many of the dramatic elements of Hellenistic mime.

In sum, there appear to be six distinct sections or fragmentary letters in 2 Corinthians. 6:14–7:1 is manifestly non-Pauline (an interpolation). But the problematic unity of 2 Corinthians is not resolved by this observation alone. There are five other fragmentary letters, which represent five different segments in the Corinthian history. By placing these letters within the larger context of the Pauline letters and of the first-century world, we can begin to piece together a probable chronology.

A Probable Reconstruction of Events

After finishing 1 Corinthians and after Timothy's visit (1 Cor 4:17; 6:10), Paul decided to modify his previous plans (1 Cor 16:3–9) and sends Titus to Corinth to speed up the collection for Jerusalem. This is done with the Corinthians' cooperation (2 Cor 8:5, 10; 9:2; 12:18). Then Jesus missionaries, emphasizing their Judaic origin, arrive in Corinth, taking the Pauline community as their base of operations. In their role as envoys they sow doubts about Paul's competence and authority.

Paul responds with Letter 1 (2:14–7:4 minus 6:14–7:1) but this is ironically unsuccessful. He wins the battle but loses the war. The Corinthians are impressed by the performance of the letter. Yet a personal visit turns into a disaster (2:1ff.; 7:5ff.; 12:14; 13:1). Paul evidently cannot compete on the terms set by the new envoys. The opposition is at its peak and Paul is ruthlessly attacked. After leaving Corinth, he sends Letter 2 (10–13) in which he takes the Corinthians and the outside agitators to task. Titus has been sent to Corinth again (2:12–13; 7:5–7). But before he returned, Paul had been arrested and imprisoned for several months (cf. the Philippian correspondence). Upon his release Paul hastens to Troas, then to Macedonia, where Paul meets Titus and learns that the situation is vastly improved (7:5–16). Paul sends Letter 3 (1:1–2:13; 7:5–16) to clarify the response that should be made to the person who offended Paul and to explain his failure to visit Corinth on his way to and from Macedonia.

In Letter 4 (chap. 8) Paul finds Titus willing to resume the matter of the collection and sends him along with two other delegates. After their departure Paul sends another letter (Letter 5, chap. 9), this one to the communities in all of Achaia. If there is any accuracy in Acts in regard to this situation, Paul finally visits Corinth again and stays there for several months (Acts 20:2–3).

The Canonical Version of 2 Corinthians

For some reason 2 Corinthians was "lost" for about 90 years. 1 Clement and Ignatius of Antioch make no mention of this letter. Marcion is the first to use it (140 CE). Marcion is the earliest "text critic" of the Christian tradition. He was the first person to compile and edit a collection of Pauline letters together with a Gospel (Luke). With his "new testament" in codex form, Marcion had a literary basis for renewal in a church he thought had greatly compromised on the original inspiration of the apostles. He wanted to purify the church from the meddling effects of the God of Israel, who was not the Father of Jesus but, in his view, a violent demiurge. Marcion also wanted to make sure that the church realized that it was in a radically new situation brought to light through the appearance of Jesus. He wanted to move away from old appearances to the revolutionary reality of God's Anointed.

There are some possible reasons why Marcion or a follower "unearthed" 2 Corinthians: the theme of the "new covenant" versus the "old covenant" (chap. 3); darkness opposed to light (chap. 4); a new order in God's Anointed (5:17); the linkage of the old covenant with slavery (chap. 3); Moses' God seems to be like the Platonic Demiurge; the apparent docetic remarks (5:16) and anthropological dualism (4:16) utilized by Marcion; the condemning of false envoys (11:13–15). In brief, this material gave Marcion considerable justification for his argument.

The first third of the second century was a most extravagant time. Some scholars have called it an age of triumphalism. The emphasis upon the extraordinary individual had reached its zenith. Trajan's Column was only one instance of the apotheosis of the individual. At the same time the Empire was undergoing significant centralization. It was also a period of canonization (e.g., Rabbinic Canon) as well as an anti-Judean period (Bar Kochba Revolt). There were shifts in eschatological thought, increased religious activity, with competing movements and mystery religions.

The Triumphal Column of Paul

From the point of view of the present reader of 2 Corinthians this "unified" text greatly resembles the column of a great individual man, endowed with power and spirit. The canonical 2 Corinthians very much bears the imprint of the second century. We can even paraphrase this "apotheosis in print" thus:

> Thanks to God for Paul, who is truthful and reconciling, triumphant in adversity; who recognizes the old is replaced by the new; who bears up in dire straits for personal glory; who is leading a triumphant procession across the world, making a collection which is a token of the universal move-

ment; who warns all to be aware of false prophets who call for a return to the ways of the Old Covenant; and he blesses all with God's power and presence.

The Opponents of Paul

Many Pauline scholars have made it quite clear that the understanding of the fragments that make up 2 Corinthians comes into focus by turning to the question of Paul's opposition. By teasing out some clues from 2 Corinthians along with a sensitive reading of Hellenistic Judaism, scholars suggest a profile for these "super-envoys."

Centering their message on "Jesus" (11:4), and emphasizing the name (4:10–14) and the notion of God's Anointed in human terms (5:16), Paul's opponents were recognized as legitimate missionaries, with proper titles (11:5, 13, 23). They retained their Hellenistic Jewish traditions (11:22; chap. 3). The tradition from Moses to Jesus was seen as a storehouse of divine power and presence, which they could tap through the means of allegorical exegesis. Through this exegesis one could gain transcendental experiences. In any case ecstasy and other miraculous achievements were seen as necessary indicators of the competence of these missionaries. By this and in attempting to prove the superiority of their religion they were like their contemporaries who were viewed as divine heroes. The older the religion or tradition was, so much the better, since there would be more divine heroes available. So the tie-in of Jesus with Moses, Elijah, Solomon, etc., was essential, for they had a definite link with the spiritual power of the past. They denounced Paul for not having the objective signs of a true missionary. They, on the other hand, had public acknowledgement and used letters of recommendation to provide continuous proof of their spiritual status. They did so to maintain a stance in the missionary competition and to aid them in gaining followers. The community or audience became the judges between them and Paul in regard to the question of competence and acknowledgement.

The Fragmentary Letters

Letter 1: A Defense of Paul's Credibility

2 Cor 2:14–6:13; 7:2–4

If one were to read the 2 Cor 2:14–6:13; 7:2–4 through without any regard to context there would be a great straining to discover a consistent line of reasoning in Paul's thought. Thus, many commentators have argued that Paul has once again become emotional and even "mystical." But this explains nothing. When one considers this section from the perspective of the possible opposition—indicated by the evident debating style and language—then the section begins to make sense. Paul is presupposing that the Corinthians appreciate the style of allegorical interpretation of the opposition. Although he does not allegorize Exodus 34, he does use it as a base of interpretation and filters it through the lens of "two" covenants. The position advocated by the opposition partakes of the order which is ending, including their use of letters of recommendation and the analysis of scripture by allegorization. The community already had the key to interpreting not only scripture (letter) but even history itself through their possession of the power and presence of God in their midst. In short, he continues to bring the point of the argument back to the Corinthians themselves, so that they may recognize on their own what they have in trust. Here Paul uses his opponents' language (covenant, competency, letter, brilliance) in order to demonstrate that the power and presence of God already present to the community can provide all that the opposition promise (and control).

Letter 2: A Parody of "A Fool's Speech"

2 Corinthians 10–13

This fragment is a defensive response to the charge that Paul is a boaster, namely, that there is a discrepancy between what he says (or writes) and his personal appearance. Paul takes a significant chance in writing this letter. He feels that he has almost lost connection with the very community he founded.

So he decides to use a comic approach in order to get the Corinthians to see the flawed assumptions upon which they have judged Paul. The use of a fool's speech (with a variety of characters) is designed to provoke self-examination in his listeners. In 12:19 Paul makes it clear why he wrote—for the Corinthians' upbuilding. Paul uses himself as the foil, the butt of jokes so that the community might discover themselves. By taking the charge of unverified boasting and carrying it to comic extremes, Paul forces the community to see the issue of competence in a different light and to re-examine the basis of their social assumptions and judgments.

Letter 3: A Letter of Reconciliation
2 Cor 1:1–2:13; 7:5–16

What has been traditionally the opening to Second Corinthians is actually a further installment in the conversation Paul had with the Corinthians. Evidently Paul has gotten word that his "fool's letter" had its intended effect. The Corinthians have grown in their understanding of Paul's perspective. A new level of relationship has been reached.

Letters 4 & 5: Collection Appeals
2 Corinthians 8 and 9

These letters are appeals for the collection in Jerusalem. While Letter 4 (chap. 8) is directed to Corinth, Letter 5 (chap. 9) is intended for a larger audience (the Roman province of Achaia). The collection for the "poor" in Jerusalem was a crucial issue for Paul. While it may have been originally meant as assistance for the poor Jesus followers in Jerusalem, Paul has transformed it into something more. Since Paul has proclaimed a message that the nations can approach the God of Israel with the trust like that of Jesus, God's Anointed, the collection Paul would bring to Jerusalem would embody that understanding. This collection would substantiate the equality of the nations with Jews before the God of Israel. It is not known whether it was so received in Jerusalem (nor does Acts aid us in this matter).

Letter 1
A Defense
of Paul's Credibility

2 ¹⁴. . . Thank God, who always makes a spectacle of us in the service of God's Anointed, and spreads through us the fragrance of knowing him everywhere. ¹⁵To God we are the sweet incense of God's Anointed both for those who are headed for deliverance and those who are bound for ruin. ¹⁶To the latter it's an odor that reeks of death; to the former it's the sweet smell of life. Who can handle this? ¹⁷We are not like many who crassly market God's message; we speak in the Anointed's service with integrity, as if in the presence of God.

3 Are we beginning to give ourselves too much credit? We don't need letters of recommendation to you or from you, as some people do, do we? ²You are our letter, inscribed on your hearts, known and read by everyone. ³You are showing

---

Letter 1 This letter is very much like a political speech, defending Paul's mission and critiquing his opposition.
2:14 An abrupt break from 2:13. The travelogue that Paul begins in 2:12–13 and continues in 7:5–7 has been interrupted here in canonical 2 Corinthians by an insertion of this earlier piece of correspondence. The thanksgiving (2:14) apparently is part of the opening of this earlier fragment. See the Introduction.
2:14–16 An image of a military triumph, well-known in the Empire, is cast as a universal parade. The triumph has a double aspect, revealing as pungently as incense both life and death. Paul leaves the image somewhat ambiguous. Does he see himself among the captives or among the victors?
2:16 This rhetorical question plays on different levels. It refers to the issue of competency of those who declare the message of the Anointed. It also refers to the question of who can stand at the coming of God.
3:1 Evidently Paul's missionary opponents possessed letters of recommendation. Such letters would document the competence of the missionary witnessed by the recommending community.
3:3 Paul is playing upon the well-known rhetorical distinction between what is conventional (*nomos*) and what is natural (*physis*). Here Paul replaces what is natural with the power and presence of God (*pneuma*). This is an instance of the long-standing cultural debate contrasting the genuine to the artificial. It is

yourselves to be a letter from God's Anointed delivered by us—written not with ink but by the power of the living God, not on tablets of stone but on tablets of human hearts.

[4]The Anointed has given us the confidence in God [to make such a claim] [5]We do not presume to claim that our competence is based on our own ability; rather, our credentials come from God [6]who authorized us to be agents of a new covenant—not one that's inscribed, but one that's alive in us. Relying on what is written kills, but the power of God's presence gives life.

[7]If the old order inscribed in stone that ends in death came with such brilliance that the Israelites could not look directly into the face of Moses because of its brightness, even though it was transitory, [8]how can the new order of life-giving power not be all the more brilliant? [9]For if there was brilliance in the old order that leads to condemnation, how much more brilliant is the new order that leads to vindication! [10]For what was once illustrious has lost its luster in comparison with the brilliance that surpasses it. [11]If what was transitory came with brilliance, how much more brilliant is that which endures.

---

not simply a matter of a "spiritual" or higher reading of a text. Along with this cultural contrast, Paul draws upon the distinction found in the eschatological visions of Ezekiel (11:19 LXX, 36:26 LXX) and Jeremiah (38:33 LXX) that contrast a covenant written on stone with a new one written on the human heart.
3:6 *What is written* (literally "letter" in Greek) conveys a wide spectrum of meaning, running from a letter of the alphabet to the law that establishes society. The "letter," seen as a tool for cultural advancement, served for many as a storehouse of the power of God. The one who could not only read but also interpret a scroll would demonstrate a competence to deliver meaning to the listeners. That person would unlock the "power" in the letter.
Note that this is an oral performance. Paul is not imagining a silent reading of texts but an oral performance; hence his speech is delivered "live."
3:7–18 Exodus 34:27–35 provides the basis of Paul's interpretation. It may well have been used by his opponents in establishing their teaching credentials. Through an allegorical reading of Exodus 34 the opponents could deliver "God's power and presence," the inner meaning of the text.
3:7–11 Paul sees contrasts rather than continuities. The tradition written in stone is transitory and deadly. Paul argues that Moses prevented the people from discovering the transitory nature of the written tradition by a "cover up," that is, by placing a veil over his face (v. 13).

¹²It is because we have this hope that we can speak so openly—¹³not like Moses who covered up his face with a veil so that the Israelites would not see the inevitable end of what is transitory. ¹⁴But their minds were shrouded. To this day when they read the old covenant the same veil remains; it is not removed unless it is taken away through God's Anointed. ¹⁵Still today whenever the writings of Moses are read a veil lies over their hearts: ¹⁶As scripture says: "But whenever he turns to the Lord, the veil is lifted." ¹⁷Now the word "Lord" here refers to God's presence and power. And where the Lord's power is present, there is freedom. ¹⁸All of us with our faces unveiled are reflecting the brilliance of the Lord so that we are being transformed into the same divine image from one aspect of brilliance to another, just as the term "Lord" really means "God's presence and power."

4 Since it is God who has entrusted this mission to us, we do not give up. ²We have disowned shameful cover-ups, we do not engage in devious behavior, nor do we counterfeit God's message. Rather, by an open disclosure of the truth we recommend ourselves to everyone's conscience before God. ³Now, if our message is "veiled," it is "veiled" because those bound for ruin don't get it. ⁴They are among those closed minds the

---

3:13 Paul suggests that there has been a "cover up"—Moses should have enabled the Israelites to see the limit of the old order but he prevents them. In effect, the missionaries who claim to disclose the meaning of the text are continuing in this cover-up. Contrast Galatians 3, where the law is limited in its role. By describing it as a slave who accompanies a child to school and serves as a disciplinarian until the child grows up, Paul argues for the temporal nature of the law.
3:16 Paul comments on the allegorical method of interpretation of his opponents. A "veil" of ignorance remains until the text of Exodus 34 has been opened up to the listeners. Exodus 34:34 becomes the key text. Just as Moses took off his veil, so also the interpreter removes the veil on the scroll.
Lord refers to God. It is not a Christological reference.
3:17 *God's presence and power*: This is the allegorical move from literal level to "spiritual." But Paul apparently adds a further connection of God's power and presence with freedom.
4:3 Paul's opponents may well have charged that his message of the Anointed did not convey the true inner meaning.

god of this age has blinded so that the light of the world-transforming news of the brilliance of God's Anointed—who is the image of God—doesn't dawn on them.

[5]We are not publicizing ourselves but Jesus, God's Anointed, as lord and ourselves as your slaves on Jesus' behalf. [6]For the God who said, "Let light shine from darkness," has enlightened our hearts to recognize the splendor of God in the face of Jesus, God's Anointed.

[7]This treasured message we bear in "ordinary earthenware," so its dynamic impact comes from God and not from us. [8]We've been pressured from all sides but not boxed in, at a loss but not at our wits' end, [9]hounded but not abandoned, knocked down but not knocked out. [10]Every day we expose ourselves to the same threats that led to the death of Jesus, so that the life of Jesus might be visible in us. [11]While we are alive we are repeatedly handed over to death on account of Jesus, so that the life of Jesus might be visible in our mortal bodies. [12]So death takes its toll on us, but life [abounds] in you.

[13]Since we have the same air of confidence as the one who wrote, "I have confidence in God and so I spoke," we also have confidence and so we speak. [14]We know that the One who raised the lord Jesus will bring us to stand with you in God's presence. [15]All this is for your benefit, so that as divine favor spreads to more and more people, their added thanksgiving swells the chorus of praise to God. [16]So we don't give up. If our outer self is decaying, our inner self is renewed day after day. [17]Our present distress is only a light burden to bear considering that it is far outweighed by the glorious future for which it is preparing us. [18]We keep our eyes not on what is visible but on what is not visible. For what is visible is fleeting, but what is not visible endures forever.

4:6 Paul contends that creation is happening now within the Corinthian community.

4:16 Paul is speaking in terms of a dichotomy. He has already contrasted "outer vs. inner" above in terms of fragile containers (4:7).

5 We know that if the earthly tent we inhabit is destroyed, we have a house provided by God, a home not made by human hands, everlasting in the heavens [2]For while we're in this tent in our present circumstances we moan, yearning to acquire our heavenly attire [3]so that, even if we've been stripped of our earthly tent, we won't be caught naked. [4]I mean that, as long as we are in this tent, we groan, weighed down over not wanting to be stripped stark naked but to be dressed up so that what is mortal will be swallowed up by life. [5]God prepares us just for this by offering us God's presence and power as a down payment.

[6]We always keep our courage up, even though we know that as long as we're home in the body we're not at home with the lord, [7]for we walk by confidence in God, not by what we can see. [8]As I say, we keep our courage up, even though we'd rather be away from the body and at home with the lord. [9]In any case, whether at home or away, we strive to please him. [10]For we all must come up to the podium of God's Anointed so that each of us may be given our award according to what we have done through the body, whether it was good or not so good.

[11]Since we know what it means to revere the Lord we try to persuade people [about this]. God sees us for what we really are and I hope you discern this too. [12]We're not trying to give ourselves too much credit again; rather, we're giving you reason to speak well of us so that you will have something to

---

5:1 *Not made by human hands/everlasting* is a rhetorical play based in Hellenistic dualism.

5:2 *moan:* Compare v. 4 variant of "groan."

5:10 The spatial metaphors (tent/heavenly dwelling) now are followed by a temporal scene—that of a future award ceremony—not a sentencing session of a court. Everybody gets something. It is not about punishment but a differentiation of prizes determined by the quality of the contribution one makes.

5:11 Paul expresses his honest relationship before God. While it is a matter of the heart it is nonetheless a public issue. As in 2 Corinthians 4 Paul has nothing to hide.

5:12 This picks up the issue of self-recommendation (2 Cor 3:1ff.). The rhetorical dualism of appearances and reality underpins this argument.

say to those who pride themselves on their appearance and not on what is in the heart. [13]If we were in an ecstatic state, it was for God. If we were in our right mind, it was for you. [14]The Anointed's love is what motivates us—because we are convinced that since one died for all, therefore all have died. [15]What this means is that he died for all so that those now alive might no longer live for themselves but for the one who died and was raised for them.

[16]From now on, therefore, we don't look at anyone from a worldly point of view. Even though we thought of God's Anointed in that way, we think of him in that way no longer. [17]Consequently, for anyone in solidarity with God's Anointed, it is as if there is a new world order. The old order is gone, look—the new order has arrived! [18]All of this comes from God who changes our relationship with the divine through the Anointed and has made us agents of this change. [19]God is, as it were, changing the world's relation with the divine through the Anointed, not charging their deficits to their accounts, and entrusting us with this message of change. [20]We act as agents of God's Anointed, as if God were making an appeal through

---

5:14 *We are convinced* indicates Paul's judgment. He delivers his conclusion. Verses 14–15 anticipate vv. 16–21. The conditions of existence have changed, with the consequences being a mutual exchange of purpose (v. 15).
5:16 This verse brings out the consequences of vv. 14–15. "The worldly point of view" is not simply a *perspective*. It indicates that a matter of judgment, value and comparison is at stake. Paul implies that even the wrongheaded valuation of God's Anointed can be a matter of judgment based upon the old regime.
5:17 *new world order:* It is not just a notion of "creation" but of a new order of the universe, a new foundation has been laid. There is a new establishment of what constitutes reality.
5:18 *changes:* The usual default translation *katallasso* is "to reconcile." This implies a return to status quo ante. But we do not have this in 2 Cor 5:14–21. A new situation is argued for in arresting images. The root meaning for this verb is "to change money" (LS 899) which leads to the sense of "exchange." If Paul is considering the founding of a new world order, could he be using the root metaphor of reminting the coinage? Whenever there was a regime change in the ancient world, there was a reminting of coinage in order to communicate to the illiterate population that a political transformation had occurred. The simple term "change" in this translation plays with this notion of such a fundamental change.
5:19 *As it were* indicates Paul's further working out of his sense of a new cosmic situation. The stress is on a novel development, even a change in the image of divine vis-à-vis the world.

us. On behalf of God's Anointed we implore you: Accept the new terms of our relationship with God: [21][It's as if] God took him, a coin in mint condition, and treated him as if he were [a] coin that had lost its value for our benefit so that through him we might be recast into the coinage of God's integrity.

6 As co-workers of God we implore you not to let the gift of God's favor go to waste. [2]As scripture says:

> At the right time I heard you;
> on a day of deliverance I came to your aid.

Look! The right time is now; see, today is the day of deliverance! [3]We try to avoid offending anyone in any way so that no fault will be found with our work. [4]In every way possible we present ourselves as God's agents—by great endurance, under heavy pressure, in anguish, and in distress, [5]by beatings, imprisonments, riots, by hard work, sleepless nights, going hungry; [6]by our sincerity, understanding, and long-suffering, by our kindness, with a spirit of integrity and genuine love, [7]by speaking the truth and by God's power; armed both for offense and defense with the weapons of justice, [8]whether honored or dishonored, blamed or praised; labeled "deceivers" we are really truthful, [9]"unknown" though really well known, "at death's door" and look, "We're alive!" Punished, but not put to death, [10]in pain we're always joyful, impoverished we enrich many, owning nothing we have everything.

[11]Corinthians, we have been completely transparent with you. Our hearts are wide open to you. [12]Your difficulties are not with us but with your own deeply felt predispositions. [13]I appeal to you as my children: open up your hearts in response. 7 [2]Make room in your hearts for us! We haven't harmed anyone, corrupted anyone, taken advantage of anyone. [3]I'm not

---

5:21 The root metaphor may well be that of reminting new coins from old. This would nicely tie in the notion of a new cosmic order. Not restoration, but a revolution. Compare P. Cair. Zen. I 59021, where *ginomai* (become) means "to be cast into new money."

7:2 This verse picks up the language of 6:13. 2 Corinthians 6:14–7:1 is a non-Pauline interpolation. See the Introduction above and the Interpolation below.

condemning you. I already told you that you are in our heart as partners whether we die or live. [4]I have great confidence in you and I have great pride in you. In the midst all of our pressures you encourage us greatly and fill us with joy . . .

Scripture Parallels

2:16	Joel 2:11 (LXX)
3:3	Ezek 11:19 (LXX); Ezek 36:26; Jer 38:33
3:7–10	Exod 34:30, 33–35
3:13	Exod 34:33,35
3:15–16	Exod 34:34
4:4	Gen 1:27
4:6	Gen 1:3
4:13	Ps 115:1 (LXX); 116:10
5:1, 4	Wis 9:15
5:10	Eccl 12:14
5:17	Isa 43:18–19
6:2	Isa 49:8
6:8	Ps 118:17

Pauline Parallels

2:14	1 Cor 15:57; 1 Cor 4:9
2:15	1 Cor 1:18
3:3, 6	Rom 2:29; 7:6
4:2	1 Thess 2: 3,5–6; 1 Cor 2:4
4:8–12	Phil 1:19–20; Rom 5:3; 8:36–39
4:13–15	1 Thess 4:16; 1 Cor 15:12–19; Rom 6:5–10
4:16–18	1 Cor 15:51–54; Rom 8:18–25
5:1–4	1 Cor 15:53–54
5:10	Rom 2:6–10
5:14–15	Rom 5:6–10
5:17	Gal 2:19–20; 6:15; Rom 7:4
6:4–10	1 Cor 4:9–13; Rom 5:3–5
7:2–4	1 Thess 2:5–8

Letter 2
A Parody of
"A Fool's Speech"

10 I, Paul, personally appeal to you in the spirit of the Anointed's gentleness and kindness—the one you say is "timid in your presence but aggressive [when he's] away from you." [2]I hope that the next time I'm there with you I won't have to be aggressive in refuting those who regard me as behaving in a worldly way. [3]Although we do live in the world, we are not involved in a worldly fight. [4]Our combat weapons are not worldly but divinely empowered to take out strongholds. We destroy entrenched positions [5]and every pretentious defense mounted against the knowledge of God. We make every thought captive to God's will, as did the Anointed. [6]We're ready to put down all resistance, until your own submission is complete.

[7]Look at what should be obvious to you. If any are convinced that they are the Anointed's people, let them consider that we belong to the Anointed as much as they do. [8]If I talk a bit too much about the authority which the Lord gave [to me] for building you up, not tearing you down, I don't have anything to be ashamed of. [9]I am not trying to frighten you through my correspondence. [10]"His letters," they say, "are

---

Letter 2 This letter is a defensive speech, performed for the most part as a comic effort.
10:1 This quotation is an accusation made against Paul. Evidently his personal appearance (10:10) in Corinth did not match the dramatic effect of his earlier letter (Letter 1). Paul would have been considered a "boaster." The rhetorical trope of appearance vs. reality will undergird this entire letter.
10:4 Paul's use of military metaphors reflects his defensive response and anticipates the boastful warrior speech (11:23–33).
10:8 In the first century if a boaster could not back up his words he would experience social sanction.

weighty and forceful, but his physical presence is unimpres-
sive and his speech is pathetic." [11][On the contrary,] they ought
to know that what we sound like in our letters is what we really are like in person. [12]We do not presume to put ourselves in
the same class or compare ourselves with some of those who
promote themselves. But, it must be said, when they become a
mutual admiration society and indulge in self-congratulation,
they don't know what they're doing.

[13]We won't claim credit excessively, but [will stay] within
the limited sphere which God assigned to us. And that sphere
reaches all the way to you. [14]We really are not overstepping our
boundaries when we reached as far as you. We were the first
to arrive with the world-transforming message about God's
Anointed. [15]Although we are not immoderately taking credit
for others' labor, we hope, when your understanding of what
it means to trust God matures, to enlarge our sphere of action
to such an extent [16]that the message spreads to places beyond
you—not to claim credit for what has already been done in
others' territory. [17]"Let those who want to claim credit, give
the credit to the Lord." [18]It is not the one who endorses himself
who is approved, but the one whom the Lord endorses.

11 I wish you'd let me play the fool for a little while. But, of
course, you will! [2]I am so deeply and passionately concerned
about you. I am protective about you. For I arranged to deliver
you to God's Anointed as if I were presenting a virgin to her

---

10:12 Paul's opponents evidently based their claims by documenting their
competence. Letters of recommendation recounted their public performances.
Paul indicates that he does not play this competitive game. At stake was the
basis of the Corinthians' judgment on what constitutes "competence."
10:13 *limited sphere* refers to missionary territory.
10:18 Paul concludes the opening of this speech with a critique of those who
measure themselves by their own standards (10:12). In interpreting Jer 9:24 (v.
17), he delivers a new basis for making a judgment.
11:1 Here begins a "fool's speech" (11:1–12:18) that takes much from ancient
mime. Paul personifies different "voices" to make his comic case.
11:2 Here Paul takes on the voice of a matchmaker.

husband. [3]But I fear that, just as the snake seduced Eve with his cunning line, your sincere [and pure] thoughts about the Anointed have been corrupted. [4]For if someone comes along, proclaiming a "Jesus" whom we did not proclaim, or you embrace some other supposedly divine power that you did not receive [from us], or some strange message you did not get from us, you are easily taken in.

[5]As I see it, I'm in no way inferior to the "super-envoys"! [6]Although I'm not a polished speaker, I'm not without knowledge. In all kinds of ways I've made it clear to you that I know what I am talking about. [7]Was it a mistake to downplay myself in order to raise your self-esteem, by proclaiming the world-transforming message of God to you free of charge? [8]I robbed other gatherings of the Anointed, as it were, and took my pay from them to serve you. [9]When I was with you and I ran short, I didn't press you for funds. The brothers arrived from Macedonia and supplied what I needed. I kept myself—and intend to keep myself—from ever becoming a financial burden to you. [10][I swear] by the truth of God's Anointed my calling attention to this will not be silenced in the districts of Achaia! [11]Why? Because I don't love you? God knows I do! [12]I'll keep on doing what I am doing to undermine the pretentions of those who want to brag that they are our equals. [13]Those people are phony envoys, specialists in deceit, who disguise themselves as envoys of the Anointed. [14]And no wonder, for Satan disguises himself as a messenger of light. [15]It's not a great surprise if his agents pose as models of integrity. Their end will match their deeds.

11:3 This is a textual variant. Compare P[46].

11:4 This is a good example of how different this letter is from the first letter. The sarcastic mood suggests a very different relationship to the audience.

11:5 Paul exaggerates the title ("envoy") his opponents used.

11:7 Payment for a missionary's performance was considered another proof of his competence. Because Paul did not charge a fee, the Corinthians seem to consider his message to be of little value.

¹⁶Again I say, let no one take me for a fool. On second thought, if you must, go ahead and accept me as a fool so that I can brag a little. ¹⁷What I am going to babble on about is not from the lord. I am going on babble on like an idiot with a braggart's swagger. ¹⁸Since many are bragging in a typically worldly way, so will I. ¹⁹Indeed, you gladly welcome fools, that's how wise you are! ²⁰You put up with it, if someone dominates you, or exploits you, or takes advantage of you, or acts better than you, or punches you in the face! ²¹To my shame I admit that I don't have the gall to do that!

Whatever they insist on bragging about—I'm talking like an idiot—I do too. ²²Are they "Hebrews?" Me too! "Israelites?" Me too! "Descendents of Abraham?" Me too! ²³Are they "servants of the Anointed"? I'm babbling like I'm out of my mind—my service far surpasses theirs! With so many more troubles, so many more arrests, even more lashes, often in danger of death. ²⁴Five times I received forty lashes minus one from my fellow Jews, ²⁵three times I was beaten with rods, once I was stoned, three times I was shipwrecked, a day and night I spent in the deep, ²⁶often on journeys, with dangers on rivers, dangers from robbers, dangers from my compatriots, dangers from the nations, dangers in the city, dangers in the desert, dangers at sea, dangers from false friends, ²⁷in toil and drudgery, often losing sleep, in hunger and thirst, often on an empty stomach, cold and naked—²⁸and apart from everything else is my daily preoccupation, the concern for all the gatherings of the Anointed. ²⁹Who among them is weak and I'm not also? Who is being led astray and I am not incensed?

³⁰If I need to brag, I'll brag about my limitations. ³¹The God and Benefactor of our lord Jesus, may he be blessed forever,

---

11:8 The metaphor underlying this sentence is that of temple robbing.
11:22–23 Paul lists the various titles of honor by which the opponents identify themselves.

Instead of listing genuine accomplishments Paul details a list of disasters. This parody of what people would expect is similar to the parodies of ancient comedy. There one can find the speeches of the "boastful soldier," that also play against the social grain and expectation.

knows that I'm not lying. ³²At Damascus the governor under King Aretas kept the citizens of Damascus on watch to trap me ³³and I was lowered down in a fish basket through a window in the wall and escaped his clutches.

12 I have to brag. Although it's pointless, I'll move on to visions and special insights about the lord. ²I know a man who belongs to the Anointed who fourteen years ago was carried away—whether in the body, I don't know, or out of the body, I don't know, God knows—carried off to heaven's third level. ³I know that this man—whether in the body or out of the body I don't know, God knows—⁴was carried off to Paradise and heard indescribable words which no one may speak. ⁵I am willing to brag about that one, but I'll not brag about "yours truly" except for my limitations. ⁶I wouldn't be a fool, if I wanted to brag because I would be telling the truth. But I hold back, so that people won't think more of me than they see in me or hear from me. ⁷So I wouldn't get a swelled head from an overabundance of transcendent experiences, I was awarded a painful disability, a messenger from Satan to pummel me so that I would not get too carried away. ⁸Three times I begged our lord for it to go away. ⁹He spoke in an oracle to me:

> My favor is enough for you, because my power achieves its ends through [your] limitations.

Now more than ever I shall brag most gladly of my limitations, so that the power of God's Anointed might reside in

---

11:33 This verse appears to be an aside by Paul or an interpolation from a later reader. He is not exactly the conquering hero! If Paul's list here is a parody of the "boastful soldier," this reference may be a parody of "the wall crown"—an honor given to the soldier who first scaled the wall of a city the army was attacking. See Furnish, *Anchor Bible*, 542.
12:1–10 Paul parodies those who establish their competence by presenting religious revelations. Some scholars suggest that 12:3–4 may actually reflect Paul's revelatory experience mentioned in Gal 1:15.
12:4 The Greek is "Paradise," that is, the Garden of Eden, now transferred to the heavenly realm.
12:7 Despite endless speculation Paul's chronic condition cannot be determined.
12:9 This parodies oracles received from healing gods such as Asclepius.

me. [10]So, for the sake of God's Anointed, I accept limitations, insults, calamities, persecutions, difficulties. For when I accept my limitations, then I am empowered.

[11]I've played the fool! You forced me into it! I should have been recommended by you. I'm in no way outranked by the "super-envoys," even though I'm nothing. [12]The marks of an authentic envoy were brought out with full sustaining power in your midst with signs, wonders, and miracles. [13]What is it that makes you feel that I treated the other gatherings of the Anointed better than you, except for the fact that I didn't press you for financial support? Forgive me that slight!

[14]Now look, I'm ready to visit you for the third time. I won't impose on you. I'm not looking for what you own. I want you. Children shouldn't save up for their parents. Parents should save for their children. [15]I'd be delighted to spend and be spent for your lives. If I love you so much, am I to be loved less? [16]All right, I didn't impose on you, but, I was cunning and took you in by deceit, [you say]. [17]Did I take advantage of you through anyone I sent to you? [18]I asked Titus to go and I sent a brother along. Did Titus take advantage of you? Did we not act with the same integrity? Did we not take the very same approach?

[19]Do you really think that all this time we've been defending ourselves to you? Before God, my dear friends, we say all these things in the spirit of the Anointed for your growth and development as a community. [20]I'm afraid that I might arrive and find you not as I'd like and I'd be found by you not as you like. I fear there might be competition, jealousy, anger, ambi-

---

12:19 Paul makes it clear why he writes—for the Corinthians' growth and development. He uses himself as the butt of jokes so that the community might discover themselves. By taking the charge of unverified boasting and carrying it to comic extremes Paul forces his listeners to see the issue of his competence in a different light and to re-examine the basis of their social assumptions and judgments. This is actually typical of the ancient diatribe, where the speaker impersonates the situation of the audience right before their eyes. The listeners can detect what their true situation is through reflecting on what the speaker presents. Here Paul humorously presents their desire for competitive honor and worth. He attempts to expose them to the consequences of their own assumptions.

tion, backbiting, gossip, swelled heads, and confusion. ²¹I'm afraid that God would embarrass me because of you when I come again. I would grieve over many who continue in their vices and have not repented of the impurity, sexual license, and debauchery which they practiced.

13 This is the third time I'll be coming to you.

> Every charge must be corroborated by two or three witnesses.

²I said it before, when I was there for my second visit, and I'll say it again now while I'm not there, to those who continue in their vices and to all the rest, that if I come again I won't be lenient, ³since you require proof that God's Anointed speaks through me. He is not powerless in dealing with you; rather he empowers you. ⁴He was crucified as one who appeared to have no power, but he lives because of God's power. We're powerless along with him, but in dealing with you we will live with him because of God's power.

⁵Test yourselves to see if your behavior is consistent with putting your confidence in God. Examine yourselves. Don't you realize that Jesus, God's Anointed is among you?—unless you have failed the test. ⁶I hope that you'll learn that we haven't failed the test. ⁷We pray to God that you do no wrong—not that we might appear to have passed the test—but that even if we were to fail the test, you would do what's right. ⁸We can't do anything against the truth but only for the truth. ⁹We rejoice when we're powerless and you're strong. This is what we pray for: your restoration [as a community of the Anointed]. ¹⁰That's why I write these things while I am away from you so that, when I'm there with you, I won't have to be severe in using the authority the lord gave me for your growth and development as a community, not for your ruin.

¹¹Lastly, brothers and sisters, rejoice, put things right, encourage each other, come to a common understanding, live peacefully, and the God of love and peace will be with you. ¹²Greet each other with respect and affection. All of God's

people send greetings to you. [13]May the favor of the lord Jesus, God's Anointed, and the love of God and the partnership of God's powerful presence be with all of you.

Scripture Parallels

10:8	Jer 24:6
10:17	Jer 9:23–24
11:3	Gen 3:13
12:7	Num 33:55
12:12	Wis 10:16
13:1	Deut 19:15

Pauline Parallels

10:3–6	1 Thess 5:8; Rom 12:2
11:4	Gal 1:6–9
11:7	1 Thess 2:9; 1 Cor 9:15
11:13–15	Gal 1:7
11:16–18	1 Cor 1:26–29
11:22–23	Phil 3:4
11:23–29	1 Cor 4:9–13
11:30	1 Cor 1:27–29
12:1	Gal 1:16; 2:2
12:14	1 Thess 2:7–8; 1 Cor 4:14, 19; Phlm 22; Rom 15:23, 28
13:12	1 Thess 5:26; 1 Cor 16:20; Rom 16:16
13:14	1 Thess 5:28; Gal 6:18; 1 Cor 16:23–24; Phil 4:23; Phlm 25; Rom 16:20

Letter 3
A Letter of
Reconciliation

1 Paul, by God's will an envoy of Jesus, God's Anointed, and our brother Timothy to God's gathering in Corinth along with all God's people throughout southern Greece: [2]Divine favor and true peace from God, our Creator and Benefactor, and from our lord Jesus, God's Anointed.

[3]Praise to the God and Benefactor of our lord Jesus, God's Anointed, the compassionate Patron and all-consoling God. [4]God supports us in times of hardship so that we can support others in their hardship in the same way we were supported by God. [5]Just as we know full well the sufferings of God's Anointed, so we also know full well God's boundless support through the Anointed. [6]If we're having a rough time, it's for your encouragement and ultimate well-being, or if we're encouraged, it's for your benefit, to enable you to put up with the same sufferings that we're experiencing. [7]Our hope for you is sure, since we know that, if you share in the sufferings, you also share in the benefits.

[8]We want you to know, brothers and sisters, about the adversity we suffered in the province of Asia. We were so deeply distressed—more than we could take—that we despaired even of life. [9]We felt as if we had been sentenced to death, so that we wouldn't rely on ourselves but on God who raises the

---

Letter 3 This letter celebrates the resolution of differences between Paul and the Corinthians. See the Introduction.

1:1 *southern Greece:* Greek reads *Achaia.*

1:8 Much ink has been spilt on speculating what happened to Paul. Was he imprisoned? Condemned to death? Some attempt to use Acts 19:23–41 to fill the historical blank. But if Acts is dated to the second century, the writer of Acts may well be using the fragmentary Corinthian material as the basis for the later narrative.

dead. [10]God has rescued us from the threat of such a death and will rescue us again. We have set our hope in God to rescue us still, [11]with the help of your prayers. The more people who pray for us, the more will give thanks for the favor graciously granted to us.

[12]This is our source of pride, made with a clear conscience: that we have conducted ourselves in the world, especially in our relationship with you, with absolute integrity and sincerity, not following worldly wisdom, but in keeping with the generous favor of God. [13]For we write to you nothing other than what you can read and understand. I hope that you will come to understand fully [14]just as you partly know us now, that we are your pride and you are ours on the day of our lord Jesus.

[15]Confident of this, I intended to come to see you sooner. Then you could have a double benefit: [16]I'd be going your way to Macedonia, and then coming back to you from Macedonia. I would then have your support for my journey to Judea. [17]If I was intending to do this, did I act insincerely, [as some of you say]? Did I decide what I wanted to do for self-serving reasons, so that I could say, "Yes, yes, I'm coming," and "No, no, I'm not "? [18]As God is true, what we say to you isn't "yes and no." [19]The "son" of God, Jesus, God's Anointed, proclaimed to you by me and Silvanus and Timothy, was not "yes and no" but, in our service to him, our proclamation was consistently "yes." [20]Whatever are God's promises, they find their "yes" in the Anointed. And that is why the affirmation of God's promises comes from the Anointed through us for the glory of God. [21]The one who is establishing us along with you in the service of the Anointed is God, who has also certified our authenticity. [22]We have received God's seal of approval and have been given the power and presence of God in our hearts as the first installment [of our fulfillment].

1:15 Paul attempts to explain the fact that he failed to visit Corinth on the way to and from Macedonia.

²³On my life, I appeal to God as my witness, I'm sparing you in not yet coming to Corinth. ²⁴It is not that we're trying to be the masters of your confidence in God; rather we are co-workers for your happiness, for you are standing firm in your trust in God.

2 So, I decided not to come to you and upset you again. ²For if I cause you pain, who would cheer me up except you who have been offended by me? ³That's why I wrote as I did, so that I wouldn't come and be offended by you who should cheer me up. I have confidence in you all, that my joy is the joy of all of you as well. ⁴I wrote to you in great distress and anxiety, with many tears, not to upset you but to let you know the love I have especially for you.

⁵I don't want to go on and on about this, but if someone has offended anyone, he hasn't offended me as much as all of you. ⁶The censure the majority agreed on is enough for him. ⁷So, now you should forgive and console him so he won't be consumed by excessive grief. ⁸Therefore, I urge you to reassure him with love. ⁹That's why I wrote: to test your worth and see if you responded appropriately to everything. ¹⁰Anyone you forgive, I do too. If I had anything to forgive, I have forgiven it for your sake in the presence of God's Anointed. ¹¹Let's not be taken in by Satan, for we know what he has in mind.

¹²When I arrived in Troas to announce the world-transforming news about God's Anointed there, an opportunity opened up for me on the lord's behalf. ¹³But I was so uneasy at not finding my brother Titus that I said good-bye to them and went on to Macedonia.

7 ⁵When we arrived in Macedonia, our bodies got no rest—all kinds of crises, public disputes, private apprehensions. ⁶But God, who consoles the discouraged, consoled us with the arrival of Titus; ⁷and not only by his arrival but by the very

---

2:12 The text reads *Troiada*. The reference is to Alexandria Troas, a city founded by Antigonus in 311 BCE in the Trojan region, not the ancient Troy.

way he was encouraged about you. He reported to us your desire to see us, your remorse, and your enthusiasm on our behalf. So I rejoiced all the more.

[8]I'm not altogether sorry if my letter upset you. Even if I were sorry, I see that the letter distressed you only for a while. [9]I rejoice now, not that you were offended, but that your remorse led to a change of heart. Your pain was so profoundly transformative that you were in no way damaged by us. [10]God's way of using pain results in a change of heart for genuine well-being with no regrets. But a self-serving sense of injury festers with lethal effects. [11]Look at how this experience of God's using pain not only produced intense concern in you, but also self-defense, indignation, fear, longing, zeal, and vindication. You have fully cleared yourselves in this matter. [12]So, although I wrote [so sharply] to you, it wasn't really about either the offender or the one offended, but that in the presence of God you might recognize your intense concern for us. [13]That's why we are encouraged.

In addition to our encouragement, we were especially delighted by Titus' joy, for his mind was put at ease by you all. [14]If I bragged to him about you, I was not ashamed. Our bragging to Titus has come true, just as everything we spoke to you was true. [15]His affection for you is enormous when he recalls how appropriately responsive you all were when you welcomed him with all due respect and reverence. [16]I rejoice that I [can now] be sure of you in every way.

Pauline Parallels

1:1–2	1 Thess 1:1; Gal 1:1–5; 1 Cor 1:1–3; Phil 1:1–2; Phlm 1–3; Rom 1:1–7
1:3–11	1 Thess 3:1–10; Rom 5:3–5
1:12	1 Thess 2:10; 1 Cor 4: 3–4;
1:15–16	1 Thess 2:17–18; 1 Cor 16:5–9; Phlm 22; Rom 15:22–29
2:1	1 Cor 4:14
2:6	1 Cor 5:3–5

Letter 4
A Collection
Appeal to Corinth

8 We want to remind you, brothers and sisters about the divine favor bestowed on gatherings of the Anointed in Macedonia. [2]In the midst of terribly trying circumstances their exuberant joy and their desperate poverty have yielded a surpassing generosity. [3]They gave what they could afford and, as I can testify, beyond what they could afford. Without any prompting [4]they begged us most urgently for the privilege of participating in this generous service for the Anointed's people [in Jerusalem]. [5]Beyond our expectations, they so devoted themselves, through God's will, first to the lord, and to us, [6]that we have urged Titus to complete this generous undertaking which he had already begun among you.

[7]Now, just as you excel in everything—in faithfulness, impressive speech, and discernment, in all-out enthusiasm, and in the love that came from us and now dwells in you—you should excel in this worthy project also. [8]I am not issuing a command, but by referring to the enthusiastic generosity of others I am also putting the genuineness of your love to the test. [[[9]For you know the generous favor of our lord Jesus the

---

Letter 4 A letter of appeal to the Corinthians for the Jerusalem Collection. See the Introduction.

8:1 This fragment is a letter of appeal for the collection. Titus (v. 6) probably delivered this to the Corinthians (2 Cor 8:17).

8:6 Paul, starting off this letter with an example of the generous Macedonians, provides the Corinthians with motivation by supplying a baseline for doing even better.

8:9 This verse seems to be a later insertion: nothing before or after this verse connects. It seems to presuppose pre-existence. Paul's argument works very well from v. 8 directly to v. 10. He does not issue a command he gives advice. The Macedonians were not rich; the analogy does not seem to work here.

The basis for the Corinthians' generosity is the self-giving of the Anointed, not his abdication of wealth.

Anointed, that for your sake he became poor, although he was rich, so that by his poverty you might become rich.]] [10]Here is my advice about this: it is in your best interest, since you led the way last year not only in what you did but in what you were willing to do, [11]to finish up your effort now, so that your initial enthusiasm for the project might be matched by bringing it to completion [by giving] out of what you have. [12]If your heart is in it, the gift is appreciated in relation to what you have, not to what you don't have. [13]I am not saying that others should have it easy while you are hard-pressed; it is a matter of achieving an equitable balance. [14]At the present time your surplus provides what others lack so that their surplus might furnish what you lack at some future time, so that there might be equality, [15]just as it was written:

> the one who gathered much did not have a surplus
> the one who gathered little did not go short.

[16]Thank God who put this same concern for you in Titus' heart. [17]Because he accepted our appeal, he was more than willing to set out to visit you. [18]We sent with him the brother who is well-known throughout all of the gatherings of the Anointed's people for his work in spreading the message. [19]Not only that, but he was also hand-picked as our traveling companion by the gatherings to help us with managing this fund to glorify God as well as to confirm our eagerness to help. [20]Our intention is to avoid having anyone find fault with us over the way we are administering this generous gift. [21]We want to do a beautiful thing—not only in the eyes of the Lord, but also in peoples' perceptions.

[22]We sent our brother along with them—whom we have tested and found to be earnest on many occasions—and who is

---

8:10 Notice Paul is giving his advice, not citing an oracle of the Lord. Compare 1 Corinthians 7. There is no instruction from Jesus or an oracle. Paul is making this up from his own wisdom.
8:18 The identity of the "brother" is unknown.
8:22 The identity of this person is also unknown.

now all the more enthusiastic because of his great confidence in you. [23]As for Titus, he is my companion and co-worker on your behalf; as for our brothers, they are envoys of the various gatherings; they all bring honor to the Anointed. [24]So in the presence of the Anointed's gatherings, show these men your love and the evidence for what we have claimed about you.

Scripture Parallels
8:15   Exod 16:18
8:21   Prov 3:4

Pauline Parallels
8:3, 6–7   Gal 2:10; 1 Cor 16:1–4; Rom 15:25–27
8:8   Phlm 8–9

Letter 5
A Collection Appeal
to All of Achaia

9 There is certainly no need for me to write about the collection for the gathering of the Anointed's people [in Jerusalem]. [2]I'm aware of your enthusiasm. I bragged about it among the Macedonians on your behalf: "Southern Greece has been ready for a year!" Your zeal has fired up many of them. [3]I sent the brothers so that our bragging about you wouldn't prove to be an empty boast, but that you might be as ready as I said you were. [4]I wouldn't want the Macedonians to come with me and find you unprepared. We'd be shamed, not to mention you, for being too confident. [5]I thought it necessary to encourage the brothers to go ahead to you and prepare in advance your promised contribution, so that it may be already in hand as a generous gift, not as a grudging one. [6]I mean,

> the one who sows meagerly will reap meagerly;
> the one who sows liberally will reap liberally.

[7]Each should give freely from the heart, not grudgingly. For,

> God loves a joyful giver.

[8]God is able to shower every benefit upon you so that anytime, anywhere you would have the wherewithal to be gen-

---

Letter 5 This letter is an appeal to Southern Greece for the Jerusalem Collection. See the Introduction.

9:1 The beginning of this letter suggests a situation different from that in chapter 8. The delegation mentioned in chapter 8 has already been sent off. The collection for God's people (Acts 11:29; Gal 2:10) becomes for Paul a concrete symbol of the nations' equality with the Jews before the true God.

9:2 *Southern Greece:* This refers to the Roman province of *Achaia*. Paul is probably referring to the communities of the Anointed in Achaia. Compare Letter 3 (1:1).

9:6 Here begins a series of sayings that may have come from a collection designed for such appeals.

erous in your support of good work of every kind. ⁹As it is written,

> He sows generously; he gives liberally to the poor.
> His benevolence endures forever.

¹⁰The One who supplies seed to the sower and bread for food will supply and multiply your resources and increase the benefits of your generosity. ¹¹We are being enriched in every way for every generous thing we do, and this produces thanksgiving to God. ¹²So, sharing in this public service to the community not only supplies the needs of the Anointed's people [in Jerusalem] but also spills over into widespread thanksgiving to God. ¹³Through the evidence of this generous act of service the Anointed's people in Jerusalem will glorify God for your active acknowledgement of the world-transforming news of God's Anointed and for your contribution to them and to all [of the Anointed's people]. ¹⁴Their hearts go out to you in their prayers because of the extraordinary goodness of God evident among you. ¹⁵Thanks be to God for such an incredible gift!

9:8 The ancient energy or benefit cycle underlies much of Paul's writing. Only the bestowing of benefits by the divine to humanity could bring about economic surplus in the understanding of the ancient world. Humans would respond to such benefits by giving thanks, thereby increasing the divine honor and insuring further benefaction. Paul does not limit the benefits of God to extraordinary individuals. On the contrary, the insight he derives from the fate of the Anointed is that the divine benefaction has been distributed among the nobodies of the world. And the nobodies can continue to operate within this surprising benefit cycle—contrary to the all-too-familiar limited benefits of the patron-client structure of the Roman social world.

Scripture Parallels

9:7	Prov 22:8 (LXX)
9:9	Ps 111:9 (LXX)

Pauline Parallels

9:1	Gal 2:10; 1 Cor 16: 1–4; Rom 15:25–27

INTERPOLATION

2 Corinthians 6:14–7:1

6 ¹⁴Don't get entangled in a partnership with unbelievers. What do justice and lawlessness have in common? What do light and darkness share? ¹⁵What agreement is there between God's Anointed and the Prince of evil? What do a believer and an unbeliever have a share in? ¹⁶What association can there be between the temple of God and idols? We are the temple of the living God, as God has said:

> "I will live among them and go about in their midst;
> and I will be their God and they will be my people."

¹⁷So,

> "Come out from among them and be separate," says the Lord.
> "Do not touch anything unclean; then I will welcome you."

¹⁸and

> "I will be a father" for you and you will be
> "my sons and my daughters."

says the almighty Lord.

7 ¹Since we have these promises, my beloved friends, let us cleanse ourselves from every stain of body, mind, and heart, and show our reverence for God by making our consecration perfect.

Scripture Parallels

6:16	Lev 26:11; Ezek 37:27
6:17	Isa 52:11; Ezek 20:34, 41
6:18	2 Sam 7:14; Jer 31:9; Isa 43:6; 2 Sam 7:8 (LXX)

Pauline Parallels

6:14–16	1 Cor 3:16–17; 5:1–2; 5:9–11; 6:12–16; 7:15–20

6:14 The language, issues, and tone of this portion of 2 Corinthians differ markedly from the rest of the letter. The anonymous writer urges his audience to maintain the purity of the group in dualistic language strongly reminiscent of the Dead Sea Scrolls.

6:15 *the prince of evil:* Greek: *Beliar,* a variant of Belial, which was one of the names of the prince of evil spirits according to ancient Judaism.

What Happened to Paul?

The only direct information about what happened to Paul comes in Gal 1:13–17. Paul describes his former behavior as a practicing Jew. In his estimation he went beyond most of his contemporaries in the observance of Jewish traditions. Saying that he was "notably zealous" for his ancestral traditions supports his remarks in Phil 3:5–6. As a Pharisee Paul's concerns over purity matters would have had their basis in his understanding of the purity and integrity of the God of Israel. His harassment of communities of Jesus believers may have come from the fact that some early Jesus communities (Syrian) were celebrating the death of Jesus as a hero and, in so doing, were invoking the God of Israel. From Paul's perspective such an association of God with a criminal who had been shamefully executed is tantamount to blasphemy. His concern for the integrity of God may well have fueled his attempts to wipe these communities out. Beyond this extrapolation from Pharisaic concerns, there is little that can be known.

Moreover, Paul characterizes his breakthrough insight (*apocalypsis*) as a prophetic experience. He uses traditional prophetic language to describe what he sees as a prophetic call:

> when the One who designated me before I was born and commissioned me to be an envoy —Gal 1:15

> Listen to me, O coastlands, and hearken, you peoples from afar. The LORD called me from the womb, from the body of my mother he named my name. —Isa 49:1

Paul did not see himself as what we today would call a "convert." He never stopped being a Jew (cf. Rom 9:3), although he had moved beyond his Pharisaic self-understanding. Instead, he takes up the vision of the Jewish prophets in their call to the nations. It could be said that what had actually changed was Paul's vision of God. Somehow his vision of God's integrity was transformed by seeing what God had done for Jesus. In accepting this shamed criminal the God of Israel had taken an outrageous step. God had accepted the impure. From that changed understanding of God, Paul

Continued on next page

concludes that a new chapter or dimension of God's action has begun. Paul will use a variety of metaphors to express how this has transformed the world. Paul sees his task as announcing this world-changing vision. Because God had accepted this shamed nobody, the usual conditions of human existence have changed utterly. In that light Paul was to go to those nations who would have been considered, generally speaking, as morally inferior by the Jewish people. Paul had undergone what we today would call a paradigm shift in his understanding of God and the nations and the world.

We cannot use Acts 9:1–9 as a basis for judgment since the text may well reflect a second century hand. In addition, the story format in Acts 9 is a literary commonplace of the scene of someone who opposes a god (cf. *The Bacchae*). It should be pointed out that Paul does uses the term *apocalypsis* elsewhere in Galatians and there it probably means a communal experience (Gal 2:2). Some scholars have linked the heavenly vision in 2 Cor 12:1–10, but that position has not found much acceptance. Moreover, Paul uses that scene in a comic way as a parody of an apocalyptic vision. Another possibility is that Paul's harassment of early Jesus communities (perhaps in Syria) may well have given him the occasion to observe their communal experience. An indirect witness of Paul's experience might be found in 1 Cor 14:23–25 where Paul speaks of the experience of an outsider who discovers that the deepest dreams of his heart are revealed in the communal action. Could the experience of Paul have been the discovery that "God really was present" among those he zealously wanted to wipe out?

> If then the whole congregation has come together in one place and everyone is speaking in ecstatic languages and outsiders or unbelievers come in, will they not say that you are mad? But if everyone is prophesying and some unbelievers or uninitiated persons come in, they will be convicted by all, called to account by all, the secrets of their hearts are exposed; and so they will fall on their faces and worship God and declare that "God really is present among you."

Paul's Correspondence to Philemon

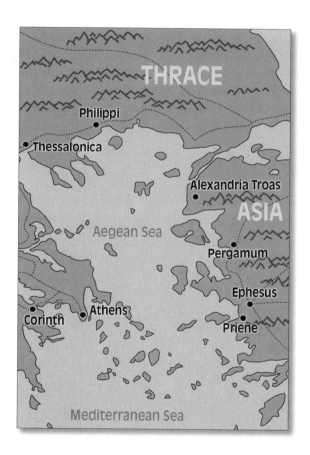

Ephesus, the second largest city of the Roman Empire, was a missionary base and a place of imprisonment for Paul. From this city Paul corresponded with the Corinthians, and, quite likely, with the Philippians and Philemon.

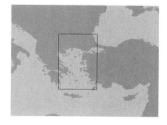

Philemon

INTRODUCTION

The Rhetoric of Paul

Paul's letter to Philemon is a rhetorical gem. Although it is the shortest of Paul's extant correspondence, the letter to Philemon demonstrates Paul's persuasive mastery in tackling a most thorny situation. In writing to Philemon, the head of a house community, Paul intercedes for Onesimus, a runaway slave of Philemon. Paul does not ask Philemon to be magnanimous in forgiving the runaway slave; on the contrary, he asks that Philemon welcome back Onesimus as a "beloved friend," as if he were Paul himself.

Paul became acquainted in prison with Onesimus sometime after the slave had fled the household of Philemon. There Onesimus not only became a follower of the Anointed but proved very useful in assisting Paul's proclamation of the world transforming message. Reluctantly Paul decided to send Onesimus back to Philemon.

Paul's plea to Philemon goes far beyond what would have been expected in the first century. In running away Onesimus has both deprived his master of his property and insulted his honor. A master would usually greet such a returning slave with severe punishment (even death) to restore the upset social hierarchy. For Paul to ask Philemon to receive Onesimus (v. 20) as he has welcomed "God's people" (v. 7) would represent a revolutionary request. In this letter Paul attempts to deal concretely with his utopian vision of freedom of those united with the Anointed within the slave society of the ancient world.

Such a request would need much to persuade the insulted slave owner from exacting a face-saving penalty. The entire letter has been constructed to give Philemon the grounds to accept Onesimus back on most unexpected terms. Paul leaves no rhetorical stone unturned in persuading Philemon.

Both the beginning (vv. 1–3) and end (vv. 23–24) of the letter provide a tip off to Paul's strategy as he appeals to Philemon within a public, not private, venue. Despite the fact that the letter is actually addressed to Philemon, the letter was delivered in the presence of the entire house community of Philemon and was known also to the associates of the imprisoned Paul. Such a social frame would lend support for Philemon who is being asked to act against the usual social protocol of master and slave.

While the entire letter can be divided into the usual format of a Pauline letter [an introduction (vv. 1–3), the thanksgiving (4–6), body (7–16), exhortation (17–22) and closing (23–25)], a rhetorical stamp can be easily delineated. The thanksgiving (vv. 4–6) functions not only vertically as a prayer before God recalling the good deeds and qualities of Philemon but also horizontally as an attempt by Paul to establish goodwill with his primary listener.

The body of this deliberative letter (7–16) provides Philemon with the reasons why he can make the decision to accept Onesimus as a "beloved friend" (v. 16). Not only does Paul note Philemon's noble character (vv. 8, 14) but also he plays upon his own condition as an "old man and a prisoner" (v. 9). Paul is quite honest with Philemon (v. 13) as he brings up the utility (v. 11) in this new and even providential (v. 15) situation. At the same time this situation has a significant emotional register (vv. 10, 12). The burden of his argument is that Onesimus is no longer what he was but is "special" to Paul and even more so to Philemon, both "as a man and as one who belongs to our lord."

What may be lost on the modern reader is Paul's wordplay. SV Paul has tried to capture what would not be lost on an ancient audience used to the niceties of rhetoricians. Thus, Paul mentions that "the hearts of the saints are refreshed" by Philemon (v. 7). He then indicates that Onesimus is his "heart"

(v. 12) and then draws the connection by asking Philemon to "refresh my heart" (v. 20). He also plays upon Onesimus' probable nickname "Useless" by employing a new nickname "Useful," as well as alluding to the root meaning of Onesimus ("useful", beneficial").

The letter's exhortation (vv. 17–22) provides a final emotional tour de force. Here Paul makes the matter quite personal, takes responsibility for anything Onesimus had done (vv. 18–19), and reminds Philemon of their relationship and even the basis of it (v. 19). His wordplay (v. 20) reinforces the brunt of his entire argument. He then flatters his listener (v. 21) as well as suggesting that he will check things out if he does get out of prison (v. 22).

The Dating and Location of Philemon

There is nothing specific in Philemon which can be used to date or locate this letter. Since the letter does not show any of the apocalyptic fervor found in 1 Thessalonians, many scholars would date it after that early letter. Many scholars have linked Paul's imprisonment with that mentioned in Philippians (1:7). Others have also suggested that the third letter of 2 Corinthians (1:8) describes the time after which Paul had been released from prison. However, an earlier fragment of 2 Corinthians (11:23) indicates that there was more than one imprisonment. Since no imprisonment situation is mentioned in Romans many scholars place Philemon and Philippians prior to the letter to Rome and possibly written from Ephesus, while others place Philemon and Philippians as the last correspondence from Rome.

The location of Philemon's house has been guessed at by making some external connections. Since the names of Epaphras, Aristarchus, Mark, Demas and Luke are mentioned in the Letter to the Colossians (1:7; 4:9–17) many scholars have concluded that the letter to Philemon came from there or in the vicinity of Colossae. However, the translators of *The Authentic Letters of Paul* are persuaded that Colossians is not from Paul and comes from a later hand. Thus it is quite debatable whether the information in Colossians is reliable or has been used to lend a sense of verisimilitude.

The Question of Slavery

The letter to Philemon has been used often by subsequent generations in the debate over slavery. Prior to the American Civil War, for example, it was employed by both abolitionists and pro-slavery supporters. The question for readers today is how to avoid anachronism in reading Philemon. Slavery was intrinsic to the social pyramid of the ancient world. Aristotle comments on it as if it were a "natural" given. Even Paul uses the current language of slavery to describe his relationship to the Anointed. Yet Paul's vision of what God has done in the Anointed led him to the conclusion that a new age had begun, a new world order was underway and he was an envoy of the new regime. In Gal 3:28 Paul envisions the new conditions of existence where there is "no longer slave or freeborn." Moreover, Paul contends that all those who stand in trust before the God of the Anointed do so without need of social or class distinctions. In Philemon Paul seems to be consistent with such a sense of solidarity. However, the practicalities of such a vision are not easily worked out. The consequences of accepting a slave as a "beloved friend" were about to be exposed through this correspondence. Paul was asking Philemon to move beyond the established social assumptions and patterns of the first century. What did it mean to receive him back as a "beloved friend?" Was Onesimus still a slave in Philemon's house? Would Philemon be able to maintain his acceptance of Onesimus in the face of what would be possibly severe social criticism by pagan neighbors? The very existence of the letter may be a clue to Philemon's positive response. But the absence of evidence in subsequent material suggests that the correspondence to Philemon may be better understood not as a definitive answer to the question of slavery but rather as an inchoate step towards human freedom.

Paul's Letter
to Philemon

Paul, a prisoner because I serve the Anointed Jesus, and Timothy, my associate, to Philemon, our dear colleague—[2]also to Apphia our sister, to Archippus who joined up with us— and to the Anointed's people who meet in your house. [3]May you have favor and peace from God, our creator and benefactor, and from our lord, Jesus, God's Anointed.

[4]I always thank my God when I remember you, Philemon, in my prayers, [5]because I keep hearing about the confidence you have with regard to the lord Jesus and your love for all God's people. [6]I pray that the sharing of your confident trust in God will result in a recognition of all of the good that we are capable of in the service of the Anointed.

[7]Your love has brought me great joy and encouragement, because the hearts of God's people have been refreshed because of you, dear friend. [8]So, although in my capacity as an envoy of the Anointed I could order you to do what is fitting, I would rather appeal to you out of love [9]– just as I am, Paul, an old man and now even a prisoner because of the Anointed Jesus. [10]I appeal to you on behalf of my child, the one whose father I became while I was in prison, Onesimus. [11]At one time he was "Useless" to you, but now he has become "Useful" both to you and to me. [12]In sending him back to you I am sending my own heart. [13]I really wanted to keep him here with me, so that he could assist me on your behalf while I am in prison for proclaiming God's world-transforming message;

---

2 *Apphia* is probably the wife of Philemon. The singular "Your" refers back to the main addressee of the letter. This singular usage continues through v. 21.
7 *hearts:* in Greek *splanchna;* it conveys our sense of "guts." Compare vv. 12, 20. Paul plays upon this word to drive his point home.
10 Greek: *Onesimus* = "useful," "profitable," "beneficial." Paul plays upon the root ("use") of this word in v. 20.
11 *Useless* was a nickname.

¹⁴but I did not wish to do anything without your consent, so that your good deed would not be done out of coercion but of your own free will. ¹⁵Perhaps the reason that Onesimus was separated from you for a while is so that you could have him back forever, ¹⁶no longer as your slave, but more than a slave, a beloved friend. He is that special to me, but even more to you, both as a man and as one who belongs to our lord.

¹⁷So, if you consider me your partner, welcome him as you would welcome me. ¹⁸And if he has wronged you in any way or owes you anything, charge that to my account. ¹⁹I, Paul, am putting this in my own handwriting: *I will pay you back*, in order to avoid saying to you that you owe me your life. ²⁰Yes, my friend, I am asking you for something "useful" in the service of our lord. Refresh my heart as one who belongs to the Anointed.

²¹I am writing like this to you because I am confident that you will comply with my wishes. I know that you will do even more than I am asking. ²²And, by the way, prepare a guest room for me, because I am hoping that, through your prayers, I will be restored to you.

²³Epaphras, who is imprisoned with me because of his service to the Anointed Jesus, sends greetings to you, ²⁴as do Mark, Aristarchus, and Luke, my colleagues.

²⁵May all of you be conscious that the gracious favor of the lord Jesus, God's Anointed, is present among you.

---

16 Paul's request is rather unusual. Instead of asking for a magnanimous response of forgiveness, Paul asks Philemon to accept his runaway slave as a "beloved friend." Contrast the advice Pliny gives to the slave owner Sabinianus over the return of his runaway slave. (Letter of Pliny to Sabinianus, *Epist. 9.21*.)

Pauline Parallels

1:3	Rom 1:7
1:9	Phil 1:7
1:17	Rom 15:7
1:19	1 Cor 16:21; Gal 6:11
1:25	Gal 6:18

Ancient Rhetoric and
the Letter to the Galatians

Understanding a writing, ancient or modern, presupposes an awareness of how the author communicates. It is crucial for a reader of ancient writings to recognize the influence and pervasiveness of rhetoric. For the inhabitants of the Greco-Roman world rhetoric was the heart of formal education. Boys, trained in rhetorical theory, were expected to think, speak, and write in rhetorical fashion. Ancient writings, such as Galatians, were composed and delivered aloud according to such ancient principles. Even those without any formal training would have been expected to recognize the appropriate rhetorical discourse.

Rhetoric is the type of discourse by which a speaker or writer attempts to persuade the audience to accomplish his or her purposes. This is effected through the treatment of subject matter, the use of evidence, argumentation, the control of emotion, and the choice and arrangement of words. That rhetoric is primarily a speech act means that even written texts of the ancient world must be read with an ear to the oral quality of the material. Such speech is linear and cumulative, so that the audience is drawn to anticipate the argument of the speaker as well as to contrast what has already been delivered.

The primary responsibility of the speaker is to discover the best means of persuading one's audience. Ancient authorities on rhetoric divided the subject up according to the five parts of composing a speech. The first task of the rhetorician was to plan the discourse and arguments to be used in it. In building his discourse, the speaker would draw upon various topics, or common areas, which would be used to amplify and illustrate the basic contentions of the address. This initial process was called invention. The arrangement or composition of diverse parts into a unified whole followed. The speaker also devoted time to the choice of words and the composition of words into well-turned sentences, in short, with style. Then there was memorization by which the speaker prepared for delivering the speech. Finally, the

Continued on next page

speaker attended to aspects of delivery, that is, to the control of voice and use of gestures.

In every rhetorical situation there are three factors: the speaker/writer, audience, and discourse. In assessing this overall situation, the ancient speaker would construct his argument through three different modes of proof. One would draw upon various forms of evidence to establish one's own credibility (ethos) before the audience. There would also be a variety of ways in which the speaker played upon the emotional reactions of the audience (pathos). Finally, through either inductive or deductive argument the speaker would advance his position (logos).

The historical situation itself determined the class of rhetorical speech. If the speaker was seeking to persuade an audience to make a judgment about events in the past, where there was a question involving justice or truth the speech was considered judicial. If there was an intent to persuade an audience to take some action in the future, where the question involved a matter of self-interest or future benefits, then the speech was termed deliberative. Exhortation or dissuasion marked this approach. Lastly, if the speaker attempted to persuade his audience to hold or reaffirm some basic values, by praising or blaming through appropriate encomium or invective, the speech would be called epideictic.

In the ancient world the judicial speech received the most attention in regard to any elaboration of arrangement. A proem or exordium (that is, an introduction) began the speech by seeking to obtain the attention, goodwill, and sympathy of the audience. Then a narration of facts, the background information, stated the proposition that the speaker wished to prove, often partitioned into separate headings. Thereupon were advanced arguments in the proof, followed by a refutation of opposing views (including a digression to explain motivations and circumstances). Finally an epilogue or peroration summarized the argument and sought to rouse the emotions to take action or judgment. The deliberative speech was regarded as a simplified version of judicial. Proem, proposition, proof, epilogue, and occasionally a narration, was the basic outline. The proof, divided into several headings, attempted to influence future decisions. With emphasis on advantages to be obtained, the exhortation was part and parcel of the proof of this speech class. While there was less interest on the speaker's part to secure a favorable judgment about himself, the audience was directly drawn into the matter. In an epideictic speech there was between the proem and epilogue a body of material divided into an orderly sequence of amplified topics dealing in various ways with the subject under consideration. It should be noted that there was often some mixing of these three forms. A deliberative speech, for example, could contain some defensive or apologetic sections. The overall tendency and direction of the speech would determine the classification.

The analysis of an ancient text, such as Galatians, according to the understanding of rhetorical theory in the Greco-Roman world can lead to the discovery of the author's intent and of the way in which it was transmitted through a text to an audience. By paying close attention to the rhetorical situation, that is, the persons, events, objects, and relations which determine the situation of the speech, and by noting the basic possibilities of speech forms as well as the use of arrangement, style and delivery, one can suggest a unified understanding of the historical material.

In recent scholarship two opposing outlines of Galatians have been presented. The question for the critical reader is: what is at stake? Is Galatians concerned with defending some past action of Paul against the accusations of some opposition (judicial)? Or is it an attempt to urge the Galatians to remain loyal to Paul and to his Gospel? Is it a matter of some future decision on the part of the Galatians (deliberative)? Is it a mixture? What is the overall direction of the argument? Examples of each in outline form follow:

Judicial

    I. Epistolary Prescript (1:1–5)
    II. Exordium (1:6–10)
    III. Narration (1:12–2:14)

Continued on next page

IV. Proposition (2:15–21)
V. Proof (3:1–4:31)
VI. Exhortation (5:1–6:10)
VII. Epistolary Postscript (Conclusion, 6:11–18)

Deliberative

I. Salutation/Exordium (1:1–5)
II. Proposition (1:6–9)
III. Proof (1:10–6:10)
   A. Narration (1:10–2:21)
   B. Further Headings (3:1–6:10)
IV. Epilogue (6:11–18)

Paul's Correspondence to the Philippians

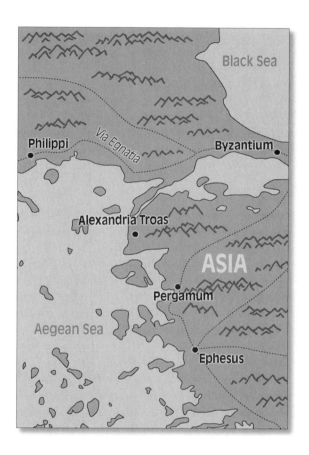

Philippi, a Roman colony on the Via Egnatia, was settled by army veterans.

Philippians

INTRODUCTION

The city of Philippi was founded in 356 BCE by Philip II of Macedon, the father of Alexander the Great. The site, in eastern Macedonia about ten miles inland from the Aegean Sea, had most recently been occupied by colonists from the island of Thasos. They had called their settlement Daton. Even earlier, Thracian settlers had known the site as Krenides ("springs"). Philip made Philippi the center of the Pangaeus gold fields, which are said to have produced 1,000 talents of gold annually. This substantial yield helped to fund his campaigns and those of his famous son. By Roman times, however, the extraction of the precious metal from the mines and streams in the region had apparently largely played out. Philippi was strategically located on the ancient overland route from Asia Minor to the West, known in the Roman period as the Via Egnatia. The road ran immediately adjacent to the forum at the center of the city. The extensive remains of Roman Philippi have been excavated by a number of archaeological efforts over the last century.

In 42 BCE the forces of Antony and Octavian defeated the army of Brutus and Cassius in the Battle of Philippi, fought just west of the city. Subsequently numerous army veterans were settled there and the city was designated a Roman colony, which made the residents Roman citizens. After the Battle of Actium in 31 BCE, Octavian settled more army veterans in Philippi and allowed many whom he expelled from Italy because they had supported Antony to establish themselves there as well. So it was a substantially Romanized city with a mixed population that Paul visited when he first took his mission into European territory.

Paul's own comments in his earliest preserved letter, 1 Thessalonians, enable us to outline the itinerary of his first visit to Macedonia and Greece. Paul reminds his readers that he had told them how he had suffered and been insulted at Philippi before he arrived in Thessalonica (1 Thess 2:2). He also indicates that when he reached Athens, after having left Thessalonica, he sent Timothy back to the new community there to nourish their faith and to encourage them to stand up to the pressure of opposition that he knew would be directed against them (1 Thess 3:1–5). Timothy returned with a good report (1 Thess 3:6) and Paul wrote 1 Thessalonians either from Athens or, more likely, from Corinth, to praise them for their perseverance and to offer further admonition. So it appears that Philippi was the first stop in a four city itinerary (Philippi, Thessalonica, Athens, Corinth) that Paul undertook in Macedonia and Greece.

The narrative in Acts 16:11–40 offers a vivid and dramatic account of Paul's first visit to Philippi, but recent scholarship has persuasively argued that this account owes more to Luke's ability to compose an engagingly plausible tale than to his access to historically reliable information about Paul's missionary experience beyond what can be gleaned from Paul's own letters.[1] In this narrative episode, as in much of Acts as a whole, Luke gives us historical fiction rather than an historical report.

The text of canonical Philippians poses two puzzling and consequential questions which affect the way one reads and understands what Paul has written. The first is whether the letter as we have it is a unity, a single letter in the form authored by Paul, or is in fact a composite put together by an unknown compiler in the second century from what were originally three separate letters of Paul to the community he had founded in Philippi. It will be argued below that persuasive evidence indicates that canonical Philippians is best understood as such a composite text. The second puzzle is that although it is clear that Paul was in prison when he wrote

1:1–3:1a, at least, it is not clear where he was imprisoned at the time. Are we to infer that he is writing from Rome near the end of his life and under the house arrest depicted in Acts 28, or is he writing earlier during one of the several imprisonments to which he refers in 2 Cor 1:8–9; 11:23, but whose exact location he does not specify?

Why These Letters Are Important
The letters Paul wrote to the Philippians offer us several windows on his mission, his relationship with the communities he founded, his religious thinking, and his rhetoric that appear only in this letter.

For instance, it seems clear that Paul had a more cordial relationship with the Philippians than with any of the other communities with whom he corresponded. In Letter 1 (4:10–20) we learn that the Philippians had sent Epaphroditus (probably to Ephesus) with a sum of money to meet Paul's financial needs and to assist him in furthering his work. No other group that he founded supported him financially, as far as we know (4:15–16).

In his correspondence with the Corinthians, he vociferously rejects the idea of receiving financial support from them for fear that it would lead them to question his integrity and create a distraction that would obstruct the reception and spread of his message (1 Cor 9:1–18). Evidently some in Corinth questioned his motives and entertained the suspicion that "he was just in it for the money."

In his letter to the Galatians we see a community seriously divided over whether Paul was a legitimate envoy of the Anointed and ready to question the truth of the message he had proclaimed. Not only did Paul receive no financial support from them, but it appears that most of them took the side of his critics and opponents who insisted that all members of the Anointed's new community, both Jews and those from the nations, were required to observe the ritual as well as the moral requirements of the Mosaic law. They insisted that circumcision continued to be mandatory, if one wanted to be among the Anointed's people, whereas Paul insisted that circumcision had become irrelevant for the Anointed's people (Gal 5:2–6; 6:15).

We hear nothing about financial support for Paul in his letter to the Thessalonians either; and in his letter to the Romans, written before he had ever been to Rome, Paul expresses the hope that they will provide him with material support for his plans to carry the message about God's Anointed to Spain (15:24), but he had received no promises.

In Letter 2 (1:1–3:1a; 4:4–9, 21–23), written from prison, we gain a distinctive glimpse of the progress of Paul's mission. He cheerfully reports that his imprisonment, perhaps contrary to the Philippians' apprehensions, had resulted in the further spread of his message. Although some people around him are taking advantage of his imprisonment to promote themselves as "preachers," Paul sees the irony of their competitive efforts: in spite of their self-serving motives, God's world-changing news is being proclaimed (1:15–18). At the time he writes this letter, it is uncertain whether he will be released from prison or executed. No matter: to live means more fruitful work; to die is gain (1:21–23). For Paul, discouragement is not an option.

Also in Letter 2 is the most well known passage in Paul's Philippian correspondence: the "Christ Hymn" in 2:6–11. Introduced in support of his appeal to his readers to look out for each other's interests, not their self-interest, the "hymn" is an eloquent affirmation of the exemplary and redemptive life of God's Anointed. (See Cameo on the "Christ Hymn" in Philippians 2:6–11, p. 193.)

Letter 3 (3:1b–4:3) begins with a startlingly harsh warning: "Watch out for those curs, watch out for those perpetrators of fraud, watch out for those who would carve up your flesh" (3:1b). The unnamed adversaries characterized in such derisive language are persons who are flaunting their credentials as certified representatives of the "authentic" Jesus movement who insist that the Philippians must maintain the traditional observances of Judaism in obedience to the Mosaic law. Paul responds by one-upping them in a brief autobiographical recitation of credentials that were superior to theirs (3:5–6), and then argues for the transvaluation of values that accompanied his response to God's world-changing news. What he had once regarded as having supreme value—those superior credentials—he now regards as worthless (3:7–9): the path to resurrection from the dead that God has opened up through the Anointed's unconditional trust in God trumps all other goods (3:10–11). What is of supreme importance now is not the preservation of his religious past, but the call of God to the life above (3:12–14, 20–21). In this passage we have Paul's most passionate and sharply worded statement about what embracing God's world-changing news meant in his own life experience.

One Letter or Three?

On the first question, there are several features of the canonical form of Philippians that seem odd, if we are to assume that it is a faithful copy of a single letter written by Paul to the church in Philippi. In 2:25–30, for instance, Paul informs the Philippians that he intends to send their emissary, Epaphroditus, back to them now that he has recovered from a nearly fatal illness. (News of Epaphroditus' illness had distressed the Philippians and he was anxious to return to his friends in Philippi.) It is odd, after reading this notice in 2:25–30, to find Paul expressing his thanks to the Philippians for the monetary gifts they had sent with their emissary in 4:10–20, near the end of the canonical letter, as if Epaphroditus had just arrived. In the canonical order of the letter, then, notice of Epaphroditus' return to Philippi comes before notice of his arrival to present the Philippians' gifts to Paul. Further, Paul's remarks in 4:10–20 have no clear connection with what immediately precedes them in the canonical text (4:2–9), nor with Paul's argument and exhortation in 3:1b–4:1. The remarks in 4:10–20 make better sense, if they were in fact a separate thank-you note written shortly after Epaphroditus' arrival bearing the Philippians' gifts. A credible sequence of events follows if 1:1–3:1a of the canonical letter was written some time later to update the Philippians on Paul's situation after Epaphroditus had recovered from a life-threatening illness and was then able to return to Philippi. Such considerations, together with others sketched below, have led a number of scholars to infer that 4:10–20 was originally the first of three letters Paul wrote to the Philippians that were subsequently combined, probably in the second century, to create a single composite letter that became the canonical form of Paul's correspondence with the Philippians.

Another feature of canonical Philippians that is puzzlingly odd is the abrupt way in which Paul's sharply-worded polemic against circumcision is introduced in 3:2. No explanation is given for the contemptuous warning given in 3:2, nor is any reason offered about why Paul thought it necessary to repeat here what he had either already spoken to them about or had previously written to them about. There is no indication of who the advocates of circumcision were either. This abrupt and unexplained change in tone and subject and its inclusion at this point in canonical Philippians without discernible connection with what precedes it or transition to what follows it has led some scholars to infer that it most probably is a fragment of another letter from the apostle to the Philippians that the compiler judged important to preserve. So he included it in his composite letter, but with no more regard for connecting it well to the undoubtedly single letter we see in 1:1–3:1a than he did in appending the thank-you note in 4:10–20 to the end of his compilation of Paul's Philippian correspondence.

One other indication of the patchwork method used by the compiler to produce the composite letter which became the canonical text is the series of phrases and remarks typical of the way Paul concludes his letters that are interspersed in the canonical form of the letter. "Finally, my friends" occurs both at 3:1a and at 4:8; the admonition to "rejoice in the lord" is found both at 3:1a and at 4:4. In 4:21–23 is another typical Pauline conclusion. Since such concluding phrases occur in other genuine letters of Paul, they may well be markers of what were originally separate letters, but read oddly when interspersed as they are in canonical Philippians.

These considerations yield the following possible identifications of the original letters or letter fragments whose joining produced the canonical text:

Letter 1: 4:10–20
Letter 2: 1:1–3:1a; 4:4–9, 21–23
Letter 3: 3:1b–4:3

Despite this evidence internal to the canonical text of Philippians, some scholars continue to defend the unity of the letter. The weightiest case made for the unity of the letter in recent scholarship is based on an analysis of its rhetorical character. It is argued that Philippians represents what literate people in the first-century CE Greco-Roman world would have recognized as a "letter of friendship." Such letters are typically "agonistic," or competitive: they reflect the fact that friends struggle against enemies or rivals. Paul's remarks in Phil 1:15–18; 1:29–30; 2:19–24; 3:2–11, for example, exhibit "typical vocabulary of friendship and enmity" that is characteristic of letters of friendship.[2] Paul also presents himself as an exemplary model in contrast, for example, to those who preach Christ for self-serving reasons (1:17) and those who insist on the continued importance of circumcision (3:2–3). The use of contrasting models is also a familiar feature of ancient friendship letters.

On the basis of such rhetorical analysis some scholars have argued that what appears to some modern readers as evidence that canonical Philippians is a composite of three originally separate letters should be recognized as common features of the ancient letter of friendship, and that Philippians should therefore be seen as a single, unified letter, not an assemblage of letters.

There is no doubt that rhetorical criticism can contribute much to our understanding of the language of the New Testament writings. But to claim that one can demonstrate the *unity* of Philippians by identifying much of its rhetoric as consistent with the rhetorical conventions of the ancient letter of friendship is to overreach. Rhetorical criticism can identify the character of Paul's language in this correspondence, but it cannot tell us how many letters he wrote to the Philippians. Paul could have used the rhetoric of friendship in three letters to the Philippians as easily as in one.

Fortunately, there is some evidence external to the canonical text of Philippians that can help to resolve the debate about the unity of the letter. Two ancient writings indicate that their authors knew of more than one letter of Paul to the church at Philippi. Polycarp, Bishop of Smyrna, wrote a letter to the church at Philippi not long before he suffered martyrdom, probably in 155 CE, in which he refers to Paul's *letters* to the Philippians:

> Neither I nor anyone like me is able to replicate the wisdom of the blessed and glorious Paul. When he was with you he accurately and reliably taught the word of truth to those who were there at the time. And when he was absent he wrote you letters [*epistolas*]. If you carefully peer into them, you will be able to be built up in the faith that was given you.[3]

If we give Polycarp credit for knowing what he is saying here, then he knows that Paul wrote more than one letter to the Philippians.[4]

The most significant ancient external evidence that the canonical Philippians is in fact a composite text is derived from an apocryphal mid-second-century document attributed to Paul known as his letter to the Laodiceans. Although scholars have known for some time that this brief apocryphal letter consists mostly of a series of comments and phrases drawn almost entirely from Philippians, it was not until Philip Sellew published his analysis of the letter that its significance for the question of the composite character of canonical Philippians was recognized.[5] What Sellew has noted is that except for his use of Galatians 1:1 and 3 in the opening line of his pseudonymous letter, the author of *Laodiceans* uses Philippians as his source for the structure of his letter as well as for its content. He follows the sequence of the portion of Paul's letter he uses as a source; he does not move back and forth between earlier and later passages in his Philippians source. Without exception, he follows Paul's order. What is most significant is the fact that all of the content of *Laodiceans* is drawn from Phil 1:2–2:14; 3:1a; 4:6–9, 22–23, all of which are from Letter 2. In other words, *Laodiceans* makes no use of any of the content of canonical Phil 3:2–4:3, or 4:10–20—the exact portions of canonical Philippians that numerous scholars have identified as probably originally separate letters, or major portions of the body of separate letters from Paul to the church at Philippi. The compiler of *Laodiceans* does skip over some passages in the parts of canonical Philippians he uses, presumably because he found nothing of interest in these passages for his purposes. But to suppose that he used nothing precisely in 3:2–4:3 and 4:10–20 because he found nothing of interest there is much less likely than that he omitted these sections of canonical Philippians because he did not know about them. The most persuasive inference to draw from this evidence is that he only had access to one of the three letters that ultimately were combined to form the letter of Paul to the Philippians that became part of the New Testament.

Paul's Location

The question about where Paul was imprisoned when he wrote at least 1:1–3:1a of what was to become canonical Philippians has traditionally been answered as probably Rome. Several references in the New Testament writings are usually cited in support of this hypothesis. Paul himself states his *intention* to travel to Rome in 15:23–24 of his letter to the believers there, and Acts narrates his adventurous journey to that city and reports that he lived there under the guard of a soldier for two years while awaiting the outcome of his appeal to Caesar of charges that certain of his ethnic kinsman (as he calls them in Rom 9:3) had brought against him when he visited Jerusalem. Further, the references to "the whole praetorium" in Phil 1:13 and to "those in Caesar's service" (or "in Caesar's household") in 4:22 seem to support such a conjecture.

There is less real evidence than there appears to be that Paul wrote to the Philippians from Rome, however. For one thing, neither the reference to "the whole praetorium" nor to "those in Caesar's service" necessarily points to Rome. In Acts 23:35, for instance, the official residence of Roman procurators and governors of Judea in Caesarea, built by Herod the Great, is referred to as "the praetorium"; and when the gospel accounts locate Jesus' appearance before Pilate and his being mocked by the soldiers in "the praetorium" in Jerusalem, the reference is to the palace Herod built there (see Mark 15:16; Matt 27:27; John 18:28, 33; 19:9). As these and other similar usages make clear, the term *praetorium* was not used exclusively in reference to the camp of the emperor's elite guard near the Porta Viminalis in Rome. Rather, by an extension of its original meaning the term came to be used of provincial governors' residences and to various other Roman military and governmental facilities throughout the empire.

A similar extension of meaning is apparent in the case of the expression "Caesar's household." For example, in the course of his account of the subversive scheming of Herod the Great's son, Antipater, Josephus says that Herod's first impulse upon learning of his son's duplicity was to put an end to him on the spot for plotting against him "and for having corrupted the household of Caesar" (*Antiquities* 17.5.8 [142]). In this passage the phrase plainly refers to Herod's family and household staff in Judea, not to the emperor's in Rome. As this example illustrates, it had become customary to refer to a provincial ruler's family and to all in his employ, from high officials to menial servants, as "the household of Caesar." Obviously, then, the occurrence of that expression in Phil 4:22 does not constitute compelling evidence that Paul wrote these lines while he was in Rome.

There is an additional reason, and probably a surprising one for many readers, for being skeptical about the conjecture that Paul wrote to Philippi from Rome: uncertainty about whether Paul in fact ever reached Rome. True, Rom 1:9–15 tells us that Paul had long *wanted* to visit Rome, and Rom 15:22–25 tells us that he was *planning* to stop in Rome on his way to Spain, once he completed a trip to Jerusalem to deliver a substantial sum of money he had collected from communities whose members were from the nations to support impoverished members of the Jewish-Christian community there. But a number of scholars, notably members of Westar Institute's Acts Seminar, have become convinced that the letters of Paul are the primary source for Luke's account of the apostle's travels narrated in Acts, and that the author was not in possession of significant independent sources of information about Paul's missionary work or about the apostle's fate. It may be that Luke based his account of Paul's arrival in Rome on the apostle's statements in his letter to the church there that he *intended* to make such a journey and assumed that Paul lived to see his intentions to visit Rome fulfilled (although under circumstances quite different from what he had in mind when he wrote his letter to the Christian community there). Furthermore, Luke had his own apologetic reasons for wanting to portray Paul in Rome, free to proclaim the gospel unhindered by Roman authority and posing no threat to Roman sovereignty. In any case, it is quite striking to notice that no other early Christian source offers unambiguous evidence that Paul ever actually reached Rome. There are several references to Paul's martyrdom in Rome, based upon what were apparently assumed to be "traditions," but no identifiable historical evidence.

For example, the earliest non-canonical reference to Paul's death is in the letter that Clement, a leader of the church in Rome, wrote to the church at Corinth near the end of the first century CE. Clement admonishes the Corinthians to repent of the envy and strife that he believes had induced them to depose the leaders of the church there and commends the noble example set by Peter and Paul, both of whom, he claims, endured hardships born of envy and strife:

> Because of jealousy and envy the greatest and most upright pillars were persecuted and they struggled in the contest even to death. We should set before our eyes the good apostles. There is Peter, who because of unjust jealousy bore up under hardships not just once or twice, but many times; and having thus borne his witness he went to the place of glory that he deserved. Because of jealousy and strife Paul pointed the way to the prize for endurance. Seven times he bore chains; he was sent into exile and stoned; he served as a herald in both the East and the West; and he received the noble reputation for his faith. He taught righteousness to the whole world, and came to the limits of the West, bearing witness before the rulers. And so he was set free from this world and transported up to the holy place, having become the greatest example of endurance.[6]

In this passage Clement speaks in general terms about the end of Paul's life, but his remarks are disappointingly vague. For neither apostle does he offer any information about the date, location, or manner of their deaths. To suppose that if Clement refers to their deaths they must have been executed in Rome, is only a conjecture unsupported by any specific evidence.

Writing in 325 CE Eusebius, Bishop of Caesarea, reports the story he has found in his sources that both Paul and Peter were put to death in Rome in the time of Nero (Paul allegedly beheaded, Peter allegedly crucified). Eusebius believes that these stories are confirmed by the fact that cemeteries named after Peter and Paul were known to be in Rome in his day. He also notes that, according to a late second-century to early third-century writer and defender of apostolic orthodoxy named Caius (whose writings are no longer extant), monuments in honor of the two apostles who founded the Roman church (a claim that we know to be historically untrue) could be seen in his (Caius's) day at the Vatican and on the Ostian Way.[7] Eusebius does not claim to have inspected the cemeteries or monuments himself, nor to have sought corroborating evidence. He simply assumes that the "tradition" about the apostles' deaths is based on fact. It is more difficult for a modern historian to see evidence of historical actuality in such stories and memorials than it apparently was for Eusebius. Such "tradition" could also be based on nothing more historical than pious commemoration. In any case, it is a fact that no eyewitness testimony about the deaths of either apostle has been preserved in any extant source of reliable historical information.* So while it is possible that Paul eventually reached Rome, we have no conclusive historical evidence that he actually did so. We have only his statement of his intentions, Luke's suppositional story-telling in Acts, "traditions" about a cemetery and a monument bearing his name in the capital city,† and fanciful late second-century tales meant to honor his memory rather than to report it.

If the hypothesis that Paul wrote Philippians from Rome seems doubtful, is it possible to identify a more probably place of origin? A rather good case can be made for the possibility that Paul wrote his letters to the Philippians from Ephesus. Paul himself says that he had been imprisoned a number of times (2 Cor 6:5; 11:23), but he never specifies where these confinements occurred.‡ The one location that Paul does mention by name as a place where he had experienced an espe-

---

*The accounts of the martyrdoms of Peter and Paul in the apocryphal Acts of Peter and Acts of Paul are miracle-filled pious fictions composed in the late second century CE. They are hagiographies, not historical accounts.
†St. Paul's Cemetery in Rome, to which Eusebius refers, may be no more evidence of his burial there than is London's St. Paul's Cathedral evidence of the apostle's missionary visit to that city.
‡Luke, in Acts, reports three such locations: Philippi (16:16–40); Caesarea (23:12–26:32); and Rome (28:16–30).

cially difficult, even life-threatening time and that could have been the place from which he wrote Philippians is Ephesus. Paul mentions that city by name in a rhetorical question that is part of his argument for his belief in the resurrection of the dead in 1 Corinthians 15: "If the dead are not raised at all . . . for what conceivable reason am I putting my life at risk all the time? . . . If I had to fight wild beasts, so to speak, at Ephesus, what good does that do me? If we who die are not raised, 'Let us eat and drink, because tomorrow we will be dead'" (1 Cor 15:29–32, SV). While the reference to "wild beasts" here is most likely metaphorical, it nevertheless suggests that the apostle faced a life-threatening situation of some kind in Ephesus. Further, in 2 Cor 1:8–9 Paul tell his readers in Corinth that he had faced distress "in Asia" that was so severe he thought he was facing the death sentence. Ephesus was the capital of the Roman province of Asia. So even though Paul does not name Ephesus in this passage, his reference in 1 Cor 15:32 to a life-threatening ordeal in that city suggests the possibility that in this somewhat later, non-metaphorical remark, he is referring to a more recent development of that same situation: what had earlier appeared to be ferocious opposition subsequently seemed likely to lead to the death sentence. It appears that in Phil 1:19–26 and 2:17 also, the possibility of Paul's death is in prospect; and while he is hopeful that the charges brought against him will not eventuate in a death sentence, the issue is still in some doubt. It may be, then, that the apostle's remarks in 1 Cor 15:32; Phil 1:19–26; 2:17; and 2 Cor 1:8–9 all reflect ongoing developments in the same crisis situation in the same city—Ephesus.

Another reason for thinking that Philippians could have been written in Ephesus is that the frequency of travel and communication reflected in the letters between the place where Paul is imprisoned and Philippi would have been more likely if the place of his incarceration was there rather than in Rome. The Philippians had sent Epaphroditus to Paul with a monetary gift (4:10–20); in the meantime they somehow learned of his serious illness while he was staying with Paul, and then Paul sent him back to Philippi. Further, Paul wrote at least three letters to the Philippians, if our analysis of the canonical text is correct. He also hopes to send Timothy to them soon and intends to visit them himself in the near future (2:19–24). It is easier to account for all of these exchanges if Paul is at Ephesus, about 300 miles from Philippi, than at Rome, more than twice as far away.

Finally, 2 Cor 1:8–2:13 tells us that Paul did follow Timothy to Macedonia once his ordeal in Asia was behind him, just as he said in Phil 2:19–14 he hoped to do; and Timothy is named as the co-sender of the letter preserved in 2 Cor 1:1–2:3; 7:5–16 that Paul sent to Corinth from Macedonia. A considerable coherence with what Paul himself says about his travel plans in other letters thus results, when we consider the possibility that Paul's letters to the Philippians were written from Ephesus.

When Were These Letters Written?

If Paul wrote these letters to the Philippians from Ephesus before he went to Jerusalem to deliver the sizable gift of money he had collected from the gentile churches for the poor of the church there, they may well have been written in the winter of 54–55. This would place them shortly before his last visit to Corinth from where in the winter of 55–56 he is thought to have written his letter to the Romans.

NOTES

1. See Richard Pervo, *Profit with Delight: The Literary Genre of the Acts of the Apostles* (Philadelphia: Fortress Press, 1987), 23–24.

2. Stanley Stowers, "Friends and Enemies in the Politics of Heaven," in *Pauline Theology*, vol. 1 of *Thessalonians, Philippians, Galatians, Philemon*, ed. Jouette M. Bassler (Minneapolis: Fortress Press, 1991), 114.

3. Polycarp, *Letter to the Philippians*, 3:2–3 in *The Apostolic Fathers*, ed. and trans. Bart D. Ehrman, Loeb Classical Library (Cambridge, MA: Harvard University Press, 2003), I, 337.

4. Interestingly, the document known for centuries as Polycarp's Letter to the Philippians is now regarded by most scholars as a com-

posite of two letters of Polycarp to the church at Philippi: a brief cover letter sent with copies of the letters of Ignatius soon after his visit to Smyrna in 110 CE, and a longer letter written decades later. This is a further indication that creating a single letter out of originally separate pieces of correspondence was not unusual in early Christian efforts to preserve copies of such correspondence in a convenient form. For details, see the Introduction to the letter in the new Loeb Classical Library edition cited above, or in Helmut Koester, *Introduction to the New Testament*, vol 2: *History and Literature of Early Christianity* (Philadelphia: Fortress Press, 1982), 306.

The Syriac *Catalogus Sinaiticus* (about 400 CE) lists two letters of Paul to the Philippians, and the Byzantine chronicler Georgius Syncellus (eighth–ninth century) refers to Paul's "first letter to the Philippians." However, neither of these references can be considered as reliable historical evidence. The repetition of "Philippians" in the *Catalogus Sinaiticus* is apparently only an instance of careless dittography. Syncellus' reference to "first Philippians" is late (eighth–ninth century) and scholars generally regard him as an unreliable source.

5. Philip Sellew, "*Laodiceans* and the Philippian Fragments Hypothesis," *Harvard Theological Review* 87 (January, 1994): 17–28. For an English translation of Laodiceans, see Edgar Hennecke and Wilhelm Schneemelcher, eds., *New Testament Apocrypha*, English translation ed. R. McL. Wilson (Philadelphia: The Westminster Press, 1964), II, 131–32. For an attempt to refute Sellew's argument, see Paul A. Holloway, *Consolation in Philippians: Philosophical Sources and Rhetorical Strategy* (Cambridge University Press, 2001), 9–11. See also his article, "The Apocryphal Epistle to the Laodiceans and the Partitioning of Philippians," *Harvard Theological Review* 91 (July, 1998): 321–25; and Sellew's "*Laodiceans* and Philippians Revisited: A Response to Paul Holloway" following, 327–29. Holloway's claims are dependent upon a particular rhetorical theory and a series of conjectures about *Laodiceans* compiler's "redactional considerations."

6. 1 Clement 5:2–7, in Ehrman, ed., *Apostolic Fathers*, Loeb Classical Library, I, 43, 45.

7. Eusebius, *The Ecclesiastical History*, II.25.5,6.

Letter 1
A Thank-You Note

4 ¹⁰I was overjoyed, because of our common service to the lord, that you have finally shown some concern about me again; actually, you were concerned about me all along, but had no opportunity [to show it]. ¹¹I am not complaining about being in want, because I have learned how to manage in whatever circumstance I find myself. ¹²I know how to do with very little and how to handle abundance. I have learned the secret of dealing with circumstances of every kind, with being well fed and being hungry, with having plenty and doing without. ¹³I can cope with anything through the one who strengthens me. ¹⁴Nevertheless, it was good of you to become my partners when I was having a hard time. ¹⁵And you Philippians know very well that from the time I first proclaimed God's world-changing news among you, when I decided to leave Macedonia none of the Anointed's gatherings entered into partnership with me in balancing the account of giving and receiving, except for you. ¹⁶Even when I was in Thessalonica, more than once you sent [gifts] to meet my need. ¹⁷What I am looking for is not your gift; what I am interested in is the

---

4:10 This verse appears to be the beginning of the body of the first of three letters Paul wrote to the Philippians that were combined, probably early in the second century CE, to form canonical Philippians. In its original form this short letter would undoubtedly have included a salutation similar to that in 1:1–2 of Letter 2 below, as all of Paul's other letters did, but was omitted when it was made a part of the canonical text. See the Introduction to Philippians.

I was overjoyed, because of our common service to the lord: Literally, "I rejoice in the lord greatly." The cryptic Pauline phrase "in the lord" conveys a range of meanings in his letters. Here it expresses his view that both the Philippians and he belong to and serve the Anointed as lord.

4:11 *how to manage:* Greek, *autarkēs*, "content," "self-sufficient," a term used by Stoics in reference to a favorite virtue. In this remark Paul is making his own use of the notion that the wise and mature man does not allow his life to be determined by outward circumstances.

dividend that increases your balance in the account [of giving and receiving]. [18]Indeed, I have received payment in full and now have more than enough. My need is fully met now that I have received from Epaphroditus what you sent, the fragrant aroma of a sacrifice that is acceptable and pleasing to God. [19]And in turn my God will amply provide everything you need from the splendid abundance of the divine resources through the Anointed Jesus. [20]To God our Great Benefactor be the highest praise forever and ever. Amen.

Letter 2
A Letter from Prison

1 Paul and Timothy, slaves of God's Anointed, Jesus, to all God's people in the service of the Anointed Jesus who are in Philippi including your leaders and their assistants.

²Divine favor and genuine peace to you from God our great Benefactor and our lord, Jesus, God's Anointed.

³I thank God every time I think of you. ⁴Whenever I pray for you all I pray with joy, ⁵because of your partnership on

---

1:1 *slaves of God's Anointed, Jesus:* Greek: *douloi,* plural of *doulos,* "slave." Paul uses this expression about himself in the salutation of a letter only here and in Rom 1:1. By using this language Paul is advancing his claim that being the slave of God's Anointed elevates one above being the slave of any other master. Whereas "slave" is a dishonorable term in ordinary society, "slave of God's Anointed" is a term of authenticity and honor in Paul's usage. Liberated from servitude to lesser powers (sin, Rom 6:16–22; cosmic powers, Gal 4:3,9; human beings, 1 Cor 7:23), all who acknowledge Jesus as lord have become "children of God" (Gal 4:7, 21–23) and heirs of the promise of eternal life (Rom 8:1–17).

all God's people in the service of the Anointed Jesus: Literally, "all the saints in Christ Jesus." Greek *hagios,* "holy," plural, *hagioi,* "holy ones, saints," was originally a cultic term designating persons or things set apart for divine service. The phrase "in Christ Jesus" here and often in Paul means being in the Anointed's service or belonging to him, as to a lord. This translation conveys the sense of the Greek, rather than a literal word for word rendering that fails to convey its sense.

leaders and their assistants: The traditional translation of these terms, "bishops and deacons," is anachronistic, because they later came to designate forms of ecclesiastical office that did not yet exist in Paul's time. Paul's terms do indicate that certain leadership roles developed early in the communities he founded, even if these did not yet constitute an ecclesiastical hierarchy. The Philippians themselves may have named these leadership positions. Paul does not refer to leaders by these terms in any other letter.

1:2 *lord:* The use of the lower case for this term here is intended to indicate that while Paul's conception accords to the risen Jesus an exalted status, he nevertheless does not yet think of the risen Jesus as the second person of the Trinity. That conception did not attain the status of orthodoxy until the adoption of the Nicene Creed in 325 CE.

Paul uses the conventional letter-writing form of his day by naming senders and recipients and extending greetings; but he expands this formula here by including Timothy as a co-sender and by designating both senders as slaves of God's Anointed, Jesus. He also expands the reference to the recipients by referring to the community's "leaders and their assistants."

behalf of God's world-changing news ever since we met. ⁶What I know for sure is that the One who began this good work among you will bring it to fulfillment at the day of the Anointed Jesus. ⁷It is surely right for me to feel this way about you all, because you have a special place in my heart; both when I was making a case for the reliability of God's world-changing news and when I was imprisoned, you all have shared God's gift [of this ministry] with me. ⁸God knows how I long for all of you with a depth of feeling like that of the Anointed Jesus. ⁹I am praying that your love [for one another] may continue to grow in understanding and discernment, ¹⁰so that you will be able to recognize what really matters, be absolutely genuine and innocent of any offense on the day of the Anointed, ¹¹and be filled to overflowing with the benefits of the integrity that Jesus the Anointed inspires in us. This is what will bring honor and praise to God.

¹²I want you to know, friends, that what has happened to me here has turned out to advance God's world-changing news more than ever. ¹³It has become apparent to the whole praetorium and to everyone else that I have been imprisoned because of my service to God's Anointed, ¹⁴and my incarceration has led most of our people here to such confidence in the lord that they now have more nerve than ever to spread the word [about God's Anointed] without fearing [what might happen]. ¹⁵Some, I know, are proclaiming the Anointed because they are envious and contentious, but others do so out of good

---

1:6 *the day of the Anointed Jesus:* By this and similar expressions (1:10, 2:16; 1 Thess 5:2, 4; 1 Cor 5:5) Paul refers to the coming of the risen Jesus at the end of the age to inaugurate the new era when this mortal body is clothed with immortality and everything is subjected to God's sovereign authority and power (1 Cor 15:24–28; 51–54).

1:7 *God's gift [of this ministry]:* Literally *charis.* In this verse and in Rom 1:5; 12:3; 15:15; and Gal 2:9, Paul uses the term *charis* to refer to his calling to be an envoy as God's particular "gift" to him.

1:12 *I want you to know* is a conventional phrase by which letter-writers often introduce the body of the letter and indicate what the letter is about. Paul also uses this and similar phrases to introduce a topic he wants to emphasize.

will. [16]The latter are proclaiming the Anointed out of love, because they understand that it is my appointed task to make the case for our claims about God's Anointed, [17]but the former are proclaiming the Anointed for self-serving reasons. Their motives are not pure: they have it in mind to stir up trouble for me while I am in prison. [18]So what? Either way, whether their motives are specious or sincere, the Anointed is being proclaimed; and that makes me glad. And I will certainly continue to be glad [19]because I know that through your prayers and the support of Jesus the Anointed through the presence and power of God, this will all work out for my release. [20]This is in keeping with my keen anticipation and hope that I am not going to be ashamed about anything. On the contrary, I am completely confident that now as always the Anointed will be exalted by my life whether I live or die. [21]What I mean is that for me living is all about the Anointed, and, if I die, I gain. [22]But if my earthly life continues that will mean that my work will be even more fruitful. Which I would prefer is hard for me to say; [23]I am torn between the two. I have a desire to depart this life and to be with the Anointed, which would be better by far. [24]For my earthly life to continue, on the other hand, is more necessary for your sake. [25]Since I am persuaded that this is the case, I know that I'm going to live and remain with all of you for the sake of the joyful growth of your trust in God, [26]so that my coming again to you will increase your confident pride in the Anointed Jesus.

[27]Just make sure that you conduct yourselves in a manner that is worthy of the world-transforming message about the Anointed, so that whether I come and see you or am away and only hear news about you, you are resolutely one in heart and mind, contending side by side with the unconditional confidence in God that the world-transforming message inspires, [28]not intimidated in the least by our opponents. Your confidence in God is an omen of their ruin but a sign of your deliverance and this is from God. [29]You have been given the privilege not only to believe in what the Anointed stands for,

but also to suffer for his cause, [30]and you are involved in the same struggle in which you have seen and now hear that I am engaged.

2 So if [you know] how uplifting it is to belong to the new community of the Anointed, if [you know] something about being motivated by love, if [you know] something about the spirit of fellowship and genuine compassion, [2]then make me completely happy by sharing the same attitude, showing the same love toward one another, and being united in heart and purpose. [3]Don't be always thinking about your own interests or your own importance, but with humility hold others in higher regard than you do yourselves. [4]Each of you should keep others' interests in mind, not your own. [5]I appeal to all of you to think in the same way that the Anointed Jesus did, [6]who

> although he was born in the image of God,
> did not regard "being like God"
> as something to use for his own advantage,
> [7]but rid himself of such vain pretension
> and accepted a servant's lot.

> Since he was born like all human beings
> and proved to belong to humankind,
> [8]he recognized his true status
> and became trustfully obedient all the way to death,
> even to death by crucifixion.

> [9]That is why God raised him higher than anyone
> and awarded him the title that is above all others,

> [10]so that on hearing the name "Jesus,"
> every knee should bend,
> above the earth, on the earth, and under the earth,
> [11]and every tongue declare: "Jesus the Anointed is lord!"
> to the majestic honor of God, our great Benefactor.

[12]In light of this, my dear friends, just as you have always listened to what I say, not only when I am present but now

even more when I am absent, demonstrate what your deliverance means with an appropriate sense of apprehension and trepidation, [13]because God is the one who arouses you both to will and to accomplish God's good purpose. [14]See to it that you do everything without complaining and arguing, [15]so that you may be above reproach and without guile, untainted children of God in the midst of a dishonest and devious generation, among whom you stand out like lights in a dark world. [16]If you hold on to the message of life, that will give me something to be proud of on the day of the Anointed: that I have not run a pointless race, nor has my labor been a waste of time. [17]But even if my life is being poured out as a libation along with the sacrificial service that your confident trust in God is, I rejoice to do this and share my joy with all of you. [18]For the same reason you should rejoice and share your joy with me.

[19]In the interest of our service to the lord Jesus, I hope to send Timothy to you soon, so that I may be encouraged when I hear the news about how you are faring. [20]No one else here is such a kindred spirit, who will be as genuinely concerned about how you are getting along as I am. [21]All of the others are looking out for their own interests, not the interests of Jesus the Anointed. [22]You already know that he has proven himself, like a child who helps his father he has served with me on behalf of the world-changing news from God. [23]So I hope to send him to you as soon as I am able to see how things are going to go for me. [24]And my trust in the Lord makes me confident that I myself also will come to see you before long.

[25]I think it is necessary to send Epaphroditus back to you—whom you sent to attend to my needs, and who has been to me a brother, a fellow-worker, and a fellow-soldier—[26]because he misses you all terribly and was concerned about your hearing that he had been ill. [27]And indeed, he was so sick that he nearly died. But God had mercy on him, and not only on him but on me as well, so that I would not have one sorrow after another. [28]So I was eager to send him right away, so that by

seeing him again you would be cheered up and I would be less worried. ²⁹Let him know with what great pleasure you welcome him home as truly one in the lord's service. You should hold people like him in high regard, ³⁰because his dedication to the work of the Anointed nearly cost him his life. He risked his life to provide the help that you all could not. **3** ¹Finally, my friends, rejoice that you belong to our lord. . . . **4** ⁴Always show how glad you are to be in the lord's service. I say it again: show how glad you are! ⁵Let your considerate regard for one another be known to all people. The lord is near. ⁶Don't be anxious about anything; instead, make your concerns known to God by prayer and petition with a thankful heart. ⁷And the peace of God which is beyond all human comprehension will stand guard over your hearts and minds because you belong to the Anointed Jesus.

⁸Finally, friends, keep your minds on what is true, what commands respect, what is just, what is pure, what is kind, what is commendable, whatever is excellent and worthy of praise. ⁹Put into practice what you have learned and received from me, what you have heard me say and seen me do, and the God of peace will be with you.

²¹Extend greetings to every one of God's people in the service of the Anointed Jesus. The brothers and sisters [here with me] send their greetings to you. ²²All God's people send their greetings, especially those who work in Caesar's service. ²³May the gracious favor of the lord Jesus the Anointed be with your heart and mind.

4:4 In the judgment of the SV translators and numerous other scholars, the editor of canonical Philippians—probably in the second century CE—inserted 3:1b–4:3 between 3:1a and 4:4. Paul's remarks in 4:4 continue the encouraging exhortation he introduces in 3:1a, whereas the sharp-edged polemical argument that begins in 3:1b disrupts that cordial appeal. See the discussion in the Introduction to Philippians, above.

Scripture Parallels

2:10–11   Isa 45:23

Pauline Parallels

1:1–2   1 Thess 1:1; Gal 1:1–3; 1 Cor 1:1–3; 2 Cor 1:1–2;
          Phlm 1–3; Rom 1:1–7
1:3   1 Thess 1:2; 1 Cor 1:4; Phlm 4; Rom 1:8
1:4   1 Thess 1:2–3; Phlm 4; Rom 1:9
2:12   2 Cor 7:15
2:19–21   1 Cor 16:10–11
4:9   3:17; 1 Thess 1:6; 1 Cor 11:1
4:21–22   1 Thess 5:26; 1 Cor 16:19–20; 2 Cor 13:11–13;
          Rom 16:16
4:23   1 Thess 5:28; Gal 6:18; 1 Cor 16:23 ; 2 Cor 13:14;
          Phlm 25; Rom 16:20b

Letter 3
Paul's Testimony and Advice

3 [1]. . . To repeat here in writing things that I have already told you is no trouble for me and will serve as a safeguard for you. [2]Watch out for those curs, watch out for those perpetrators of fraud, watch out for those who would carve up your flesh. [3]We are the ones who know what circumcision really means; we are serving [God] with our whole heart and mind and base our confidence on the Anointed Jesus and do not put our trust in religious credentials. [4]I say this even though I also have grounds for putting my trust in religious credentials. If any of these other people think that they have grounds for putting trust in religious credentials, I can top them. [5]I was circumcised eight days after my birth, I belong to the people of Israel by birth and am descended from the tribe of Benjamin, a Hebrew descended from Hebrews. With respect to the law I was a Pharisee. [6]My zeal about this led me to persecute the Anointed's people. In regard to the requirements of the law, I was flawless. [7]But all of these things that

---

3:1b This remark is often taken as an indication that Paul had previously written to the Philippians about the same matter he addresses in this chapter. If so, that earlier letter has not been preserved. It is also possible that Paul is here repeating in writing what he has previously told them orally. See the similar remark in 3:18.

3:2 *Watch out for . . . :* Paul uses very derogatory terms in a series of three phrases to characterize those in the Jesus movement who insisted that the requirements of Jewish religious law must be observed by "all God's people" (1:1b), including those from the nations.

3:3 This translation omits the Greek term *theou* = "of God" from this verse, as does P[46], the oldest extant manuscript of Paul's letters. Other manuscripts also omit this term. This results in a reading that is closely parallel to Paul's remark in Rom 1:9: "God is my witness, whom I serve wholeheartedly. . . ."

3:3 *religious credentials:* Greek: *sarx,* "flesh." Paul lists in this passage those matters of physical descent and religious observance that once constituted his identity and status as a devout Jew. They amount to what we would call his religious credentials.

3:7 Paul uses economic terms figuratively here.

I once thought were valuable assets I have come to regard as worthless because of God's Anointed. [8]Indeed, I now regard everything as worthless in light of the incomparable value of realizing that the Anointed Jesus is my lord. Because of him I wrote off all of those assets and now regard them as worth no more than rubbish so that I can gain the [incomparable asset of] the Anointed, [9]and be found in solidarity with him, no longer having an integrity of my own making based on performing the requirements of religious law, but now having the integrity endorsed by God, the integrity of an absolute confidence in and reliance upon God like that of the Anointed [Jesus]. This integrity is endorsed by God and is based on such unconditional trust [in God]. [10]My aim now is to know the Anointed's unconditional confidence and trust and the power of his resurrection—to join him in his sufferings and to live out the meaning of his death, [11]in the hope that I may attain the goal of the resurrection from among the dead.

[12]I am not saying that I have already attained the resurrected state nor that I have already become a perfected being, but I continue to pursue that prize in the hope that I may gain possession of it, because it is for this purpose that the Anointed

---

3:8 *worth no more than rubbish:* Greek, *skubala,* a common word for excrement, filth; but also a common word for gleanings, chaff, leftovers, refuse, the wreckage of a ship, and other things that had no worth. Paul's language here is emphatic rather than crude: what he once prized, he now regards as worth nothing.

3:9 *integrity:* Greek, *dikaiosunē,* "righteousness." What Paul is referring to here is not his moral principles or ethical conduct but his impeccable observance of the requirements of Jewish religious law by which he had maintained his standing as a righteous Jew. Paul has changed his mind about what God counts as integrity.

3:9 *like that of the Anointed Jesus:* Literally, "that which is through the faith of Christ." The subjective genitive here refers to the confidence in and reliance upon God that Christ had—his own "faith," not to faith in Christ, which would require the dative case. Most modern English translations of this phrase are theologically motivated mistranslations. Paul always speaks about "faith" in God, not "faith" in Christ.

3:10 *live out the meaning of his death:* Paul means that he has already "died" to a merely earthly existence. Cp. Gal 2:19, "I was crucified with the Anointed." See also Rom 6:5–11.

Jesus has taken possession of me. [13]I do not regard myself as having reached this goal, my friends; I just concentrate on one thing: I forget about the things I have left behind me and I strive with all my strength toward what lies before me. [14]I run as hard as I can toward the finish line to win the prize—the call of God through the Anointed Jesus to the life above. [15]So then, those of us who are mature in our understanding should adopt this way of seeing things, and if you see things differently right now, [I am confident that] God will enlighten you about this also. [16]In any case, we must be true to what we have come to see. [17]You should all follow my example, my friends, and should keep your eyes on those who are dealing with life as I do. We are your models. [18]As I have told you often before and tell you again now with great sadness, many have adopted a way of life that is opposed to everything the cross of the Anointed stands for. [19]They are heading for destruction. Their god is the belly and they take pride in their shameful behavior. They have their minds set on a merely earthly existence. [20]The commonwealth to which we belong, on the other hand, is in heaven, from where we are expecting the one who will deliver us, our lord, Jesus the Anointed. [21]He will transform our weak and mortal body into a body as glorious as his, by the power he has to make everything subject to his will. 4 [1]And so, my dear friends, whom I long to see, my pride and joy, be firmly committed to the lord's service, dear friends.

[2]I urge Euodia and Syntyche to settle their differences as befits those who belong to the lord. [3]Yes and I ask you too, my true colleague, to give them your help. They contended side by side with me in the work of spreading God's world-changing news along with Clement and the rest of my co-workers, all of whose names are in the Book of Life.

3:20 In Roman law the slave has no family and no country. The person liberated through an unconditional trust in God like that of God's Anointed now does belong to a new country as the slave of a true lord.
4:3 *my true colleague:* Extensive attempts to identify this unnamed person have not been convincing.

Pauline Parallels

3:4–6	Gal 1:13–14; 2 Cor 11:21–22
3:13b–14	1 Cor 9:24–27
3:17	1 Thess 1:6; 1 Cor 11:1

The "Christ Hymn"
in Philippians 2:6–11

This famous passage has long been seen as an affirmation of the pre-existence and divinity of Christ that goes all the way back to Christianity's "first theologian," the Apostle Paul. In this structured passage, for more than a hundred years now characterized as a "hymn," Christ Jesus—named in Paul's introductory clause, but not in the "hymn" itself—is said to be "in the form of God" (King James Version and many others)—or "being in very nature God" (New International Version), or "being essentially one with God" (Amplified New Testament), or "His state was divine" (Jerusalem Bible)—and "did not consider it robbery to be equal with God" (King James Version)—or, did not regard it as "something to cling to" (Jerusalem Bible) or "something to be grasped" (New International Version)—but "emptied himself" (of his divinity) and became incarnated in the form of human beings, assumed the humble role of a servant and suffered death on the cross in obedience to God's will. God then raised him on high as the lord to whom every knee will bend and whom every tongue will acknowledge. This reading of the passage assumes that a descent-ascent pattern gives the "hymn" its basic structure.

In this way the passage has been read as reflecting what had come to be the orthodox version of the story of redemption: that the eternal Son of God descended from heaven, emptied himself of his divinity and became incarnate in human flesh. In obedience to God's will he died on the cross to save us from our sin, was raised from the dead and returned

Continued on next page

to his place at the right hand of God from where he will rule, world without end, his saving mission accomplished.

The work of several scholars, taken together, has now cast this passage in a different light, that of an exalted affirmation of Jesus as God's Anointed without the coloration of orthodox christology. One study has convincingly demonstrated that the key to understanding the statement in 2:6 is recognizing its use of an idiomatic expression—not literal language—that should be translated, "he did not regard being like God as something to exploit," or "to use for his own advantage."[1] Translations that fail to note the idiomatic character of the language in this remark and attempt to translate the term *harpagmos* literally can now be seen as mistranslations.

Another study shows that the allusive phrasing of the hymn, especially in vv. 6–8, makes use of synonymous terms and pleonasm[2]—"the use of more words than are necessary for the expression of an idea; redundancy."[3] The synonyms and repetitions in this part of the hymn are not designations of the stages of the figure's descent from the divine realm, as has traditionally been assumed, but celebrative language that lauds the figure's attitude and behavior, as Paul's introductory admonition in 2:5 clearly implies.

Several of the terms used in vv. 6–8 echo the terminology found in the story of the creation and fall of Adam in Genesis 1 and 3 in the Greek translation of the Hebrew Bible (the Septuagint) that Paul and all of the authors of the writings that comprise the New Testament knew and used. Adam is said to have been created in the image and likeness of God (Gen 1:26–27); and he succumbs to the "Serpent's" seductive suggestion that, if he asserted himself, he would become equal to God (Gen 3:5). The similarity of the language in Phil 2:6-8 to the language in these Genesis passages points to another way of reading the "Christ Hymn:" as contrasting the First and Second Adam—a contrast Paul explicitly draws in Rom 5:12–14, and in 1 Cor 15:21–23, 45–50.[4] The contrast between the First and Second Adam reflected in the "Christ Hymn" can be charted in this way:

First Adam	Second Adam
bearing the image of God	bearing the image of God
he regarded being like God as something to use for his own advantage	he did not regard being like God as something to use for his own advantage
with vain pretention he asserted himself	he rid himself of vain pretentions
and rejected his lot as a servant	and accepted his lot as a servant
he exalted himself	he humbled himself
his disobedience led to his death	he was obedient to the death even death by crucifixion
he was condemned by God and cast out of paradise	he was exalted by God and named lord of all[5]

The meaning of this passage is also related to its structure. One influential analysis of the structure of the "hymn," first published in 1928, saw the "hymn" as organized into six strophes of three lines each.[6] The one line of the "hymn" that did not fit in this structure, "even death by crucifixion," was thought to be a Pauline addition to a pre-Pauline composition. This structural analysis assumes that the basic pattern of the "hymn" is that of the descent and ascent of the figure it celebrates. The first three strophes recount the descent, the last three the ascent.

A more recent structural analysis sees the "hymn" as organized in four strophes. This analysis is based on close attention to the parallelism within the passage and offers an arrangement in which each strophe expresses a complete thought that is reinforced by repetition of important terms.[7] This analysis of the "hymn's" structure is consistent with the view that the hymn intends to contrast the First and Second Adams. The First Adam, as all who have heard the story of his creation and fall in Genesis know, mishandled his status as a creature and blundered into self-exaltation that resulted in his self-destruction. The Second Adam rightly handled his status as a creature and was approved by God as a model of how a human being should conduct himself, and was exalted as the prototype and lord of a re-created human race.

Continued on next page

The SV Paul translation reflects this four strophe analysis of the structure of the "hymn." The structure of the passage together with its idiomatic, allusive, and celebrative (not literal) language indicate that its author did not intend to speak about the descent and ascent of a divine being, but about the exemplary earthly life of Jesus as a human being. God endorsed that exemplary life by raising Jesus on high as the Second Adam, who represents the remedy for the failure of the First Adam.

NOTES

1. Roy W. Hoover, "The *Harpagmos* Enigma: A Philological Solution," *Harvard Theological Review* LXIV (1971): 95–119.

2. Casey Wayne Davis, *Oral Biblical Criticism. The Influence of the Principles of Orality on the Literary Structure of Paul's Epistle to the Philippians*, Journal for the Study of the New Testament Supplement Series 172 (Sheffield Academic Press, 1999), 74, 87–88,114–15, 163–64. Davis, however, allows his literary analysis to be overruled by the orthodox christology that he sees in this passage. He remarks that *"en morphe theou huparchon* should be synonymous with *to einai isa theou* but the synonymy is negated by the context" (p. 163).

3. *Webster's New World Dictionary.*

4. Compare the comment of Oscar Cullmann: "All the statements of Phil 2:6ff. are to be understood from the standpoint of the Old Testament history of Adam" in *The Christology of the NewTestament* (Philadelphia: The Westminster Press, Revised Edition,1963), 181.

5. Adapted from an unpublished paper by John H. Elliott, cited in Bruce Malina and John Pilch, *Social Science Commentary on the Letters of Paul* (Minneapolis: Fortress Press, 1999), 307.

6. E. Lohmeyer, *Kyrios Jesus: Eine Untersuchen zu Phil. 2:5–11*, Sitzungsberichte der Heidelberger Akademie der Wissensch.,Phil.-hist. Kl., Jahr. 1927–28, 4, Abh. (Heidelberg, 1928).

7. Charles H. Talbert, "The Problem of Pre-existence in Philippians 2:6–11," *Journal of Biblical Literature,* LXXXVI (June, 1967): 141–53.

Paul's Correspondence to the Romans

Rome was the capital and center of the Roman Empire.

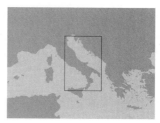

Romans

INTRODUCTION

Paul's letter to the Romans figures greatly in the history of Western Civilization. While Christian theology can easily be characterized as a series of footnotes to this letter, Western social and political thinking can also be seen as marginal glosses on Paul's address to Rome.

The letter to the Romans represents a pivotal moment in the life of Paul and the developing Jesus movement. Paul writes to Rome around 55–57 CE presumably from Corinth (Rom 15:25–27). While intending to deliver to Jerusalem the collection he had just completed among the assemblies of the Anointed in Greece and Asia Minor, Paul looks ahead as he writes to "all of God's beloved in Rome." Although he is unsure of his reception in Jerusalem (Rom 15:31), he intends on stopping off in Rome as he sets his sights on a new mission territory: Spain (Rom 15:24). The collection was very important to Paul. In his mind the reception of the collection would confirm the basic equality of the nations with Jews before God. Working on that fundamental understanding, Paul anticipates visiting the Roman communities before he journeys to what was then considered the fullest expression of Roman conquest and culture.

The Text of Romans

In its canonical form the letter to the Romans includes several possible interpolations and several appendages. The concluding benediction, for example, (16:25–27) has a suspect history. It appeared at various positions in ancient manuscripts. Because of its formal, liturgical tone and vocabulary not found elsewhere in Romans, most scholars regard this ending as a later addition. Further, the SV translators judge 13:1–7 to be an interpolation. See explanatory comments on Interpolations.

Chapter 16:1–23 probably is a separate letter of recommendation for Phoebe (16:1–2), a leader of the Anointed's people in Cenchreae, with accompanying greetings to and from various members of the early communities (16:3–16, 21–24). There has been great debate whether this letter of recommendation was sent originally with Romans 1–15. Some scholars have argued that since the letter of recommendation contains names associated with Greece and Asia Minor (Prisca and Aquila) it was circulated (with the previous fifteen chapters) around Ephesus. But other scholars have considered that the people so named had returned to Rome (cf. Acts 18:2) after having been expelled under the emperor Claudius in 49 CE. The letter of recommendation would thus have accompanied Paul's letter to Rome. If this letter of recommendation was carried along with the letter for Rome, then Phoebe may well have delivered Paul's address.

The Rhetorical Format of Romans

The letter to the Romans is the longest of Paul's correspondence. Its position in the Canon is not due to an early date; rather, size and its magisterial content may have led to situating it at the head of the Pauline material. Despite its length the letter shares the familiar structure of a Pauline Letter (Salutation 1:1–7; Thanksgiving 1:8–15; Body 1:16–11:36; Exhortation 12:1–15:32; Closing 15:33).

Yet Romans exhibits some unusual rhetorical elements. Unlike other Pauline letter openings this one is quite extensively constructed. Moreover, although 1 Corinthians has a lengthy collection of material, the body of argument in Romans differs markedly in its rhetorical approach. Further, there is extensive use of diatribe throughout the letter (see Cameo on Diatribe, p. 257). The question of the rhetorical format of Romans is crucial for understanding Paul's meaning. The very texture of the text can give the reader significant clues to the letter's intent.

Some scholars suggest that Paul produced Romans as his "last will and testament" due to his anxiety over what he might face in Jerusalem. Thus, his letter takes on the aspect of a theological apology. Others have argued that it provides the foundation for Paul's authority to preach in Rome. Still others have thought it an attempt to seek support for Paul's Jerusalem visit. While such positions touch on significant issues in the letter, they neglect Paul's vision of the future: his mission to Spain. It is anachronistic to consider this letter as Paul's final word on his work. Rather, Paul's argument builds upon establishing a common understanding of mission so that the Roman communities can assist him in moving to the "ends of the earth."

The vitality and momentum of the letter to the Romans are caught when we sense the rhetorical effort of Paul. Although not a Cicero, Paul was adept in crafting a letter (see Philemon, a rhetorical gem). From the very beginning of the letter we can detect a change in length and elegance from the other letter openings of Paul. The introductory verses (1:1–7) achieve what the ancients considered a "polished" style. The letter to the Romans has entered into competition with the elegant sounds of the empire. Such formality of speech would represent an intention to demonstrate that the subject matter of the discourse was on equal (or greater) footing with imperial claims. In these opening words Paul is establishing himself as an envoy in grandiloquent terms. He represents a new and alternative regime and his rhetoric matches his mission. The performance of this letter opening would have offered to the Roman communities the opportunity to become co-conspirators with Paul in acknowledging that a regime change had occurred and that they were acclaiming the true ruler of the universe. Paul's *euangelion* (usually translated as *gospel;* cp. 1:16) is thus a dynamic communication overturning the world itself.

Such an ambassadorial style is indicative of *epideictic* or *demonstrative* oratory (see Cameo on Ancient Rhetoric, p. 159). This rhetorical format allows the speaker to establish a sense of common values that is recognized by the listeners. It would provide the grounds for Paul's intended visit to Rome and his mission to Spain.

Paul amplifies and enhances this demonstrative speech through the use of *diatribe* (see Cameo on Diatribe, p. 257). Although diatribe was a form of speech used by Cynic and Stoic philosophers, it was not employed for simple speculation, nor for any systematic analysis. On the contrary, diatribe was primarily a teaching tool, attempting to engage the listener directly.

As a skilled rhetorician Paul would have imagined in advance his prospective audience. He would have thought out the basic points to be made, along with noting the possible objections. He would have anticipated the expectations of his listeners. He would then pepper his argument with their probable objections (e.g., 3:1, 3, 5), observations from the audience's perspective (2:2), speech directed at a fictional figure (2:2–29), and personification (7:7–25). All of this is done to get the listeners not only to imagine the argument more easily but to unpack the assumptions they uncritically hold. With Paul diatribal speech goes deep—to the fundamental human questions.

Romans was not written by Paul as his final word. On the contrary, Paul shares with a new audience a roadmap of his imagination. For Paul all roads did not lead to Rome. Rome is not his destination; it is just a stopover for further work. The completion of his work in Asia Minor and Greece, along with the collection for the "people" in Jerusalem, gives Paul the occasion to expand his horizon. The Messianic breakthrough which he has experienced is far from over. Now the task is to extend the mission to the western end of the known world. Through the use of this long-distance performance Paul invites the Roman communities to explore the world-shattering implications of their life together as the Anointed's people.

The Cultural Texture of Romans

It is difficult for modern readers to imagine what the early Jesus movement was like, especially before the fall of the

Temple (70 CE). During Paul's time both within and outside of Israel there were numerous ways of being Jewish. The followers of Jesus would have still been considered a sect within the diversity that was Second Temple Judaism. While there were some two million Jews in Israel, there were more than four million around the Mediterranean. Scholars account for such an enormous Jewish population due to extensive missionary outreach. The earliest communities of Jesus believers in Rome may well have come out of this phenomenon. In fact, there may have been some 15,000 to 60,000 Jews living in Rome during the first century. Despite a high degree of xenophobia from the Roman elite, the rights of the Jewish community were repeatedly recognized in Rome. The emperor Claudius, however, in 41 CE, prohibited meetings in synagogues. And, in 49 CE, Claudius expelled Jews from Rome because of disturbances "at the instigation of Chrestus" (Suetonius). These actions may have been a reaction to disputes among Jews over messianic (*Christos*) claims by Jesus followers. We also are far from certain that the entire Jewish population was removed. In fact, the letter to the Romans suggests that the situation in Rome was much more complicated. Certainly the letter indicates that Jewish leaders were already returning to Rome.

Since the Jews in Rome lived in densely populated and lower economic areas their tenement apartments and homes could accommodate between twenty to forty people. In light of the large population of Jews in Rome the number of synagogues in Rome could have been quite significant. Those addressed by Paul may well have been affiliated with some of those synagogues. On the other hand, if there had been a decrease or absence of Jewish leadership due to Claudius' order, gatherings of non-Jewish Jesus followers may well have increased during that time period. Returning Jewish Jesus followers may well have experienced a changed social situation.

Diaspora Judaism offered an honorable religious tradition, ancient in lineage, which provided the basic tools to construct a civilized society. Both practical and mystical, Hellenistic Judaism invited the nations to experience a relationship with the God of the universe as embodied in the Torah. To the Jews, who had been favored by God with the enlightenment of the Torah, the nations were generally perceived as morally inferior and at a religious disadvantage. The nations lacked the full expression of God's will and thus the benefits that would follow from such divine patronage.

Romans 1:18–32 illustrates the synagogal appraisal of the nations. Romans 9–11, on the other hand, speaks to a mixed audience and Rom 11:13ff. directly addresses the nations who might have recently gained ascendency.

It should also be made clear that for Hellenistic Jews and Roman citizens law (*nomos*) was a positive force, enabling people to build a civilized world. Whether it was Torah or the Twelve Tables of ancient Rome, law provided the time-honored basis for establishing, ordering, and ennobling human life. Internalizing such legal traditions and customary requirements would bring out the best in human beings. Power and authority would flow down from the divine realm securing those who maintained control and promising a utopian outcome to the loyal.

We should not overlook the fact that Paul sent his letter to the very heart of the Empire. Paul's audience would not have missed the political nuances of Paul's words. "Favor" and "peace" were imperial slogans ever since Augustus established the miracle of the Pax Romana. The emperor embodied the virtues of loyalty (*pietas/pistis*) and justice (*dikaiosunē*) and proclaimed a story (*euangelion*) of remarkable success. Entitled "son of God" (*filius divi*), the emperor guaranteed the prosperity of the world through his official role and upheld an elitist pyramid of power, where the reigning 5% lived off the labor underneath. Romans' formal introduction (1:1–7) and surprising claim that a ruler would die for his enemies (5:6ff.) would have offered a shocking counterpoint to the prevailing realm.

Such sounds would have been heard as fundamentally dissonant and treasonous. Not only does Jesus' earthly lineage have royal ties (1:3); there is also a play upon the imperial apotheosis. Jesus has been deified as "'son of God' in power."

His name ("Jesus—the Anointed—our lord") is acclaimed, just as Augustus' name was hymned, and echoes from Paul's lips to those who in this name confidently rely upon God.

The World-transforming News of God

It is often assumed that the term *euangelion* occurs only within the context of the New Testament. Of course, many scholars have made a distinction between the use of this word by Paul and the writers of the Gospels, but this still limits "gospel" to its use within the canon. In fact, the term was already part and parcel of the Roman propaganda machine that helped establish and maintain the Augustan revolution. An example of this usage is found in a decree issued by of the Provincial Assembly of Asia, in 9 BCE, recorded in the Priene Inscription. This inscription presents the benefits of Roman peace as the reason for the worship of the emperor. *Euangelion* refers to the world-wide claim of the Roman Empire. This message defined and envisioned the order of the world. *Euangelion* thus cannot be read in isolation from its Roman imperial context.

Priene Inscription

Whereas the Providence (*Pronoia*) which has regulated our whole existence, and which has shown such care and liberality, has brought our life to the climax of perfection in giving to us Augustus, whom it filled with virtue for the welfare of men, and who, being sent to us and our descendents as a Savior (*soter*), has put an end to war and has set all things in order; and having become manifest (*phaneis*), Caesar has fulfilled all the hopes of earlier times, . . . not only in surpassing all the benefactors (*euergetai*) who preceded him but also in leaving to his successors no hope of surpassing him; and whereas, finally the birthday of the god has been for the whole world the beginning of good news (*euangelion*) concerning him [therefore, let a new era begin with his birth, and let his birthday mark the beginning of the new year].[1]

The opening salutation (1:1–7) by Paul to the Roman communities, in effect then, takes on the Empire. The slave of a newly declared ruler (1:4) has been designated to deliver the newsflash (*euangelion*) that peace and prosperity (1:7) have arrived with this unlikely lord. Then, in his thanksgiving (1:8–15), Paul attempts to connect with his audience by praising their well-known loyalty (*pistis*) and by expressing his desire to share his work with them. He hopes that this will be mutually beneficial.

Paul wants especially to share with them the world-transforming message of God. When Paul uses the word *euangelion* (usually translated as "gospel") he does not have in mind any manuscript or extended narrative. For Paul the *euangelion* is the oral communication of God's power touching those who trust in it. A breakthrough (*apocalypsis*) occurs to those who are open to the message. It is like a light going on in a darkened room. All of a sudden one can see things for the first time. Life has texture and color, depth and contrast. Paul discovered that God directly relates to humanity in a surprising and fundamental way. God's "reliability" (*dikaiosunē*) rests on trust alone. God trusts us so that we can respond in kind (1:17). Even the written tradition speaks to that: "The one who decides to live on the basis of confidence in God is the one who gets it right" (Hab 2:4; Rom 1:17).

The first major section of the body of Romans can be broken down into five subsections (1:16–17; 1:18–32; 2:1–29; 3:1–31; 4:1–25). After delivering the basic theme of the letter (1:16–17), Paul presents the shadow side of the breakthrough of God's justice (1:18–3:20). Precisely because the genuine relationship with God appears in full light the human predicament comes under critical assessment. Paul begins his argument by employing a standard synagogal critique of the nations (1:18–32). It is crucial to see that the disorder noted comes about through a basic failure to acknowledge God present through creation. Because the nations gave up on this natural capacity to know God, they fell into idolatry and uncivilized behavior. Notice also that Paul is not referring to any specific individual. It is an argument based upon the Jewish stereotype of the non-Jew. Nevertheless, the people from the nations listening to this letter probably would have agreed with this assessment of their life before being involved with God's Anointed.

Paul then turns in good diatribal fashion to addressing a fictitious listener (2:1–29). His constant questioning demonstrates that the person who claims superiority over others is no better off. The one who claims the competitive advantage of Jewish enlightenment and tradition embodies the telling contradiction between appearance and reality. Again, these remarks are not made to anyone in particular. Paul uses the figure of the Jew to address a prevailing assumption held even by followers from the nations, namely, that the non-Jewish Jesus believers were not on equal terms with fellow Jews before God. Paul wants them to know that the real issue is what really makes a Jew, that is, a genuine human being (2:29).

Paul does not discount the Jewish tradition. But he argues that this does not support any privilege. He produces a scriptural collage (3:10–18) to document that even the Torah speaks to the accountability of all. The justice of God has come about in remarkable fashion. What God has revealed through the death of Jesus transcends the competitive world of social advantage (3:21–26). True relationship with the God who will not give up on the condemned is accessible to everyone by trust alone.

The figure of Abraham, a first century model of how one from the nations becomes a Jew, takes on a deeper dimension (4:1–25). He exemplifies genuine trust (4:3). God's promise to Abraham, delivered before he underwent the requirement of circumcision, speaks not only to that ancient "father," but to all who hear those words of hope. Paul can say that the divine promise is alive, reaching all those who presently trust in the God of Jesus and Abraham. Genuine life is not just possible, it is a reality.

The Life of Trust

Paul begins the next major section (5:1–8:39) of his letter with a startling illustration of what God's loyalty is all about. The ancient world knew of heroic martyrdom. Jews and Romans honored those who would die for a noble cause. Paul may well have taken over the notion of Jesus' heroic death from Syrian Jesus followers who attempted to make sense of the shameful fate of Jesus. But Paul deepened this thinking by putting the death of Jesus in a different league. Here was the surprising instance of a ruler joining the rebels, taking on the enemies' fate (5:8–10). Here the unending loyalty of God was demonstrated to the utmost. Such a vision of God upsets the first century world of power and authority. The God of Israel is no longer at the top of the pyramid of power; rather, this God has entered into solidarity with the nobodies of the Empire.

Such a revolutionary vision allows Paul to reimagine the very origins of humanity (5:12–21). Paul moves back in time beyond Moses and Abraham to the mythical Adam. No longer a symbol of a fated humanity, Adam now intimates what a true human can be (5:14). For the loyalty of one man became the opening for an awesome surprise. Abundant life, not the confines of death, is now the watchword.

The use of mythic language by Paul should not be overlooked. By invoking the primordial figure of Adam, Paul reaches for language that speaks to the fundamental conditions and limits of human life. To the modern ear the word *myth* refers to something that is untrue or fictional. But *myth* is more than such a simplistic reduction. *Myth* refers to the deep stories that humans tell each other, not only to structure their world, but also to give a sense of orientation and identity. Myths are stories that tell people where they are from, where they are going and who they are. Mythic language is thus invoked whenever people sense that they are entering a situation beyond their control, going beyond the borders of ordinary life. Mythic language gives people the ability to locate themselves in a wider field of power and meaning. Already it has been pointed out that the Roman Empire proclaimed a world-wide message (*euangelion*) that declared what powers governed and ordered the world. The figure of Abraham in chapter 3 also engaged the listener in mythic possibilities of identity and meaning. Abraham provided an access point for those who would relate to the ultimate power of the Universe. Now Paul has moved from Abraham to Adam. Paul pushes his imagination to the very beginnings of the human story. At the same time this allows Paul to re-imagine what went wrong with the story.

It is within the revision of the story of Adam that Paul introduces *hamartia* (usually translated as "sin"). The SV translators have chosen to stress the mythic sense of the word as "the corrupting seduction of power." For Paul *hamartia* is a personified force that enters and obstructs the human story. It is more than a single act or specific actions; rather it refers to a fated condition that gains momentum over time. Even the best attempts by humans to contain this force through law (7:6–23) meet with self-contradiction and misery. But the surprising breakthrough brought about by God's acceptance of the publicly shamed Jesus throws an entirely different light on this mythic scenario. From this radically altered perspective, divine favor no longer is bestowed upon those who possess a competitive advantage over others. Instead the abundant generosity of God comes to those who trust this remarkable message.

From this re-imagined scenario Paul presses on to speak of the reality of this new life already enjoyed by the Romans. Alluding to the Romans' baptism into the Anointed Jesus (6:3–4), he makes it quite clear that such commitment changes life forever (6:9–14). Paul's use of the metaphor of slavery comes from the ancient conviction that humans are not isolated but always in relationship. The question is whether to return to the dead end of their former life or to deepen their experience of God's abundance by living out each day in hope (6:19). Paul even uses the image of a married woman who becomes free through the death of her husband (7:1–5) to demonstrate that those in the company of the Anointed are no longer bound by the customs and codes of this world. Rather, they are connected to reality through the surprising presence and power of God (7:6).

Employing diatribe again (7:7–25) Paul puts in perspective the "best" the Roman world has to offer. He personifies the individual (the "*ego*") who has internalized the cultural expectations promised by the law (both Jewish and Roman). Assuming that the successful embodiment of law would produce freedom, the individual is shocked to realize an internal rebellion. Self-contradiction is the fate of social success. The individual who would be in total control is found to be a miserable captive.

The way out is the community of loyalty experienced already by the Romans (8:1–17). Because of God's unimaginable act for the Anointed, the Romans share in God's power and presence, allowing them to become what the world so desperately desires. Paul sees their ecstatic baptismal experience (8:15) as the moment of human maturity. He, then, situates their role in the entire process of creation (8:18–25). Genesis is not over; rather, those who trust are now part of this cosmic birth. Paul has turned the typical apocalyptic imagery of the endtime into a labor of liberation. Even through a rapid series of troubling rhetorical questions (8:31–39), Paul is confident that no force of alienation can keep the love of God from the trusting heart.

The Kinfolk of Paul

Because of his confident vision, Paul is perplexed by fellow Jews who reject the compelling message (chaps. 9–11). Yet he refuses to give up on either his experience or his kin. In trying to understand why only some respond, he introduces the Jewish notion of the remnant (9:6–13; that no matter the disastrous situation some Jews will survive through God's will). But Paul does not use this tradition to give advantage to some Jews over other Jews. Instead, he turns the remnant theory on its head by casting the nations as the "nobodies" (9:25–26).

Their inclusion demonstrates God's surprising mercy. The nations, however, should not think they have any competitive advantage over the unreceptive Jews (11:17–24). In this new chapter of God's dealing with the world and Israel there are no distinctive advantages (10:12). But there will be more surprises (11:1–12). In the end Paul has no "solution" to his Jewish dilemma. Unlike subsequent generations of Christians, he leaves his kin in the hands of a God wiser and more merciful than anyone can imagine (11:33–36). If the Roman communities were still affiliated with synagogues, Paul's thinking would have provided a remarkable roadmap of toleration.

Some Words to the Wise

In the letter's final portion (chaps. 12–15) Paul delivers a broadside of advice. Paul's remarkable vision of God meets the ordinary demands of life together. Despite the lengthy list of exhortations, the basis for behavior is fundamental: God's unending solidarity with the lost (14:7–9). The "nobodies" lived-out response to God's mercy is true worship (12:1), entailing a critical assessment of the "powers that be" (12:2), as they maturely search out God's wisdom. For Paul living in solidarity with the Anointed does not provide the occasion for asserting moral superiority, for gaining advantage, or for asserting one's rights at another's expense. That is still living in the old world of power and control, forgetting the very meaning of the death of the Anointed (14:15). It is a time to surprise each other in compassionate ways that have yet to be imagined.

NOTE

1. Frederick C. Grant, ed., *Ancient Roman Religion* (Indianapolis: Liberal Arts Press, 1957), 174.

Paul's Letter to the Romans

1 Paul, slave of God's Anointed, Jesus—summoned as an envoy [and] appointed to announce God's world-changing news, [2]which was anticipated by the prophets in holy scriptures. [3]This news is about the "son of God"—who was physically descended from David, [4]appointed and empowered as "son of God," in accordance with the spirit of holiness, from the time of his resurrection from the dead—Jesus, the Anointed, our lord. [5]Through him I have received the gracious favor of my calling to promote in his name the obedience that comes from a confident reliance upon God among all of the world's nations. [6]You yourselves are among those who are called, since you belong to Jesus the Anointed. [7][I am writing this] to all of God's beloved in Rome, called to be God's own people: may gracious favor and peace from God our Great Benefactor and from our lord Jesus the Anointed be with you.

[8]First of all, through Jesus, the Anointed, I thank God for all of you, because your confident trust in God is being broadcast throughout the world. [9]God is my witness, whom I serve whole-heartedly by spreading the world-changing news of the "son of God," that I always mention you when I pray,

---

1:1 In calling himself a *slave of God's Anointed,* Paul is evoking and comparing himself with a title of dignity familiar to his readers in Rome: "slaves of Caesar" were members of Caesar's household, all of whom were regarded as enjoying an elevated status in the Roman system and some of whom rose to positions of great power and wealth. Analogously, Paul claims an elevated status in the imperial government of the world's true lord, God's Anointed

envoy: Paul sees himself as an envoy of the world-transforming message of the Anointed. The polished style of the opening of the letter reflects his position. The rhetoric of the letter is indicative of ambassadorial speech (see the Introduction to Romans).

news: This is the announcement of a major paradigm shift. It plays upon the Roman notion of *euangelion,* which was used to mean the proclamation of the great deeds and events of the empire.

[10]imploring that now at last I may succeed in coming to you, God willing. [11]I'm longing to see you so that I may share some inspiring benefit that will strengthen you—[12]or to put it more pertinently, that when we come together, we might be mutually encouraged by each other's confident trust in God, both yours and mine. [13]I think you ought to know, my friends, how often I planned to visit you—but have been prevented until now—in the hope that I may work as fruitfully among you, as in the rest of the world. [14][By virtue of my calling] I am under obligation both to Greeks and barbarians, both to the wise and the foolish; [15]that's why I'm eager to proclaim God's world-changing news also to you in Rome.

[16]I'm not embarrassed by this news, because it has the power to transform those who are persuaded by it, first Jews and then Greeks. [17]God's character is shown by this news to be trustworthy and that leads to having confidence in God, just as scripture says: "The one who decides to live on the basis of confidence in God is the one who gets it right."

[18]At the same time heaven's just indignation is being shown against all disregard of God and God's justice on the part of those who try to repress the truth (about God) by their wrongdoing. [19]What can be known about God is all around them for God has made this clear to them. [20]Indeed, God's invisible qualities—eternal power and divine nature—can be visibly apprehended, ever since creation, through the things God made. As a result, they have no excuse. [21]Even though they knew about God, they failed to honor or give God what God is due. Instead, their thinking became warped and their muddled minds grew clouded. [22]Although they portrayed

---

1:16 *embarrassed:* Paul lived in an honor/shame society. A person's social identity was formed particularly through one's primary social group (such as the extended family or community). To be "embarrassed" or "shamed" meant that one would lose worth in the eyes of others.

1:17 The emphasis in this verse is not upon life in the future but upon the virtue that one lives. If one lives out of confidence in God then one is on the true path. One has made a genuine connection. This line delivers the choice listeners can opt for.

themselves as enlightened, they became fools. ²³They traded the majesty of the immortal God for imitations—a likeness of a mortal man, as well as of birds, cattle, and reptiles.

²⁴So God handed them over in their cravings to self-destructive behavior so that they degraded their bodies among themselves. ²⁵They traded the truth about God for a lie; they adored and were devoted to the creature, instead of the creator—who is praised forever. Amen!

²⁶For this reason God handed them over to disgraceful passions. Their women exchanged natural sexual relations for what is unnatural; ²⁷in the same way, the men abandoned natural sexual relations with women and became inflamed with desire for each other—men engaging in shameless acts with men and paying the price personally for the error of their ways. ²⁸And since they did not see fit to recognize God, God handed them over to an unfit mind, to do what is not fitting. ²⁹They became preoccupied with every kind of injustice, immorality, greediness, and depravity; they are consumed by jealousy, murder, strife, deceit, and spite. They have become gossips, ³⁰slanderers, and despisers of God. They are haughty, arrogant, and pretentious. They invent evil schemes and rebel against their parents. ³¹They are senseless, faithless, heartless, and merciless. ³²Although they know full well God's judgment that those who do such things deserve to die, they not only do these evil deeds themselves, but even support those who do them.

2 [[The bottom line is: all you who judge, you have no defense, for when you judge others you condemn yourselves, for you do the very things you condemn.]]

1:24 *cravings:* Paul has begun with the mind (v. 21), then the passions (v. 24), then the lower parts (vv. 21, 24, 26). This is a traditional tri-partite schema of the human figure; also see Rom 3:10–18.

2:1 Some scholars consider 2:1 a gloss on the Pauline text. This brings out the basis of judgment underneath the passage. It may have been originally a marginal note, exposing the basis of judgment and then was incorporated into a later manuscript.

[2]Now, we all know that "God judges rightly those who do such evil deeds."

[3]Do you suppose, any of you who judge those who do such things even while you are doing the same things, that you will escape God's judgment? [4]Do you so belittle the wealth of God's generosity, restraint, and patience that you are unaware that the point of God's goodness is to get you to turn your life around?

[5]But actually because of your stony and stubborn hearts you're compounding the consequences for yourselves that come due on the day of God's just indignation, when divine judgment will be made clear [6]and when God will pay back each person according to what each person has done.

[7]For those who by persisting in doing the right thing strive for praise, honor and immortality, what they get is a glorious life. [8]But for those who from self-serving ambition reject the truth and embrace wrongdoing, what they get is furious anger. [9]There will be distress and anguish for every single human being who does evil, first the Jew and then the Greek; [10]but praise, honor, and peace for everyone who does what is good, first the Jew and then the Greek, [11]because God has no favorite people.

[12]All those ignorant of the law of Moses who are guilty of wrongdoing will perish despite their ignorance of the law. All those who know the law of Moses will be condemned by the law. [13]For those who receive the law of Moses are not the ones approved by God but those who do what it says.

[14]When the nations who do not have access to the law of Moses do naturally what the law requires, they embody the law in themselves, even though they do not possess the law. [15]They demonstrate that the values engraved in the law of Moses are "written on their hearts." This is confirmed by the

---

2:2 This reflects the conclusion the listeners would draw from the indictment of those who are not in true relationship with the God of Israel.
2:3 This is a diatribal question, designed to get the listeners to reconsider their assumptions. See Cameo on Diatribe, p. 257.

witness of their conscience and by their habit of debating among themselves what is right and what is wrong. ¹⁶This will become clear when God exposes what is hidden of the human condition through the Anointed Jesus, as I understand God's world-changing news.

¹⁷As for you now, you call yourself a Jew, you rest your hopes on the law of Moses, and you boast about your relation with God. ¹⁸Since you are trained in the law, you claim to know God's will and to discern what really matters. ¹⁹You're convinced that you're a guide for the blind, "a light for those in darkness," ²⁰an instructor of the foolish and a teacher of the young. You appear to embody the knowledge and truth that are in the law. ²¹When you are teaching others, do you learn anything yourself? When you rant against stealing, are you yourself a thief? ²²When you speak out against adultery, are you an adulterer? As someone who detests idols, have you made an idol of your own religion? ²³You boast about the law; do you then dishonor God by breaking the law? ²⁴It's just as it is written: "Because of you God's name is held in contempt among the peoples of the world."

²⁵Now, it is the case that to be circumcised is indeed valuable, provided that you adhere to the law. But if you're a lawbreaker who happens to be circumcised, then you've become like someone uncircumcised. ²⁶Suppose someone uncircumcised practices the virtues required by the law; won't his being uncircumcised count the same as if he were circumcised? ²⁷As a result, someone remaining uncircumcised, who lives by the law, stands in judgment on you, the law-breaker, who has the written tradition and is circumcised. ²⁸To be a Jew, after all, is not just to be one in public, nor is circumcision just something external and physical. ²⁹To be a Jew is rather to be one in-

---

2:16 *world-changing news:* Paul is not talking about "his" proclamation of the "world-changing news." Some scholars have gone so far as to argue that v. 16 in toto is not Pauline but a 2ⁿᵈ century insertion. As a later addition to the text it may be from the same source as the doxology added at the end (Rom 16:25–27), where Paul talks about "my gospel."

wardly, and true circumcision is a matter of the heart—transformed by God not conformed to tradition. Such a person gets praised, not by mortals, but by God.

3 *Interlocutor:* What's the advantage in being a Jew? Or what's the benefit of circumcision?

Paul: [2]A great advantage with many benefits. Above all, the Jews were entrusted with the words of God.

Interlocutor: [3]So what if some of them were unreliable? Surely, their unreliability doesn't invalidate God's reliability, does it?

Paul: [4]Absolutely not! Surely God must be true even if everyone else is false, "so that," as scripture says, "in all you say your justice shows and when you are accused you win your case."

Interlocutor: [5][Well, Paul,] if our misdeeds highlight God's reliability, dare one conclude that God who punishes us is unjust—if one may speak irreverently?

Paul: [6]Absolutely not! If that were so, how could God judge the world?

Interlocutor: [7][Wait a minute, Paul], if God's truthfulness is made more evident by my lying, so that God is glorified even more, why am I still being condemned as a sinner?

Paul: [8][To follow your argument], then why should we not "do evil so that good may come from it," as some people who slander us claim that we say? Such slanderers are rightly condemned.

Interlocutor: [9][Well, Paul,] are we Jews then better off than other people?

3:1 SV has introduced *Interlocutor* and *Paul* to make clear that Paul is using a diatribal technique to illustrate a point at issue. Paul anticipates objections on the part of his audience and brings up the questions he imagines his listeners will have. Such a question and answer format serves to develop the argument. See Cameo on Diatribe, p. 257.

Paul: Not at all! We have already charged that Jews and Greeks alike are all prone to wrongdoing. [10]Here is what's in the scriptures:

> There is no virtuous person, not even one.
> [11]there is no one who understands,
>   no one who is searching for God.
> [12]They have all turned away,
>   together they have become worthless.
> There is no one who shows kindness,
>   not a single one.
> [13]Their throats are open graves,
>   they deceive with their tongues.
> Viper's venom is under their lips.
> [14]Their mouths are full of cursing and bitterness.
> [15]Their feet rush to shed blood,
>   [16]ruin and misery line their paths,
> [17]the way of peace is unknown to them.
> [18]There is no fear of God in their eyes.

[19]We know that whatever scriptures say is spoken to those under its authority so that every mouth may be silenced and the whole world be accountable to God. [20]Therefore, no human being will be acceptable in God's sight on the basis of traditional religious observances; since through the tradition of the law comes knowledge of human waywardness. [21]Only now has God's reliability been made clear, independent of the tradition from the law, although the whole of scripture offers evidence of it.

[22]God's reliability has now been made clear through the unconditional confidence in God of Jesus, God's Anointed, for the benefit of *all* who come to have such confidence—no exceptions!

3:9 This text can be read either in the middle or passive voice. But the answer "Not at all" is the same.

3:18 Paul actually constructs a "human" out of the various verses of scripture. The audience would have considered this a rhetorical delight.

3:22 This line gives us a hint of how Paul can use the scriptural tradition to prove his point.

²³After all, everyone has messed up and failed to reflect the image of God. ²⁴At the same time, we are all accepted by God freely as a gift through the liberation that comes when we identify with the Anointed Jesus, ²⁵whom God presented publicly as the one who conciliates through his unconditional confidence in God at the cost of his life, in order to show God's reliability by overlooking, by divine restraint, how we messed up. ²⁶This shows God's reliability at this decisive time, namely, that God is reliable and approves the one who lives on the basis of Jesus' unconditional confidence in God.

> *Interlocutor:* ²⁷[Well, then, Paul], Is there anything left to boast about?

> *Paul:* There are no grounds for boasting.

> *Interlocutor:* By what criterion [do you claim this]? Traditional religious practices?

> *Paul:* No—by the criterion of confidence in God. ²⁸We contend that a person is acceptable to God through an unconditional confidence in God without regard to traditional religious practices.

> *Interlocutor:* ²⁹[But Paul] surely God is only the god of the Jews?

> *Paul:* And not also of all other people? Yes, of course, all other people as well, ³⁰since 'God is one.' God will approve the circumcised on the basis of unconditional confidence in God, and the uncircumcised on the same basis.

> *Interlocutor:* ³¹Are we then nullifying the law through this so-called confidence in God?

> *Paul:* Certainly not! We are affirming the law.

3:23 Note the allusion to Gen 1:27. It's not only that human beings have obscured the divine image in which they were created; they have also lived at a lower level than their elevated status in the creation called for.
3:25 This is a retrospective view of the meaning of Jesus' life. Paul may well be using a pre-Pauline understanding of the death of Jesus, namely the notion that Jesus died a hero's death. Paul moves beyond that understanding to a consideration of what sort of God accepts the crucified criminal.

4 *Interlocutor*: What, then, shall we say? That we have found Abraham to be our forefather by virtue of his religious credentials? [2]If Abraham became a righteous man by virtue of his admirable deeds, then he does have something to boast about, doesn't he?

Paul: Not in the sight of God, though. [3]Because what does the scripture say? "Abraham put his trust in God, and God counted that the right thing to do." [4]Now, the wage paid to a worker is not counted as a gift, but as what he has earned; [5]and to the one who does no work but who puts his unconditional trust in the One who accepts the non-religious, his confidence in and total reliance upon God is counted as doing the right thing. [6]This is the good fortune of those whom God counts acceptable on a basis other than what they have done, just as David says:

[7]Fortunate are those whose violations of the law are forgiven and whose waywardness is overlooked.
[8]Fortunate is the man whose irresponsible behavior the lord will not hold against him.

[9]Is this good fortune available only to the circumcised, or is it available also to the uncircumcised? We say that in Abraham's case his trust in and reliance upon God was counted as the right thing to do. [10]When was he credited with getting this right? Was it after he was circumcised, or before he was circumcised? It was not after he was circumcised, but before he was circumcised. [11]He accepted the mark of circumcision as a way of certifying that putting his trust in God while he was still uncircumcised was the right thing to do. This was so that he would be the prototypical "father" of all of the uncircumcised who put their trust in and rely upon God and they too

---

4:2 Paul's Jewish contemporaries assumed that Abraham gained God's favor through his virtuous acts. We see in Jub 23:10, "Abraham was perfect in all his deeds with the Lord, and well pleasing in righteousness all the days of this life." In effect, claiming the lineage of Abraham gave one a competitive advantage over others (e.g., the nations).

would be counted as getting this right. [12]He would also be the "father" of the circumcised who are not only circumcised but also follow in the footsteps of our "father" Abraham, who put his trust in God before he was circumcised.

[13]Now it seems quite clear that the promise that Abraham or his descendents will inherit the world did not come by the agency of the law, but by virtue of his getting confidence in and reliance upon God right. [14]If people inherit the world on the basis of the law, then Abraham's confidence in God is irrelevant and the promise God made to him amounts to nothing.

[15]What the law actually produces is [God's] just indignation; but where the law is not involved, the question of [the nations'] violation of the law does not arise. [16]That's why becoming heirs results from putting confidence in and relying upon God, so that the promise is entirely a matter of [God's] free gift and is guaranteed to all of Abraham's descendents, not only to those who claim to be heirs by virtue of covenant law, but to those who share Abraham's confidence and reliance upon God. He is the father of us all, [17]just as it is written, "I have appointed you to be the father of many nations." [Thus Abraham is the father of us all] in the sight of the God in whom he put his trust—the God who has the power to bring the dead to life, and to call into existence things that did not exist. [18]Beyond all human hope, he confidently continued in the hope that he would become the father of many nations just as he was told, "So shall your descendents be." [19]His confidence in God did not waver when he considered that he was impotent—he was already almost a hundred years old—nor when he considered that Sarah was far too old to bear a child. [20]He did not regard God's promise as incredible, but his confidence in God grew strong and he gave God the glory, [21]because he was fully convinced that God could do what God had promised. [22]That's why God counted Abraham's confidence in God to be right. [23]That "God counted" was not written in scripture only for Abraham's benefit, [24]but for ours also. We are destined to be counted right who put our confidence in the one who raised

Jesus our lord from among the dead, ²⁵who was given up to
death because of our wayward offenses and raised so that we
could be counted right in the sight of God.

5 So then, since we have been counted as right in the sight
of God on the basis of putting our unconditional confidence in
God, we are at peace with God through our lord, Jesus, God's
Anointed. ²He is the one through whom we have gained access
to the divine favor that has given us our [new] standing and
we boast in our hope of [seeing] the splendor of God's majesty.
³And that's not all. We also boast about hardships, because we
know that hardship produces fortitude ⁴and fortitude shows
character, and character reinforces hope. ⁵This hope will not
embarrass us because our hearts have been filled with the love
of God through the gift of God's presence and power.

⁸But what shows God's own love for us is that God's
Anointed died on our behalf even while we were not measur-
ing up to what God expects of us. ⁹Since we have been counted
as right in the sight of God at the cost of the Anointed's life,
it is all the more assured that we will be rescued through him
from the just indignation (of God). ¹⁰For if while we were living as if we were rebels against God's rule our relationship
with God was changed through the death of God's "son," now
that we have been reconciled we can be even more assured
that we will be spared [from, facing condemnation] through
his life [as the risen lord]. ¹¹But that's not all. We also boast in
God through our lord, Jesus, God's Anointed. He is the one
through whom we have now been given the new relationship.

¹²What this means is that just as through one man the cor-
rupting seduction of power entered the world and death en-

5:6–7 See the Interpolations.
5:12 *the corrupting seduction of power:* Greek: *hamartia,* usually translated as
"sin." Paul refers to *hamartia* here as if it were a spiritual power that effectively
holds sway over the human mind and heart and seduces humans into a way of
life that is ultimately, if not always immediately, self-destructive. See Introduction.

tered with it, so death spread to all human beings inasmuch as all human beings proved to be corruptible. [13]The corrupting seduction of power was in the world before the law was given [to Moses], but corruption was not counted against people in the absence of that law.

[14]Nevertheless the regime of death reigned [over all human life] from Adam to Moses, even over those whose who were not corrupted in the same way as Adam was. That Adam is a type of the Adam who would come in the future. [15]But God's generosity far surpasses Adam's costly blunder. If death came to many through the costly blunder of that one man, God's favor and gift freely given through the selfless generosity of the one man Jesus, God's Anointed, is far more abundant. [16]The free gift does not have an effect that is [merely] comparable to the consequences of the corruption of that one man. The judgment that followed from one [false step] led to condemnation, but the gift that followed many blunders led to being counted right in the sight of God. [17]For if through one blunder death reigned through that one man, how much more will those who receive the far greater favor and gift of being counted right in the sight of God reign in life through the one man, Jesus, God's Anointed.

[18]So then, just as one man's blunder led to a death sentence for all humanity, so one man's getting it right leads to an affirmation of life for all humanity. [19]Just as through one man's rebellious mindlessness many were led to become wayward, so also by one man's trusting mindfulness many will be led to getting it right. [20]Law was introduced as an afterthought to make the blunder even more offensive, but where corruption increased, God's generous favor proved to be even more abundant, [21]so that, just as the corrupting seduction of power

---

5:20 *an afterthought:* Characterizing the law as "an afterthought" and that it would only "make the blunder more offensive" would be unsettling to listeners—both Jewish and Roman—who would assume a positive and constructive understanding of law.

reigned in death, so also the power of God's generous favor, through what God counts as getting it right, could be shown to lead to unending life through Jesus, the Anointed our lord.

6 How then should we respond [to our changed relationship with God]? Should we continue to live as before so that God's generous favor can become even more remarkable? ²That would be ridiculous!

How can we who have "died" to the seductive power of corruption continue to live as if we were still in its grasp? ³Or do you not grasp the fact that all of us who were immersed in baptism as a way of identifying with the Anointed Jesus were symbolically immersed into his death?

⁴What that means is that we were buried with him when we were symbolically immersed into his death so that, just as the Anointed was raised from the dead by the power and splendor of God, we also might live a new kind of life. ⁵If we have truly identified with him in a death like his, then we will certainly be united with him in rising to a new kind of life like his. ⁶This we know: the old version of the human condition has been crucified with him, so that the life that was corruptible might be brought to an end and that we might no longer be in bondage to the seductive power of corruption. ⁷Now the one who has died [with the Anointed] has been freed from the seductive power of corruption. ⁸And if we really died with the Anointed, we are confident that we will also live with him, ⁹since we know that, because the Anointed has been raised from the dead, he is not going to die again; death no longer has any power over him. ¹⁰When he died he died to the lure of corrupting power once and for all, but the life he lived he lives to God. ¹¹In the same way you must think of yourselves as if you were dead to the appeal of corrupting power, but as alive to God in solidarity with the Anointed Jesus.

¹²Don't allow the seductive power of corruption to reign over your earthly life inducing you to submit to worldly desires. ¹³Don't put any part of your body at the disposal of that

power as an instrument for doing wrong, but put yourselves at God's disposal as people who have been brought to life from the dead and present your bodies to God as instruments for doing right.

¹⁴For the lure of corrupting power will not lord it over you, because you are no longer living under [the condemnation of] the law, but under [the freedom] of God's generous favor.

> *Interlocutor:* ¹⁵What you are really saying, Paul, is that if we do not live under [the condemnation] of law but in [the freedom] of God's generous favor, then it makes no difference if we submit to sin's seductive, corrupting power—right?
>
> *Paul:* That would be ridiculous! ¹⁶You know, don't you, that what gets your attention gets you, either the regime of corrupting power that results in death, or the mindfulness that puts you right in the sight of God. ¹⁷Thank God that although you were slaves of the power of corruption you have become obedient from the heart to the pattern of teaching with which you were entrusted. ¹⁸Once you were liberated from that corrupting power, you became slaves in the service of what is right.

¹⁹I am speaking in common, ordinary terms to accommodate your limited powers of comprehension. Just as you once put the members of your body at the disposal of immorality that leads to moral anarchy, so now you must put the members of your body in the service of what is right and leads to complete moral integrity. ²⁰When you were enslaved by the corrupting seduction of power you were "liberated" from the demands of moral virtue. ²¹So what were you getting out of this? Things which you now find shameful, because they end in death. ²²But now that you have been liberated from the corrupting seduction of power and have committed yourselves to the service of God, what you gain is complete moral integrity and in the end the unending life of God's new world.²³The corrupting seduction of power has a pay-off: death. God offers a free gift: the unending life of God's new world in solidarity with the Anointed Jesus, our lord.

7 Are you unaware, my friends—after all I am speaking to people who know something about the law—that the law has jurisdiction over a person only as long as that person is alive? [2]For example, a married woman has a legal obligation to her husband while he is alive, but if her husband dies, that obligation comes to an end. [3]Consequently, if a woman becomes involved with another man while her husband is alive, she will be called an adulteress; but if her husband dies, she is freed from legal obligation to him, so that if she marries another man, she is not an adulteress. [4]Just so, my friends, you symbolically died to the jurisdiction of the law when you identified yourselves with the crucified body of the Anointed, so that you could be free to commit yourselves to another, to the one who was raised from the dead, in order that we may be productive in the service of God. [5]When we were living a merely earthly life, the powerful attractions of corrupting ambition, conjured up by the law, were having their effect in our bodies to make them productive for the regime of death. [6]But now we have been freed from obligation to the law, since we "died" to what held us under obligation, so that we might serve God in a new spirit of freedom, not in the old prescriptive tradition.

[7]Am I saying that the law itself is corrupting? Certainly not! My point is that I would not have become aware of what the seductive power of corruption is, were it not for the law. For example, I would not have been aware of what's wrong with excessive desire for what others have, if the law had not said, "You shall not covet." [8]But the power of corruption used this prohibition to deceive me and to arouse all kinds of excessive desire in me. Without the law the power of corruption is as good as dead. [9]There was a time when I was living without reference to the law. But when that prohibition came to my attention, the power of corruption came to life and my earlier innocent self "died." [10]I discovered in my own experience that the very commandment whose purpose was to lead me to life

led me to death. ¹¹For the power of corruption used this moral command to deceive me and by this means put my naïve self to death. ¹²It is clear, then, that the law is grounded in the sacred and that the moral command is pure and just and good.

¹³Am I claiming that what is good caused my death? Certainly not! What I am saying is that the power of corruption showed how destructive it really is through using what is good to bring about my death, and, by taking advantage of the commandment to achieve its purpose, became utterly corrupting.

¹⁴We know that the law has its origin in the divine realm, but I am a creature of the earth, sold as a slave and in bondage to the power of corruption. ¹⁵I don't understand what I find myself doing. I do not accomplish what I intend, but what I actually do I deplore. ¹⁶If what I do is not what I intend, then I am really concurring with the law that it is good. ¹⁷In that case it can no longer be thought that I am the one who is doing this; what's doing this is the corrupting power that has taken up residence in me. ¹⁸I recognize that the good does not reside in me, I mean my earthly life. I have the capacity to intend what is right, but I cannot make it happen. ¹⁹I do not accomplish the good I intend, the bad I do not intend is what I actually bring about. ²⁰If I bring about what I do not intend, then it is no longer I who produces this, but the corrupting power that has taken up residence in me.

²¹So I take it to be a fact of life: that when I intend to do the good, the bad is right there at my side. ²²I rejoice in the law of God so far as my inner self is concerned, ²³but I observe another law in my outward acts at war with the law of my mind and this other law—the law of corrupting power—takes me captive. ²⁴What a sorry creature am I! Who will rescue me from this earthly self which is captive to death? ²⁵Thanks be to God, the rescue has come through Jesus, God's Anointed, our lord. So then, left to myself I am mentally devoted to God's law, but in my worldly life I'm enslaved to the law of corruption.

8 [[So now those who are in solidarity with the Anointed Jesus are no longer under a sentence of death.]] [2]For the rule of the spirit of life that was in the Anointed Jesus has liberated you from being ruled by seductive corruption and death. [3]For by sending God's own "son"—a participant, like us, in an earthly life attended by seductive corruption—to deal with that corrupting power, God did what the law of Moses—weakened by the conflicted character of earthly existence—was incapable of doing: God condemned the corrupting power that attends our earthly life, [4]so that the just requirement of the Mosaic law might be fulfilled in us who live not according to the ambitions of a self-serving earthly life, but according to God's purposes and power. [5]Those who are oriented to a self-serving life have their minds set on worldly things, but those who are oriented to God's presence and power have their minds set on God's purposes and power. [6]To set your minds on worldly things means death, but to set your mind on God's power and purpose means life and peace. [7]Because the mind that is set on worldly self-advancement is at odds with God, it does not submit to God's law; it's incapable of doing that. [8]It is not possible for those who are pre-occupied with worldly self-advancement to please God. [9]You are not pre-occupied with worldly self-advancement but with God's power and purpose. If anyone does not have the spirit that was in the Anointed, that one is not one of his. [10]But if the Anointed lives in you, although your body is in the grip of death because of the seductive power of corruption, your spirit is alive because of God's reliability. [11]And if the power of the One who raised

---

8:1 Some scholars think that 8:1 makes excellent sense where it stands, provided we recognize that it connects neither with 7:25a nor with 7:25b but with 7:6. This seems to reflect a modern literary sense, not taking into account the oral effect of ancient speech. In light of that consideration others regard 8:1 as a gloss, since 8:2 seems the more natural sequel to 7:25.

8:2 *You* is singular here. This reflects the diatribal style and provides an answer to the question of the overwhelmed "ego" in 7:24. One can notice that the person of the verbs change in chap. 8 to the plural and especially to the first and second person plural. Paul underscores the reality of the community of trust, experienced by his listeners.

Jesus from among the dead resides in you, the One who raised the Anointed from among the dead will give life to your mortal bodies through the power and presence of God that resides in you.

[12]So, brothers and sisters, we are under no obligation to worldly life, to live according to what it expects of us. [13]Because if you live in accord with worldly expectations, you are surely doomed. But if by the power of God you continue to eliminate the malignant practices of your mortal life, you will live. [14]For all who are led by the power and purpose of God are the children of God. [15]You have not received a slave's spirit that will lead you back to a state of fear, but you received a spirit of adoption by virtue of which we call out, "Abba! Father!" [16]God's power and presence joins us in affirming that we are God's children. [17]And if we are God's children then we are also heirs, heirs of God and co-heirs with the Anointed, since we experience the same abuse as he did in the hope that we may share his exaltation.

[18]I regard the sufferings of the present pregnant moment as nothing compared with the future splendor to be revealed to us. [19]For the whole creation eagerly anticipates the disclosure of who God's children really are. [20]For the purpose of the creation was suppressed through no fault of its own, but by the One who subjugated it [21]in the hope that the creation itself would be liberated from its subjection to degeneration and participate in the splendid freedom of the children of God. [22]We know that the whole creation has been moaning with birth pangs till now; [23]and not only the creation, but we who have savored the first taste of God's power also sigh within ourselves while we await our adoption, the release and transformation of our bodies from their earthly limitations and fate. [24]This hope [of adoption] has saved us. Hope is not about what our eyes can see. For who hopes for what he sees? [25]But

---

8:19 *eagerly anticipates*: in the Greek *apokaradokia*. This word makes a first appearance here in Paul. Such a vision contrasts with the Roman imperial propaganda, which announced a new Golden Age through the iconography of a fertile Mother Earth.

if we are hoping for what we do not see, then we are eagerly looking forward to it through our perseverance. [26]In support of this hope God's power comes to the aid of our weakness— we do not know what we should pray for as we ought, but God's power intervenes with yearnings beyond words. [27]The One who searches human hearts knows what the divine intention is. God's power and presence intervenes on behalf of the people of God in accordance with the purposes of God.

[28]Now we know that for those who love God—those who are called to live in accordance with God's purpose—God always collaborates for a good outcome. [29]That is, God provided for those who were called, and God decided in advance that they would take on the form of God's "son," so that he would be "the first" among many brothers and sisters. [30]And those about whom God had decided in advance, God also called; and those God called, God also affirmed as getting it right; and those God affirmed as getting it right God also has transformed into something splendid.

[31]What should we say in view of all this? If God is for us, what does it matter who is against us? [32]How can we think that the One who did not spare God's own "son" (from suffering and death), but allowed this to happen to him for our sake, will not also graciously give us, along with him, the whole world? [33]Who is going to impeach those whom God has chosen? God—who vindicates us? [34]Who is going to condemn us—the Anointed Jesus who died—to make it even more absurd—who has been raised, who is at the right hand of God and who is interceding for us? [Preposterous!] [35]What can possibly separate us from the love of God's Anointed? Could it be distress, or anguish, or persecution, or famine, or destitution, or danger, or the sword? [36]As scripture says,

> On your account we are being put to death the whole day
>> long,
> We are treated as if we were sheep fit to be slaughtered.

[37]To the contrary, we completely overcome all of these adversities through the one who loved us. [38]I am convinced that there

is nothing in death or life, nothing in the present or in the future, nothing from fallen angels nor from political authorities, nor from any other powerful force,[39]nothing above the earth nor below the earth, nor any other created thing that can separate us from the love of God that has been made known to us through the Anointed Jesus, our lord.

9 I am telling you the honest truth—as one who belongs to the Anointed, I am not lying. I can say with a clear conscience certified by the power and presence of God—[2]that there is great sorrow and unrelieved distress in my heart. [3]I would go so far as to pray that I myself be damned and permanently cut off from the Anointed, if that would benefit my brothers and sisters, my kinfolk by physical descent. [4]They are Israelites. They were given the sonship, the splendor of God's presence, the covenants, the legal tradition, the sacred rituals, the promises. [5]They were also given the patriarchs, and the Anointed is physically descended from them. May the God who rules over all be blessed forever. Amen.

[6]It's not as if God's promise has fallen short of fulfillment, because not all those who are physically descended from Israel are Israel, [7]nor are all the physical children of Abraham his true descendents; but as scripture says, "Those who will be acknowledged as your descendents will be through Isaac." [8]That is, the children of God are not the children of physical descent, but the children of the promise are the ones who are considered to be Abraham's descendents. [9]This is the wording of the promise: "About this time of the year I will return and Sarah will have a son." [10]But that's not all. Rebecca also [received a promise] when she became pregnant by one man, our forefather Isaac. [11]She was told—before they were born and had not done anything either worthy or worthless in order that the purpose God had chosen might continue to unfold,

---

9:3 *damned:* In Greek *anathema.* This refers to social ostracism from a community.

¹²based not on human accomplishment but on God's choice—
"The older will serve the younger," ¹³just as scripture says,
"I preferred Jacob and rejected Esau."

¹⁴What then should we conclude from this? Does this mean
that God's preference is unfair? Not at all! ¹⁵Remember that
God said to Moses, "I will have mercy on whomever I may
choose to have mercy and I will have pity on whomever I may
choose to have pity." ¹⁶So then it is not a matter of someone
desiring mercy or striving for it; what matters is that God is
the one who shows mercy. ¹⁷Remember that scripture says to
Pharaoh, "I brought you to power for just this reason: that my
power might be demonstrated through you and that my name
might be proclaimed throughout the world." ¹⁸So then, God
has mercy on whomever God wills, and hardens whomever
God wills.

¹⁹You [interlocutor] will then ask me, "Why then does God
still regard anyone as deserving blame? Who has ever man-
aged to resist God's will?"

²⁰[Paul:] The pertinent question is, "Who do you think you
are to talk back to God?" What is molded does not say to
the one who molded it, "Why have you made me like this?"
²¹Or, does the potter not have the right over the clay to make
from the same lump both an elegant vessel and a common
pot?

²²[Paul, from another perspective], what if God, wanting to
demonstrate the reality of the divine predisposition and
show divine power, patiently put up with vessels about to
be destroyed ²³in order to show the wealth of the divine
grandeur for vessels of mercy which God had prepared for
splendor in advance. ²⁴We are those vessels of mercy whom
God has called, not only from among the Jews but also from
among the nations.

9:24 *nations:* Paul uses the traditional notion of the remnant in a novel way.
Usually the remnant referred to those Jews who survived the disasters of their
people. Here Paul inserts the nations as the "remnant."

²⁵It's just as God says in Hosea:

> I will call those who are not my people, "my people,"
> and I will call "my beloved" a people who were not loved.
> ²⁶And in the place where it was said to them, "You are not my people,"
> there they will be called "children of the living God."

²⁷And Isaiah cried out about Israel:

> Even if the number of the children of Israel are as numerous as the sand of the sea, only a remnant will be saved [from final judgment and death]. ²⁸Because the Lord will thoroughly and decisively carry out divine judgment upon the earth.

²⁹And just as Isaiah predicted,

> If the Lord of the [heavenly] armies had not left us descendants,
> we would have become like Sodom and have been made like Gomorrah.

³⁰What shall we conclude from this? That the nations who did not pursue getting it right [in the sight of God] have [nevertheless] attained it—that is, the getting it right that is based on confidence and unconditional trust in God; ³¹but that, although Israel did pursue the law of righteousness, they did not succeed in fulfilling the aim of the law. ³²For what reason? Because they did not pursue it on the basis of putting their complete confidence and trust in God, but on the basis of faithful observance of their religious tradition. They stumbled over the stone that offends them, ³³just as it is written:

> Look, I am placing in Zion a stone that will cause them to stumble and a rock that will offend them,
> and those who put their confidence in it will not be put to shame.

10 Friends, my heart's desire and my prayer to God for them is for their ultimate well-being. ²I can testify about them from my personal experience that they have a certain zeal for God, but it lacks discernment. ³Because they miss the point about God's integrity and seek to establish their own, they do not accept what God's integrity means. ⁴God's Anointed represents the kind of integrity that is the goal of the law for all who put their confidence and trust in God. ⁵Moses writes about the kind of integrity that is based on the law that "the one who participates in these [religious practices] is under obligation to live by them." ⁶But the kind of integrity that is based on complete trust and confidence in God says, "Do not say in your heart, 'Who will ascend into heaven?'—that is, to bring God's Anointed down? ⁷Or, 'Who will descend into the abyss?'—that is, to bring God's Anointed up from the realm of the dead. ⁸But what does scripture say? 'The word [of God] is very near you'—it's on your lips and in your heart." That refers to the word about complete confidence and unconditional trust in God that we preach—⁹that if you say, "Jesus is lord!" and have complete confidence in your heart that "God raised him from the dead," you will be on your way to fulfillment. ¹⁰For it is in the heart that one comes to have the confidence in God that leads to integrity, and it is with the mouth that one acknowledges what leads to salvation. ¹¹Remember that scripture says, "None of those who put their confidence in God will have cause for embarrassment." ¹²There is no distinction between Jew and Greek, because the same one is lord of all and is generous to all who appeal to him. ¹³As scripture says, "Everyone who appeals to the name of the lord will be delivered."

¹⁴How, then, could people appeal to one in whom they have no confidence? And how could they put their confidence in someone they have never heard of? And how could they hear without a preacher? ¹⁵And how could they preach if they have not been sent by a higher authority? Just as it is written, "How

---

10:13 *Everyone who appeals:* This phrase would carry the echo of an appeal to the Emperor.

well-timed are the footsteps of those who announce good news?" ¹⁶But not all of them have paid attention to this news. It is as Isaiah says, "Who has put any confidence in what he has heard from us?" ¹⁷In other words, confidence comes from hearing the message, and the message comes through what is said about God's Anointed. ¹⁸But I ask, "Is it not true that they have heard?" They certainly have. [As scripture says],

> The sound of their voice has reached to the ends of the earth,
> and what they have said to the outer limits of the inhabited world.

¹⁹But I ask, "Could it be that Israel did not understand?" First of all, Moses says,

> By those who are not a nation I will provoke you to zealous hostility,
> By a morally obtuse nation I will provoke you to anger.

²⁰And Isaiah boldly says,

> I was discovered by those who were not looking for me,
> I became well-known to those who did not ask about me.

²¹But about Israel he says,

> All day long I have extended my hands
> to a recalcitrant and contentious people.

11 I have to ask, then: "Has God given up on the people of Israel?" Of course not! I am an Israelite myself, a descendent of Abraham, a member of the tribe of Benjamin. ²God has not given up on the people of Israel whom God already embraced in faithful love. Or do you not know what scripture says about Elijah, how he appealed to God against Israel:

> ³Lord, they have killed your prophets, they have torn your altars down to the ground, and I am the only one left, and they are searching for me to kill me.

⁴But what did the oracle say to him in reply?

11:4 *oracle:* This word is used only here in the NT. It means a divine oracle.

> I have reserved for myself seven thousand who have not so
> much as bent a single knee to Baal.

⁵So also in this decisive time there is a remnant freely selected
by God's favor. ⁶And if by God's free favor, then [selection] is
no longer based on faithful observance of religious tradition,
because in that case God's favor would no longer be a gift.

⁷So what does this mean for Israel? This means that what
Israel aspires to it has failed to obtain. Those who were freely
selected obtained it, but the rest became obtuse, ⁸just as it is
written,

> God put them in a state of chronic stupor, they have eyes
> that do not see and ears that do not hear right down to the
> present day.

⁹And David says,

> Let their table-fellowship become a snare and a trap
> something that trips them up, and their payback.
> ¹⁰Let their eyes cloud over so that they do not see
> and let their backs be doubled over all the time.

¹¹I have to ask, "Did they get tripped up in order to fall into
utter ruin?" Of course not! Rather, by their misstep, God's
fulfillment [is being offered] to the nations, in order to provoke Israel into zealous competition. ¹²Now if [Israel's] misstep means wealth for the world and if [Israel's] loss means
wealth for nations, how much more [wealth] will Israel's being
brought to fulfillment mean?

¹³I am talking to you from the nations now. In view of my
being an envoy to the nations, I make large claims about my
ministry ¹⁴in the hope that I may somehow provoke my kinsmen to zealous competition and [in this way] lead some of
them to God's fulfillment. ¹⁵If their rejection [of the world-
changing message] means global transformation, what would
their acceptance [of the world-changing message] mean but a
return to life from among the dead!

¹⁶Now if the first portion [of the dough] belongs to God, so
does the whole batch of dough; and if the root belongs to God,

so do the branches. [17]But if some of the branches of the olive tree were broken off and although you, my friend—a wild olive shoot—were grafted in among the rest of the branches and benefited with them from abundant oil of the olive tree's root, [18]don't brag about the engrafted branches. But if you do brag, don't forget that you don't sustain the root, but the root sustains you. [19]Then you'll still probably say, "Branches were broken off so that *I* could be grafted in." [20]That's so. They were broken off because they did not put their whole trust in God; but you remain firmly in place only if you do. So don't become obsessed with your self-importance; but watch out. [21]For if God did not let the natural branches off, God will not let you off either. [22]So pay attention to the kindness and the severity of God: severity toward those who have fallen away, but God's kindness toward you—if you continue [to rely upon] God's kindness; otherwise you too, my friend, will be cut off. [23]And if they do not persist in their refusal to put their whole trust in God, those branches that have fallen will be grafted in, because God has the power to graft them in again. [24]For if you have been cut from a naturally wild olive tree and grafted into a cultivated olive tree, how much more easily will these natural branches be grafted back into the olive tree from which they came?

[25]So that you will not overestimate your own wisdom, friends, I want you to know about God's previously undisclosed plan: that a certain closed-mindedness has come over part of Israel until the full complement of the nations gets in, [26]and in this way all Israel will be brought to God's fulfillment, just as it is written,

> The liberator will come from [Mt.] Zion,
> he will eliminate godless behavior from Jacob.
> [27]And this will be my covenant with them
> when I do away with their waywardness.

[28]So far as God's world-changing news is concerned, their hostile opposition has turned out for your benefit, but as far

as [God's] free selection is concerned, they are loved, because of their ancestors. ²⁹God has no regrets about the gifts and the invitation offered to them. ³⁰Just as you were defiant toward God at one time, but now have received mercy because of their defiance, ³¹so now they are defiant toward God because of the mercy you have received, so that [ultimately] they may receive God's mercy. ³²This shows that God has made defiance inescapable for all humankind, so that God could have mercy on all.

>³³How inexhaustible are the riches
>and wisdom and knowledge of God!
>How inscrutable are God's judgments
>and untraceable God's ways!
>³⁴Who knew the mind of God,
>or became God's adviser?
>³⁵Or who gave to God first
>so as to oblige God to return the favor?
>³⁶For everything comes from God, exists through God, and
>ultimately serves God's purposes.
>The glory belongs to God for all time. Amen.

12 So, I appeal to you, friends, as recipients of the wondrous mercy of God, to dedicate every fiber of your being to a life that is consecrated and pleasing to God, which is what enlightened worship ought to be. ²Don't accept the life of this age as your model, but let yourselves be remodeled by the recovery of your true mind, so that you can discern what is consistent with God's purposes—what is good, worthwhile, and completely genuine.

³So as one whom God has favored with the gift of my calling, I say to every single one of you: don't entertain any false sense of superiority, but be realistic in your self-estimation, according as God has assigned to each of you a particular ability to express what living with complete confidence in God means. ⁴Just as each of us has one body with many parts that do not all have the same function, ⁵so although there are

many of us, we are the Anointed's body, interrelated with one another. ⁶We have different capabilities according to the gifts with which God has endowed us. If your gift is prophecy, then prophesy in a way that reflects your confidence in and reliance upon God. ⁷If your gift is providing service, then serve. If you can teach, then teach. ⁸If you are good at exhortation, you should offer encouragement. The one who is able to contribute money should do so generously. The one who gives aid should do so willingly. The one who does deeds of compassion should do so cheerfully.

⁹Make sure that your love is without pretense; abhor what is evil; stick closely to what is good. ¹⁰Be devoted to one another as members of the same family. Take the initiative in honoring one another. ¹¹Don't let your enthusiasm fade; radiate the presence of God's power; serve our lord. ¹²Be joyful in your hope; be patient in adversity; be persistent in prayer. ¹³Treat the needs of the Anointed's people as your own; take hospitality seriously.

¹⁴Ask for God's blessing on those who harass you; ask for God's blessing, not God's curse on them. ¹⁵Celebrate with those who have something to be happy about; commiserate with those who are in sorrow. ¹⁶Treat one another as equals. Don't entertain notions of your superiority; on the contrary, associate with ordinary people. Don't become wise in your own eyes. ¹⁷Don't repay anyone who has injured you by injuring them; instead, focus on what is honorable in the eyes of all people. ¹⁸If possible—insofar as it depends on you—be at peace with all people. ¹⁹Don't try to retaliate on your own, dear friends, but leave that to God's just indignation, because scripture says, "Justice is my business; I will put things right," says the Lord. ²⁰But (so far as you are concerned) as scripture says, "If your enemy is hungry, give him something to eat, and if he is thirsty, give him something to drink; because if you do this, you will pile red hot coals [of shame?] on his head." ²¹So don't let yourselves be defeated by what is evil, but defeat what is evil with what is good.

13 ⁸You have no obligation to each other, except to love one another, because the person who loves the other has fulfilled the [Mosaic] law. ⁹The commandments, "Do not commit adultery, do not commit murder, do not steal, do not covet," and any other commandment, are summed up in this single sentence: "You must love your neighbor as yourself." ¹⁰Love does no wrong to the neighbor; therefore, love is what fulfills the law.

¹¹I don't have to tell you that we are living in the most decisive moment in human history. The hour has already passed for you to be roused from your sleep, because the time of ultimate fulfillment is nearer now than when we first put our unconditional confidence and trust in God. ¹²The night is almost gone, the day is almost here. Let us rid ourselves of the preoccupations of the darkness and clothe ourselves with the armor of the light. ¹³Let us conduct ourselves in ways befitting those who live in the full light of day, not in gluttony and drunkenness, not in promiscuous sexual behavior nor in uninhibited self-indulgence, not in contentiousness and envy. ¹⁴But adopt the manner of life of our lord, Jesus, God's Anointed, and make no concession to the lifestyle of this age and its pursuit of self-gratification.

14 You should welcome those who are uncertain about what trusting God involves, but not to argue with them about their dietary scruples. ²One person believes that it is permissible to eat anything one likes, but the uncertain individual eats only vegetables. ³Those who eat whatever they like should not look down on those whose scruples restrict their diet, and those whose scruples restrict what they eat should not condemn those who eat whatever they like, because God has accepted them both. ⁴What gives you the right to criticize a household slave who is owned by someone else? It's in

---

13:8 Romans 13:1–7 appears to be a later insertion. See the Interpolations.

the eyes of his master that he stands or falls. In this case, the household slave will be upheld, because his lord has the authority to support him. [5]One person values one day as more sacred than another, whereas another person treats every day alike. Each of us should be fully persuaded in our own minds about how we regard days. [6]Those who especially value a particular day regard that as a way of serving the lord; and those who eat whatever they like regard that as a way of serving the lord, because they give thanks to God. Likewise those who restrict their diet regard that as a way of serving the lord, and they also give thanks to God. [7]We [who belong to the Anointed's people] do not live on our own terms or die on our own terms. [8]If we live, we live in service to our lord, and if we die, we die in service to our lord. Therefore whether we live or die, we belong to the lord. [9]This is the reason the Anointed died and came to life again: that he might be lord both of the dead and the living. [10]Why do you criticize your brother? Or why do you look down on your sister? For we will all appear in God's court, [11]because it is written,

> I assure you, says the Lord,
> to me every knee shall bend,
> and every tongue shall praise God.

[12]So then, all of us will give an account of ourselves to God.

[13]So then, let us agree not to put each other down anymore. This is what you should do instead: refrain from putting what is considered offensive or what constitutes a hindrance in the path of any of the Anointed's people. [14]I know and am persuaded by the lord Jesus that no food is forbidden, except that if someone regards some food as forbidden, for that person it is forbidden. [15]If one of the Anointed's people is upset by the food you eat, you are no longer acting out of love. Don't bring one for whom the Anointed died to ruin by the food you eat. [16]Don't let what you regard as a good thing be reviled. [17]For the Empire of God is not about food and drink, but it is about the integrity and peace and joy that comes

through God's presence and power [among us]. [18]Those who serve the Anointed in this way please God and win the respect of the community. [19]So then, we should pursue what makes peace possible and what is constructive for all of us. [20]Don't bring God's project to ruin because of disputes about food. [Some of you say,] "It's all right to eat every kind of food," but it is not all right for us to cause others to fall because of what we eat. [21]It's a good thing not to eat meat or to drink wine or to do anything that alienates your friends. [22]Keep your convictions about these things between yourself and God. People who have no reason to condemn themselves for the behavior they approve are the fortunate ones. [23]But if people eat food they have misgivings about, they condemn themselves, because they are not acting on the basis of their convictions. Everything people do that is not based on their convictions makes matters worse.

15 We who are strong [in our confidence about the liberation that trusting God involves] have an obligation to help bear the burdens of the weak [the inhibitions of those whose understanding is inadequate], and not just do as we please. [2]All of us should accommodate our neighbors so as to contribute to their good and to strengthen the whole community. [3]For the Anointed did not just do as he pleased; to the contrary, as it is written, "The insults of those who scorn you have fallen on me." [4]Keep in mind that whatever was written in earlier times was written to educate us so that through perseverance and through the encouragement of the scriptures, we might hold on to the hope [for the salvation of the nations]. [5]May the God who enables us to persevere and encourages us enable you to agree with one another by thinking in the same way as the Anointed Jesus did, [6]so that with one unanimous voice

---

15:1 *inhibitions of those whose understanding is inadequate:* Paul appears to be referring those who are incapable of grasping or who are inhibited from acting on the liberating implications of their convictions. SV has attempted to suggest the sense of the terms "strong" and "weak."

you may praise the greatness of the God and benefactor of our lord, Jesus the Anointed.

⁷Accept one another in the same way that the Anointed has accepted you, so that God's glorious purpose may be accomplished. ⁸I maintain that the Anointed became the servant of the Jewish people to demonstrate God's veracity in confirmation of God's promise to our ancestors, ⁹and so that the nations might praise God's mercy, just as it is written,

> Therefore I will acknowledge you among the nations,
> and sing songs in your honor.

¹⁰And again,

> Rejoice, nations, with God's people.

¹¹And again,

> Praise the Lord, all of you nations
> and let all peoples praise the Lord.

¹²And again Isaiah says,

> The root of Jesse will spring up,
> the one who will rise to rule the nations,
> the nations will place their hope on him.

¹³May God, the source of our hope, fill you with such joy and peace through your complete confidence in God, that by the presence and power of God in your midst your hope will be absolutely boundless.

¹⁴I myself have come to believe that you all are filled with good intentions, well furnished with knowledge of every kind, and quite capable of providing one another with good advice. ¹⁵But I have written to you rather boldly, partly to remind you, because of the calling I have received from God ¹⁶to be the ambassador of the Anointed Jesus to the nations, serving God's world-transforming message as if I were a priest, so that the nations might be acceptable to God, as if they were an offering cleansed and consecrated by God's purity and power. ¹⁷This is why I take some pride in the role I have played in the service of the Anointed to advance God's

purposes. [18]For I will not presume to speak about anything except what the Anointed has accomplished through me to win obedience from the nations, by what I have said and done, [19]by the power of signs and wonders, by the presence of God's power; so that from Jerusalem all the way around to Illyricum I have accomplished my mission of proclaiming God's world-transforming news about the Anointed. [20]So I have made it my aim not to proclaim God's world-transforming message where the Anointed had already been made known, so that I would not base my work on the foundation put down by someone else, [21]but just as it is written,

> Those who were never told about him will see,
> and those who never heard of him will understand.

[22]This is why I have repeatedly been prevented from coming to visit you. [23]But now, since there are no more good locations [for my mission] in these areas, and since for many years now I have wanted to pay you a visit, [24]I hope to see you while I am passing through on my way to Spain and to have your support for my travel there—but only after I have had the time to fully enjoy your company.

[25]However, before I come to see you, I am going to Jerusalem on a mission for the people of God there. [26]I am going there because [the Anointed's people in] Macedonia and Achaia want to express their sense of community by aiding the needy among Jesus followers in Jerusalem. [27]They were willing to do this, since they have an obligation to them, because if the nations have come to share in the non-material things of the Anointed's people in Jerusalem, they feel they should reciprocate in material things. [28]So when I have completed this task and have safely put these funds in their hands, I will be off to Spain and will stop to see you en route. [29]And I am sure that when I come to see you, I will arrive with all of the abundance of the Anointed's blessing.

[30]I appeal to you, friends, through our lord, Jesus, God's Anointed and through the presence and power of God's love,

to join me in your prayers before God [31]that I may be delivered from those in Judea who refuse to accept [God's world-transforming message], that the good will and support that I am conveying for the Jerusalem community will be well received by the Anointed's people there, [32]and that through God's will my visit with you will be a joyful one and that together we may be refreshed.

[33]The God of peace be with all of you. Amen.

Scripture Parallels

1:16	Ps 119:46
1:17	Hab 2:4
1:19	Wis 13–15
1:20	Job 12:7–9; Ps 8:4
1:21	4 Esdr 8:60; 2 Kgs 17:15; Ps 94:11; Wis 13:1
1:23	Ps 106:20; Jer 2:11; Wis 11:15; 12:24
1:27	Lev 18:22
2:4	Wis 11:23
2:5	Deut 9:27
2:6	Prov 24:12; Ps 62:12
2:9	Deut 28:53
2:11	2 Chron 19:7; Sir 35:12
2:15	Jer 31:33; Isa 51:7
2:20	Ps 50:16–21
2:24	Isa 52:5
2:29	Deut 30:6; Jer 4:4; 9:25; 31:33
3:4	Ps 50:6 (LXX)
3:10	Eccl 7:20; Ps 14:1–3
3:11	Ps 53:1–4
3:13	Ps 5:9
3:14	Ps 10:7
3:15	Isa 59:7–8; Prov 1:16
3:18	Ps 36:1
3:20	Ps 143:2
4:3	Gen 15:6
4:7–8	Ps 32:1–2

4:9	Gen 15:6
4:10	Gen 17:9–10
4:13	Gen 15:4–6
4:17	Gen 17:5 (LXX)
4:18	Gen 15:5 (LXX)
4:19	Gen 17:17
4:23	Gen 15:6
5:5	Ps 25:20
5:12	Gen 2:17; 3:14,17; 4 Esdr 3:21, 26; Wis 2:24
5:19	Isa 53:11–12
7:7	Exod 20:17; Deut 5:21 (LXX); 4 Macc 2:5
7:10	Lev 18:5
7:11	Gen 2:17; 3:13
8:20	Gen 3:17–19
8:22	4 Esdr 10:9
8:29	Gen 1:27
8:31	Ps 118:6
8:32	Gen 22:16
8:33	Isa 50:8; Job 34:29
8:34	Ps 110:1
8:36	Ps 44:22 (LXX)
8:39	Ps 139:8
9:3	Exod 32:32
9:4	Exod 4:22; Jer 31:9; Exod 16:10; 24:16; Gen 6:18; 9:9; 15:8; 17:2, 7, 9; Exod 2:24; Sir 44:12; Exod 20:1–17; Deut 5:1–21
9:5	Ps 41:14
9:7	Gen 21:12 (LXX)
9:9	Gen 18:10, 14
9:12	Gen 25:23 (LXX)
9:13	Mal 1:2–3 (LXX)
9:15	Exod 33:19 (LXX)
9:17	Exod 9:16
9:20	Isa 29:16; 45:9; 64:8
9:21	Wis 15:7; Jer 18:6
9:25	Hos 2:23

9:26	Hos 2:1 (LXX)
9:27	Isa 10:22; 1:9; Deut 5:28 (LXX)
9:28	Isa 28:22
9:29	Isa 1:9 (LXX)
9:31	Wis 2:11
9:33	Isa 8:14; 28:16
10:5	Lev 18:5
10:6–8	Deut 9:4; Deut 30:11–14; Prov 30:4
10:11	Isa 28:16
10:13	Joel 3:5 (LXX)
10:15	Isa 52:7
10:16	Isa 53:1
10:18	Ps 18:5 (LXX)
10:19	Deut 32:21 (LXX)
10:20	Isa 65:1 (LXX)
10:21	Isa 65:2 (LXX)
11:2	Ps 94:14
11:3	1 Kg 19:10, 14
11:4	1 Kg 19:18
11:8	Isa 29:10
11:9	Ps 68:23 (LXX); 69:22–23
11:26	Isa 59:20; Ps 14:7
11:27	Jer 31:33 (LXX); Isa 27:9 (LXX)
11:34	Isa 40:13 (LXX)
12:15	Sir 7:34
12:16	Prov 3:7 (LXX)
12:17	Prov 3:4 (LXX)
12:19	Lev 19:18; Deut 32:35 (LXX)
12:20	Prov 25:21 (LXX)
13:9	Deut 3:17–21 (LXX); Exod 20:13–17 (LXX); Lev 19:18 (LXX)
13:10	Wis 6:18
14:11	Isa 45:23 (LXX)
15:3	Ps 68:10 (LXX)
15:9	Ps 17:50 (LXX)
15:10	Deut 32:43 (LXX)

15:11   Ps 117:1
15:12   Isa 11:10 (LXX)
15:21   Isa 52:15 (LXX)

Pauline Parallels

1:1–7   1 Thess 1:1; Gal 1:1–5; 1 Cor 1:1–3; 2 Cor 1:1–2;
Phlm 1–3; Phil 1:1–2

1:8–15   1 Thess 1:2–10; 1 Cor 1:4–9; 2 Cor 2:14–17;
Phlm 4–7; Phil 1:3–11

1:16–17 2 Cor 10:1–6; Phil 1:12–18

1:18–23 1 Thess 2:15–16; 1 Cor 1:18–25; 3:18–23;
2 Cor 2:15

1:24–28 1 Cor 5:1–5; 5:9–13; 6:9–11; 6:12–20

1:29–32 Gal 5:16–26; 1 Cor 5:9–13; 6:9–11; 2 Cor 12:19–21

2:1–5   Gal 2:11–14

2:6–11   2 Cor 5:6–10

2:17–24 Gal 1:13–14; 2:11–14; 6:11–17; 2 Cor 11:21b–29;
Phil 3:2–11

2:25–29 Gal 3:10–14; 5:1–12; 6:11–17; 1 Cor 7:17–24;
Phil 3:2–11

3:9–20   Gal 2:15–21; 3:10–14; 3:21–25

3:21–26 Phil 3:2–11

3:27–31 1 Cor 1:26–31; 2 Cor 10:13–18; 11:16–21; 11:21–
12:10; Phil 3:2–11

4:1–8   Gal 3:15–20

4:13–15 Gal 3:15–20

5:1–5   2 Cor 1:3–11; 4:7–12; 6:1–10; 12:1–10

5:5   2 Cor 5:5

6:11–14 Gal 3:21–25

6:15–23 Gal 5:1–12; 5:13–15; 6:7–10; 1 Cor 7:17–24

7:1–6   Gal 2:15–21; 3:21–25; 1 Cor 7:8–9; 7:10–11; 7:39–
40; 2 Cor 3:1–18

7:6   2 Cor 3:6

7:7–13   Gal 3:21–25; 1 Cor 15:51–58

7:14–25 Gal 5:16–26; 1 Cor 3:1–4

8:1–8   Gal 5:16–26; Phil 2:1–11

8:9–17   Gal 2:15–21; 4:1–7; 1 Cor 3:16–17; 6:12–20;
Phil 2:1–11

8:18–25   Gal 4:1–7; 2 Cor 4:16–5:5

8:26–27   1 Cor 2:6–16; 4:1–5

8:28–30   1 Thess 1:15–20; 1 Cor 1:4–9

8:31–39   1 Thess 3:1–5; 1 Cor 4:1–5; 2 Cor 4:7–12; 6:1–10

9:1–5   Gal 3:19–20; 2 Cor 3:7–18; 11:21–29; Phil 3:17–21

9:6–13   Gal 4:21–31

9:30–33   Gal 2:15–21; 5:1–12; 1 Cor 1:18–25; Phil 3:2–11

10:1–4   Gal 1:13–14; 3:19–25; Phil 3:2–11

10:5–13   1 Thess 1:2–10; Gal 3:10–14; 3:26–29; 1 Cor 12:1–3;
12:13; 15:1–19; Phil 2:1–11

10:14–17 1 Thess 2:13–16; Gal 3:1–5; Phil 4:8–9

10:18–21 1 Thess 1:2–10

11:1–6   Gal 2:15–21; 2 Cor 11:21–29; Phil 3:2–11

11:13–16 Gal 2:1–14; 1 Cor 5:6–8; 2 Cor 5:14–21

11:17–24 1 Cor 1:26–1; 4:6–7

11:25–32 Phil 3:17–21

11:33–36 1 Cor 2:6–16; 8:4–6

12:1–2   1 Thess 4:1–8; 1 Cor 1:10–17; 2 Cor 10:1–2;
Phlm 8–14; Phil 2:14–18; 4:10–20

12:3–8   1 Cor 10:14–22; 12:4–31

12:9–21   Thess 4:9–12; 5:12–22; 1 Cor 13:4–7; 2 Cor 13:11–
13; Phil 2:1–11; 4:4–7

13:8–10   1 Thess 4:9–12; Gal 5:13–15; 1 Cor 13:1–3;
Phlm 1–20

13:11–14 1 Thess 5:1–11; Gal 5:16–26; 1 Cor 5:9–13; 6:9–11;
2 Cor 12:19–21

14:1–4   1 Cor 8:1–3; 10:23–11:1; 11:17–22

14:5–12   1 Thess 5:1–11; Gal 4:8–11; 1 Cor 4:1–5; 7:17–24;
Phil 1:19–26

14:13–23 1 Cor 4:1–5; 8:–13; 10:23–11:1

15:1–6   Gal 6:1–6; 1 Cor 1:10–17; 10:23–11:1; 14:1–5;
2 Cor 13:5–13; Phil 2:1–11

15:7–13   Gal 3:6–9; 3:10–14; Phlm 15–20
15:14–21 1 Thess 1:2–10; 1 Cor 2:1–5; 3:10–15; 2 Cor 10:13–
18; 12:11–13; Phil 1:3–11
15:22–29 1 Thess 2:17–20; Gal 2:1–10; 1 Cor 16:1–4; 16:5–9;
2 Cor 1:15–22; 1:23–2:4; 8:1–9:15; 12:14–13:4;
Phlm 21–22
15:30–33 1 Thess 5:25

A Letter of
Recommendation

An Explanatory Comment

As noted in the Introduction Rom 16:1–23 appears to be a separate letter that accompanied the major address to the Romans. This brief letter bears the marks of a letter of recommendation for Phoebe. Numerous scholars have claimed that the recommendation of Phoebe implies that she was the one who delivered Paul's letter to Rome. Evidence from ancient letter-writing practice supports this conjecture. As Robert Jewett notes, "Ancient epistolary practice would . . . assume that the recommendation of Phoebe was related to her task of conveying and interpreting the letter in Rome as well as in carrying out the business entailed in the letter" (*Romans*, p. 943).

16 I recommend to you our sister Phoebe, who is a leader of the Anointed's people in Cenchreae, ²in the hope that you will cordially welcome her as one who belongs to the lord, in a manner worthy of the Anointed's people; and that you will assist her in whatever undertaking for which she may need your help, because she has provided help to many people, including myself.

³Extend my greetings to Prisca and Aquila, my fellow-workers in the service of the Anointed Jesus. ⁴They risked their necks to save my life. Not only I, but all of the Anointed's communities of the nations are grateful to them. Extend my greetings to the community that meets in their house.

⁵Greet my dear friend Epaenetus, the Anointed's first follower from Asia.

⁶Greet Mary who has worked hard on your behalf.

⁷Greet Andronicus and Junia, my compatriots and fellow-prisoners. They are persons of distinction among [the Anointed's] envoys and they identified themselves with the Anointed before I did.

[8]Greet Ampliatus my dear friend in the lord's service.

[9]Greet Urbanus, our fellow-worker in the Anointed's service, and my dear friend Stachys.

[10]Greet Apelles whose service for the Anointed was put to the test; and greet the family of Aristobulus also.

[11]Greetings to my kinsman Herodion. Greetings to those who belong to the lord in the Narcissus family.

[12]Greetings to Tryphaena and Tryphosa, who work for our lord. Greetings to my dear friend Persis, who has done many things in our lord's service.

[13]Greetings to Rufus, one of our lord's chosen, and to his mother and mine.

[14]Greetings to Asyncritus, Phlegon, Hermes, Patrobus, Hermas, and to their friends.

[15]Greetings to Philologus and Julia, Nereus and his sister, and to Olympas and all of the Anointed's people who are with them.

[16]Greet each other with respect and affection. All the communities of the Anointed send their greetings to you.

[21]Timothy, my fellow worker, sends you greetings, as do Lucius and Jason and Sosipater, my kinsmen.

[22]I, Tertius, who wrote this letter in the service of the lord greet you.

[23]Gaius who is host to me and to the whole community of the Anointed here sends his greetings, as do Erastus, the city manager, and his brother Quartus.

Pauline Parallels

16:1–2 1 Cor 16:10–12; 16:15–18; 2 Cor 3:1–3; 8:16–4; Phlm 8–20; Phil 2:9–24; 2:25–3:1

16:3–16 1 Thess 5:26; 1 Cor 16:19–20; 2 Cor 13:11–13; Phlm 23–24; Phil 4:21–22

16:21–23 1 Thess 5:26; 1 Cor 16:19–20; 2 Cor 13:11–13; Phlm 23–24; Phil 4:21–22

INTERPOLATIONS

Romans 5:6–7

An Explanatory Comment

Romans 5:6–7 appear to be an interpolation. These verses stand in contrast to the tone, format, and flow of the surrounding material (vv. 1–11). They deliver an apparent reflection on what Paul has already written.

5 ⁶For while we were still helpless, at the appointed time, God's Anointed died for the ungodly. ⁷For it is unlikely that anyone would die for a devout man, although someone might perhaps be brave enough to die for a good man.

∞

Romans 13:1–7

An Explanatory Comment

Romans 13:1–7 appears to be a later insertion. It stands in great contrast to what Paul has just recommended in 12:1–2. He encourages his listeners not to conform to the life of the present age. Instead he calls for a remodeling of their minds. He urges the Romans to live lives of "enlightened worship." Paul thus urges wisdom and critical discernment. In 13:1–7 Paul reverts to the cultural stereotypes, and abandons the revolutionary approach he has just outlined in chapter 12. Indeed, the apocalyptic perspective of Paul appears to have disappeared. The language in 13:1–7 reflects the wisdom language found in Jewish synagogues of the period. Furthermore, upon removing these verses, the argument from 12:21 to 13:8 flows more logically.

13 ¹Every person should voluntarily submit to those who have the authority to govern. For there is no legitimate authority except that authorized by God, and those authorities that exist have been established by God. ²It follows that the person who resists such authority resists what God has arranged and those who resist will bring condemnation upon themselves. [3]Rulers are not an intimidation to good behavior, but to bad. Do you want to avoid living in fear of the person in authority? Then do what is good and he will praise you for it, [4]because he is the servant of God to uphold what is good on your behalf. But anyone who is bent on criminal behavior should be afraid, because the person in authority does not carry the sword for no reason. He is the servant of God who carries out just condemnation against the person who commits criminal acts. [5]For this reason it is necessary to submit [to those who have the authority to govern] not only for fear of punishment, but also as a matter of conscience. [6]This is also why you pay taxes. [Those in authority] are God's ministers whose mission is to collect taxes. [7]Pay everyone what they are entitled to: taxes to the one entitled to collect taxes, customs fees to the one entitled to collect custom fees, respect to the one who is entitled to respect, and honor to the one entitled to honor.

Pauline Parallels

13:1–7   1 Cor 4:1–5; 6:1–8; 8:7–13

❧

Romans 16:17–20, 25–27

16 [17]I appeal to you, friends, to watch out for those who create dissension and entrap people by opposing the doctrine that you have been taught. You should avoid them! [18]People of that sort do not serve our lord Christ, but their own base desires. By their seemingly persuasive and unctuous language they beguile the minds and hearts of the naïve. [19]Your loyal obedience is known to everyone and for that I congratulate you. But I want you to be wise about what is good, and uncontaminated by what is evil; [20]then the God of peace will quickly

---

16:20 This is a very abrupt shift. Was v. 20b an original conclusion that was placed after v. 20a? Verses 25ff. were added to some mss which did not have the ending of v. 20b.

crush Satan beneath your feet. The grace of our lord, Jesus, be with you.

²⁵Now to him who has the power to uphold you according to my gospel and the proclamation of Jesus Christ, according to the revelation of the mystery kept secret for countless ages, ²⁶but now made known through the prophetic writings in accordance with the command of the eternal God for the obedience of faith for all nations, ²⁷to the only wise God be the glory forever through Jesus Christ. Amen.

16:24 Some ancient manuscripts add: ²⁴The grace of our Lord Jesus Christ be with your all. Amen.

Pauline Parallels
16:17–20 1 Thess 2:1–8; 1 Cor 5:1–5; 5:9–13; 2 Cor 6:14–
7:1; 11:12–15
16:20   1 Thess 5:28; Gal 6:18; 1 Cor 16:23–24;
2 Cor 13:14; Phlm 25; Phil 4:23

The Rhetorical Structure of Romans 6–7

The rhetorical structure of Romans 6–7 is determined by a series of five questions. They are meant to take up the objections Roman followers have to his convictions about how believers are to live their lives in obedience to God:

1. How then should we respond [to our changed relationship with God]? Should we continue to live as before so that God's generous favor can become even more remarkable? That would be ridiculous! (6:1–2a)

2. What you are really saying, Paul, is that if we do not live under [the condemnation] of law but in [the freedom] of God's generous favor, then it makes no difference if we submit to sin's seductive, corrupting power—right? *Paul:* That would be ridiculous! (6:15)

3. Are you unaware, my friends—after all I am speaking to people who know something about the law—that the law has jurisdiction over a person only as long as that person is alive? (7:1)

4. Am I saying that the law itself is corrupting? Certainly not! (7:7)

5. Am I claiming that what is good caused my death? Certainly not! (7:13)

Cf. Thomas H. Tobin, SJ, *Paul's Rhetoric in its Contexts. The Argument of Romans* (Hendrickson Publishers, 2004), 191.

Diatribe

Modern scholars use the term *diatribe* (literally, to pass the time in lecturing) to describe the format and strategy of certain portions of rhetorical discourse. Such discourse can be found in the works of Cynic and Stoic philosophers. The speeches of Epictetus are excellent examples of *diatribe*. The speaker uses a variety of rhetorical conventions in order to engage the audience. The speaker can thus use: a series of rhetorical questions, indicting the addressees; an inductive method, causing the listeners to reconsider their experience; vivid speech in an attempt to place the issue in question right before the listeners' eyes. The speaker also can anticipate probable objections by the audience through giving voice to an anonymous interlocutor and then answering them in the argument. The argument by no means is presented as a systematic treatise; rather, its vigorous, colloquial, and dramatic expressions attempt to confront the listener directly.

Such provocative rhetorical conventions are used within a larger dialogical context where a teacher-student relationship is presupposed. The speaker leads the listener to a deeper realization of the issues under consideration. Thus, it is a matter not only of various elements of style but also of detecting the underlying strategy of communication. The various rhetorical components are designed to induce the listeners to a deeper basis of thought and reflection, to bring them into the argument, thereby giving them the opportunity to recognize their unspoken assumptions.

In Gal 3:1–5, for example, Paul directly confronts his listeners, attacking their present understanding and, in a series of antitheses, rhetorically asks how they came to their experience of God's power and presence.

> You clueless Galatians! Who has cast an evil eye on you, putting you under a spell? Your own eyes saw Jesus, God's Anointed, graphically portrayed on a cross. ²Tell me this: Did you experience God's presence and power by relying on traditional religious practices or by being

Continued on next page

convinced by what you heard? [3]How stupid can you be? Do you really think that what was begun by God's presence and power can be completed by a merely earthly life? [4]Has everything you experienced meant nothing to you? Surely it meant something! [5]Is the one, who empowers and works miracles among you, able to do so because you rely on traditional religious practices or because you are convinced by the message you heard?

Romans 3:1ff. uses an imagined interlocutor throughout. Paul anticipates the possible objections to his arguments by members of the Roman gatherings.

I: [1]What's the advantage in being a Jew? Or what's the benefit of circumcision?

P: [2]A great advantage with many benefits. Above all, the Jews were entrusted with the words of God.

I: [3]So what if some of them were unreliable? Surely, their unreliability doesn't invalidate God's reliability, does it?

P: [4]Absolutely not! Surely God must be true even if everyone else is false, "so that," as scripture says, "in all you say your justice shows and when you are accused you win your case."

I: [5][Well, Paul,] if our misdeeds highlight God's reliability, dare one conclude that God who punishes us is unjust—if one may speak irreverently?

P: [6]Absolutely not! If that were so, how could God judge the world?

I: [7][Wait a minute, Paul,] if God's truthfulness is made more evident by my lying, so that God is glorified even more, why am I still being condemned as a sinner?

P: [8][To follow your argument,] then why should we not "do evil so that good may come from it," as some people who slander us claim that we say? Such slanderers are rightly condemned.

I: [9][Well, Paul,] are we Jews then better off than other people?

P: Not at all! We have already charged that Jews and Greeks alike are all prone to wrongdoing.

Roman 7:7–24 shows another aspect of diatribe. Here Paul uses the diatribal convention of personification. The

"I" in Romans 7 is not Paul but a personification of the social ego constructed out of the aspirations and assumptions of the dominant Roman culture. Paul exposes the limits of this "I" showing how it cannot effect what it fervently desires. There is a stark contradiction between dreams and reality. The "I" is a *prosōpon*, that is, a role, which is embedded in the relationship to appearances and reality, tied to a network of social expectations and compelling social forces. Paul reveals through this contradictory monologue the limits of this understanding. The "I" of Rom 7:7ff. does not represent the solitary modern ego but a *persona dramatis* or even a *persona socialis*, thereby becoming a spokesperson (*prosōpon*) for the contradiction and truth at the basis of human existence.

> [14]We know that the law has its origin in the divine realm, but I am a creature of the earth, sold as a slave and in bondage to the power of corruption. [15]I don't understand what I find myself doing. I do not accomplish what I intend, but what I actually do I deplore. [16]If what I do is not what I intend, then I am really concurring with the law that it is good. [17]In that case it can no longer be thought that I am the one who is doing this; what's doing this is the corrupting power that has taken up residence in me. [18]I recognize that the good does not reside in me, I mean my earthly life. I have the capacity to intend what is right, but I cannot make it happen. [19]I do not accomplish the good I intend, the bad I do not intend is what I actually bring about. [20]If I bring about what I do not intend, then it is no longer I who produces this, but the corrupting power that has taken up residence in me.
>
> [21]So I take it to be a fact of life: that when I intend to do the good, the bad is right there at my side. [22]I rejoice in the law of God so far as my inner self is concerned, [23]but I observe another law in my outward acts at war with the law of my mind and this other law—the law of corrupting power—takes me captive. [24]What a sorry creature am I! Who will rescue me from this earthly self which is captive to death?

GLOSSARY

Anointed, The, God's Anointed. Greek: *christos.* Traditional translation: "Christ." The Greek term *christos* is a translation of the Hebrew term *meshiah,* and refers to one who is appointed and empowered by God to carry out a special task. When Paul refers to Jesus as "God's Anointed," he means that Jesus was designated (Rom 1:4) as the one through whom the way to God's new world has been opened to all.

Confidence, confident trust in God. Greek: *pistis.* Traditional translation: "faith." By this term Paul does not mean merely intellectual assent to a theological proposition, or believing what is contrary to knowledge, but a confident trust in and reliance upon God (which is to recognize the true nature of our existence as creatures), and to embracing and living in accordance with "God's world-changing news about the Anointed." See Cameo essay on Galatians 2:16, p. 65.

Corrupting seduction of power. Greek *hamartia.* Traditional translation: "sin." Usually the mythic sense of the word *hamartia* is overlooked in translation. For Paul *hamartia* is a personified force that enters and obstructs the human story. It is more than a single act or specific actions; rather it refers to a fated condition that gains momentum over time.

Creator and Benefactor. Greek: *patēr.* Traditional translation: "Father." The term "Father" resonated within an ancient patriarchal society and culture as an effective and appropriate way of referring to the divine source of all life, the generous and caring provider for, and strong protector of human life. In a democratic society and culture which has come to affirm the equal rights and dignity of men and women, the God Paul refers to as "Father" is better conveyed by the closely equivalent expression "Creator and Benefactor." This expression also refers to the divine source of our life and to the goodness and generosity that enables us to flourish.

Gathering of the Anointed's people, the Anointed's community.
Greek: *ekklēsia.* Traditional translation: "church." The Greek
term *ekklēsia* refers to an assembly or gathering. In Greek
ekklēsia could provoke significant political memories. Such a
term in the Empire would recall an earlier age when Greek
citizens would meet and freely decide their political fate. Paul
uses the term in the address line of several of his letters. In
Paul's correspondence the term refers to comparatively small,
informal groups who often gathered in the homes of one of
their members. This translation alerts the reader to the fact
that the groups to whom Paul wrote were at an early formative
stage, not yet ecclesiastical institutions.

God's people, God's own people. Greek: *hagioi, hoi hagioi.*
Traditional translation: "saints." By this term, found several
times in the opening and closing lines of his letters, Paul is referring to people who have responded favorably to his preaching and whom he thus regards as devoted to the service of
God's Anointed, Jesus—not to a select few individuals canon-
ized by the church hierarchy as persons of exceptional holiness
who have demonstrated the power to perform miracles.

God's presence and power. Greek: *pneuma, pneuma hagion.*
Traditional translation: "Spirit" [of God]," Holy Spirit." These
terms refer primarily to Paul's sense of the presence and
power of God in his own experience, and that of his converts.
This translation is also informed by the fact that "the spirit of
Yahweh" in the Hebrew Bible/Old Testament invariably refers
to morally defined power that is effective in directing Israel's
life in history [TDNT, Vol. 6, p. 365].

Later, in the second and third centuries CE, Christian theology came to regard "the Holy Spirit" as the Third Person of
the Trinity. To credit this ontological concept to Paul would be
anachronistic.

God's world-changing news, message. Greek: *euangelion.*
Traditional translation: "gospel." The term *euangelion* occurs
only three times in the Septuagint (Greek translation of the
Hebrew Bible), and while the related verb, *euangelizomai,* occurs in three significant passages in Second and Third Isaiah

(40:9; 52:7; and 61:1) and in a few other texts, it appears that Paul's frequent use of *euangelion* as the term for the message he proclaimed (46 times in his letters) was most likely influenced, not by these infrequent biblical occurrences, but by its use in inscriptions in the Roman period. The Priene inscription, for example, uses the term *euangelion* in reference to the news of the world-changing achievements of Caesar Augustus. Paul uses *euangelion* in an analogous way to refer to the world-changing news of what God has done through Jesus, God's Anointed. See the Introduction to Romans and the text of the Priene inscription cited there.

Heaven's messengers. Greek: *angeloi*; singular, *angelos*. Traditional translation: "angels," "angel." The Greek term *angelos* means "messenger." In the New Testament period "angels" were thought to be heavenly beings who serve God in a number of ways, often as messengers who sometimes conveyed God's will to humans in visions or dreams.

In the Anointed's service, belong to the Anointed; in the lord's service, belong to the lord." Greek: *en christō; en kuriō*. Traditional translation: "in Christ;" "in the lord." This was Paul's way of referring to his relation to God's Anointed — and the relation of all who embraced his message about the Anointed — before the term "Christian" came into general use.

Law. Greek *nomos*. In the first century *nomos* conveyed a complex meaning. For Hellenistic Jews and Roman citizens *nomos* was a positive force, enabling people to build a civilized world. Whether it was the Jewish Torah or the Twelve Tables of Rome, law provided the time-honored basis for establishing, ordering and ennobling human life. *Nomos* meant custom and tradition. Internalizing such legal traditions and customary requirements would bring out the best in human beings. Power and authority would flow down from the divine realm securing those who maintained control and keep the traditions and customs, thereby promising a positive outcome to the loyal.

Nations, The. Greek: *ethnē*, plural of *ethnos*. Traditional translation: "gentiles," "gentile." The Greek term (in the plural) refers to "nations" or "peoples." Paul's usage of this term reflects the conventional Jewish way of distinguishing "them" from "us." Similarly, Greeks thought of the world as populated by Greeks and barbarians. Paul understands "God's world-changing news" as involving the end of such "them" and "us" views. As he told the Galatians, "You are no longer Jew or Greek, no longer slave or freeborn, no longer male and female. Instead you all have the same status in the service of God's Anointed, Jesus" (Gal 3:28). Paul insistently claims that God has called him to proclaim God's world-changing news about Jesus as God's Anointed to the nations.

Slave, Greek: *doulos.* Traditional translation: "servant," "slave." Slavery was widespread in the ancient Roman world. The advice Paul's offers in a number of his letters reflects that socio-economic, political, and legal fact. But Paul also sees all human beings as slaves of some lord. That's the reality of the power structure of the whole cosmos. When he refers to himself, and the members of the communities he founded, as "a slave of God's Anointed," the word becomes a term of authenticity and honor: liberated from all lesser servitudes, all who acknowledge Jesus as lord have become "children of God" and are in line to inherit eternal life.

Suggestions for Further Study

Books on Paul

F. C. Baur, *Paul the Apostle of Jesus Christ. His Life and Work, His Epistles and Teachings.* Two Volumes in One. Peabody, MA: Hendrickson, 2003. Reprinted from the first two volume English Edition, 1873–1875. Translated from the original German edition, 1845.

J. Christian Beker, *Paul the Apostle. The Triumph of God in Life and Thought.* Philadelphia: Fortress, 1980, 1984.

Guenther Bornkamm, *Paul.* Translated by D. M. G. Stalker. New York: Harper & Row, 1969 (original German edition), 1971.

Daniel Boyarin, *A Radical Jew. Paul and the Politics of Identity.* Berkeley: University of California, 1994.

Rudolf Bultmann, *Theology of the New Testament.* Volume I, Part II: "The Theology of Paul." Translated by Kendrick Grobel. New York: Charles Scribners' Sons, 1951.

John Dominic Crossan and L. Jonathan Reed, *In Search of Paul. How Jesus's Apostle Opposed Rome's Empire with God's Kingdom.* HarperSanFrancisco, 2004.

Arthur J. Dewey, *The Letter and Spirit in Paul.* Lewiston/ Queenston/Lampeter: Edwin Mellen Press. 1996.

James D. G. Dunn, *The New Perspective on Paul.* Revised edition. Grand Rapids: William B. Eerdmans, 2008.

Robert W. Funk, "The Apostolic *Parousia*: Form and Significance," pp. 249–68 in *Christian History and Interpretation: Studies Presented to John Knox.* Ed. W. R. Farmer, C. F. D. Moule, and R. R. Niebuhr. Cambridge: Cambridge, 1967.

_____, "Language as It Occurs in the New Testament: Letter," pp. 224–305 in *Language, Hermeneutic, and Word of God.* New York: Harper & Row, 1966.

Dieter Georgi, *Theocracy: In Paul's Praxis and Theology.* Trans. David L. Green. Minneapolis: Fortress Press. 1991.

Mark D. Given, ed., *Paul Unbound. Other Perspectives on the Apostle.* Peabody, MA: Hendrickson, 2010.

Richard A. Horsley, ed., *Paul and Empire: Religion and Power in Roman Imperial Society*. Harrisburg, PA: Trinity Press International. 1997.

Robert Jewett, *A Chronology of Paul's Life*. Philadelphia: Fortress, 1979.

————, *Paul The Apostle to America: Cultural Trends and Pauline Scholarship*. Louisville: Westminster/John Knox, 1994.

John Knox, *Chapters in a Life of Paul*. New York and Nashville: Abingdon-Cokesbury, 1950.

Helmut Koester, *Paul and His World. Interpreting the New Testament in Its Context*. Minneapolis: Fortress, 2007.

Davina C. Lopez, *Apostle to the Conquered. Reimagining Paul's Mission*. Minneapolis: Fortress Press, 2008.

Johannes Munck, *Paul and the Salvation of Mankind*. Translated from the original German edition, 1954, by Frank Clarke. London: SCM, 1959.

Richard I. Pervo, *The Making of Paul. Constructions of the Apostle in Early Christianity*. Minneapolis: Fortress, 2010.

Calvin J. Roetzel, *Paul: The Man and the Myth*. Minneapolis: Fortress. 1999.

E. P. Sanders, *Paul and Palestinian Judaism. A Comparison of Patterns of Religion*. Philadelphia: Fortress, 1977.

Daryl D. Schmidt, ed., *Translating Paul. FORUM*, New Series 5,2, 2002.

Udo Schnelle, *Apostle Paul. His Life and Theology*. Translated by M. Eugene Boring. Grand Rapids: Baker Academic, 2005. Original German edition 2003.

Alan F. Segal, *Paul the Convert. The Apostolate and Apostasy of Saul the Pharisee*. New Haven: Yale University, 1990.

Mahlon H. Smith, ed., *Unmasking Paul. FORUM*, New Series 7,2, 2004.

Krister Stendahl, *Paul Among Jews and Gentiles*. Philadelphia: Fortress, 1976.

Joseph B. Tyson *Marcion and Luke-Acts: A Defining Struggle*. Columbia: University of South Carolina Press, 2006.

John L. White, *The Apostle of God: Paul and the Promise of Abraham*. Peabody, MA: Hendrickson Publishers. 1999.

Books on Ancient Letters
and on Paul's Letter Collection

William G. Doty, *Letters in Primitive Christianity*. Philadelphia: Fortress, 1973.

Hans-Josef Klauck, *Ancient Letters and the New Testament. A Guide to Context and Exegesis*. Translated and edited from the original German edition, 1998, by Daniel P. Bailey. Waco: Baylor University, 2006.

Bruce J. Malina and John J. Pilch, *Social Science Commentary on the Letters of Paul*. Minneapolis: Fortress, 2006.

David Trobisch, *Paul's Letter Collection. Tracing the Origins*. Minneapolis: Fortress, 1994.

William O. Walker, Jr., *Interpolations in the Pauline Letters*. Journal for the Study of the New Testament Supplement Series 213. Sheffield Academic Press 2001.

John L. White, *Light from Ancient Letters*. Philadelphia: Fortress, 1986.

1 Thessalonians

Jouette M. Bassler, ed., *Pauline Theology. Volume I: Thessalonians, Philippians, Galatians, Philemon*. Minneapolis: Fortress, 1991.

Karl Paul Donfried, *Paul, Thessalonica, and Early Christianity*. Grand Rapids: William B. Eerdmans, 2002.

Karl P. Donfried and Johannes Beutler, eds., *The Thessalonians Debate. Methodological Discord or Methodological Synthesis?* Grand Rapids: William B. Eerdmans, 2000.

Robert Jewett, *The Thessalonian Correspondence: Pauline Rhetoric and Millenarian Piety*. Philadelphia: Fortress, 1986.

Abraham J. Malherbe, *Paul and the Thessalonians. The Philosophic Tradition of Pastoral Care*. Philadelphia: Fortress, 1987.

_____, *The Letters to the Thessalonians*. The Anchor Bible, New York: Doubleday, 2000.

Galatians

Hans Dieter Betz, *Galatians*. Hermeneia—A Critical and Historical Commentary on the Bible. Philadelphia: Fortress, 1979.

Michael F. Bird and Preston M. Sprinkle, eds., *The Faith of Jesus Christ. Exegetical, Biblical, and Theological Studies.* Peabody, MA: Hendrickson, 2009.

Susan M. (Elli) Elliott, *Cutting Too Close for Comfort. Paul's Letter to the Galatians in its Anatolian Cultic Context.* London: T. & T. Clark, 2008.

Richard B. Hays, *The Faith of Jesus Christ. An Investigation of the Narrative Substructure of Galatians 3:1–4:11.* Society of Biblical Literature Dissertation Series, No. 56. Chico, CA: Scholars Press, 1983.

J. Louis Martyn, *Galatians.* The Anchor Bible. New York: Doubleday, 1997.

Mark D. Nanos, ed., *The Galatians Debate.* Peabody, MA: Hendrickson, 2002.

Sam K. Williams, *Galatians.* Abingdon New Testament Commentaries. Nashville: Abingdon, 1997.

1 and 2 Corinthians

Hans Conzelmann, *1 Corinthians.* Translated from the German edition, 1969, by James W. Leitch. Hermeneia — A Critical and Historical Commentary on the Bible. Philadelphia: Fortress, 1975.

Joseph A. Fitzmyer, *First Corinthians.* The Anchor Yale Bible. New Haven: Yale University, 2008.

Victor Paul Furnish, *II Corinthians.* The Anchor Bible. New York: Doubleday, 1984.

Dieter Georgi, *The Opponents of Paul in Second Corinthians.* Translated from the original German edition, 1964. Philadelphia: Fortress, 1986.

David M. Hay, ed., *Pauline Theology. Volume II: 1 & 2 Corinthians.* Minneapolis: Fortress, 1993.

Richard B. Hays, *First Corinthians.* Interpretation. A Bible Commentary for Teaching and Preaching. Louisville: John Knox, 1997.

Richard A. Horsley, *1 Corinthians.* Abingdon New Testament Commentaries. Nashville: Abingdon, 1998.

Jerome Murphy-O'Connor, *St. Paul's Corinth. Texts and Archaeology.* Good News Studies, Volume 6. Wilmington: Michael Glazier, 1983.

Charles H. Talbert, *Reading Corinthians. A Literary and Theological Commentary on 1 and 2 Corinthians.* New York: Crossroads, 1992.

Philemon

John Knox, *Philemon Among the Letters of Paul.* New York and Nashville: Abingdon Press, 1935, 1959.

Eduard Lohse, *Colossians and Philemon.* Hermeneia—A Critical and Historical Commentary on the Bible. Translated from the original German edition, 1969, by William R. Poehlmann and Robert J, Karris. Philadelphia: Fortress, 1971.

Norman R. Petersen, *Rediscovering Paul. Philemon and the Sociology of Paul's Narrative World.* Philadelphia: Fortress, 1985.

Philippians

Roy W. Hoover, "The *Harpagmos* Enigma: A Philological Solution." *Harvard Theological Review* 64,1 (1971): 95–119.

Helmut Koester, "The Purpose of the Polemic of a Pauline Fragment (Philippians iii)," *New Testament Studies* 8 (1961–62): 317–32.

B. D. Rahtjen, "The Three Letters of Paul to the Philippians." *New Testament Studies* 6,2 (January 1960): 167–73.

John Reumann, *Philippians.* The Anchor Yale Bible. New Haven: Yale University, 2008.

Philip Sellew, "*Laodoceans* and the Philippians Fragments Hypothesis." *Harvard Theological Review,* 87 (January, 1994): 17–28.

Charles H. Talbert, "The Problem of Pre-existence in Philippians 2:6–11." *Journal of Biblical Literature* 86 (1967): 141–53.

Romans

C. E. B. Cranfield, *Romans 1–8.* International Critical Commentary. London: T. & T. Clark, 1975.

———, *Romans 9–16.* International Critical Commentary. London: T. & T. Clark, 1979.

Arthur J. Dewey, "Εἰς τὴν Σπανίαν. *The Future and Paul,*" pp. 321–49 in L. Bormann et al., eds., *Religious Propaganda and Missionary Competition in the New Testament World: Essays Honoring Dieter Georgi.* NovTSup 74. Leiden: Brill. 1994.

Karl P. Donfried, ed., *The Romans Debate*. Revised and expanded edition. Peabody, MA: Hendrickson, 1991.

David M. Hay and E. Elizabeth Johnson, eds., *Pauline Theology. Volume III: Romans*. Minneapolis: Fortress, 1995.

Robert Jewett, *Romans*. Hermeneia—A Critical and Historical Commentary on the Bible. Minneapolis: Fortress, 2007.

E. Elizabeth Johnson and David M. Hay, eds., *Pauline Theology. Volume IV: Looking Back, Pressing On*. Society of Biblical Literature Symposium Series. Atlanta: Scholars Press, 1997.

Leander E. Keck, *Romans*. Abingdon New Testament Commentaries. Nashville: Abingdon, 2005.

Steve Mason, "Paul's Announcement (*to euangelion*): 'Good News' and Its Detractors in Earliest Christianity." And " 'For I am Not Ashamed of the Gospel' (Rom 1:16): The Gospel and the First Readers of Romans." In *Josephus, Judea, and Christian Origins. Methods and Categories*. Peabody, MA: Hendrickson, 2009, pp. 283–302; 303–28.

Krister Stendahl, *Final Account. Paul's Letter to the Romans*. Minneapolis: Fortress, 1995.

Stanley K. Stowers, *A Rereading of Romans. Justice, Jews, and Gentiles*. New Haven: Yale University, 1994.

Thomas H. Tobin, *Paul's Rhetoric in Its Contexts. The Argument of Romans*. Peabody, MA: Hendrickson, 2004.

Sam K. Williams, "The Righteousness of God in Romans." *Journal of Biblical Literature* 99 (1980): 241–90.